A Texas Guide to Haunted Restaurants, Taverns, and Inns

Robert James Wlodarski
and
Anne Powell Wlodarski

REPUBLIC OF TEXAS PRESS
Dallas • Lanham • Boulder • New York • Toronto • Oxford

Library of Congress Cataloging-in-Publication Data

Wlodarski, Robert James.
A Texas guide to haunted restaurants, taverns, and Inns /
by Robert J. Wlodarski and Anne Powell Wlodarski.
p. cm.
Includes bibliographical references and index.
ISBN 1-55622-827-9 (pbk.)
1. Haunted hotels--Texas. 2. Haunted places--Texas.
3. Ghosts--Texas. I. Wlodarski, Anne Powell. II. Title.

BF1474.5.W57 2000
133.1'09764--dc21 00-051714
CIP

Published by Republic of Texas Press
An imprint of The Rowman & Littlefield Publishing Group, Inc.
4501 Forbes Boulevard, Suite 200
Lanham, MD 20706

Distributed by NATIONAL BOOK NETWORK

™ The paper used in this publication meets the minimum requirements of American National Standard for Information Sciences—Permanence of Paper for Printed Library Materials, ANSI/NISO Z39.48-1992.

Manufactured in the United States of America.

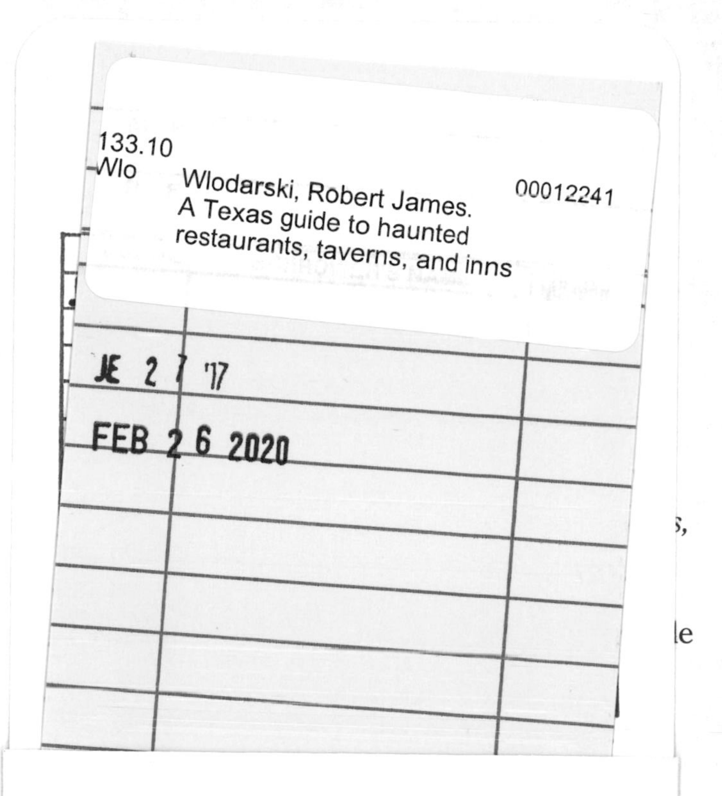
133.10
Wlo
Wlodarski, Robert James.
00012241
A Texas guide to haunted
restaurants, taverns, and inns
JE 27 '17
FEB 26 2020

Contents

Acknowledgments

That this work is finally completed is due in large part to the following people who we gratefully acknowledge:

Special thanks to our spirited friend Ginnie Bivona of Republic of Texas Press for once again believing in our research and writing and contributing her energy and skills into making this book a reality; and to the excellent publishing staff for their usual excellence in the development and production of the book. Hopefully everyone's hard work will make this book an important travel companion for those in search of haunted places to eat, drink, or to rest their weary bones in the state of Texas.

To our many good friends including owners, innkeepers, and staff who we met along the way, for their enthusiastic support and cooperation including:

Anya Adams and Michael Price of Sundance Square (web site: www.sundancesquare.com) for their help in obtaining photographs and other information pertaining to Jamba Juice in the Jett Building located in Fort Worth.

Kimberly Apelgren, Coordinator, and Jane Montz, Reference Librarian of the Austin History Center Association, Inc.

Shawna Bates of the Gage Hotel, for her help in obtaining additional ghost stories and photographs of the hotel.

Dennis Hauck, the author of the *National Directory of Haunted Places*, for his book that inspired yet another of our paranormal adventures into the unknown.

Bud Kennedy for his help in obtaining specific information about the Jett Building in Fort Worth.

Martin Leal, our ghost hunting friend in San Antonio and member of the International Ghost Hunters Society, who went out of his way to help us acquire photographs of a number of the San Antonio establishments listed in this book. When you're in San Antonio, be sure you take his inspiring Hauntings History of San Antonio ghost tours, which are offered every day of the year

(210-436-5417) (web site: http://hotx.com/mydog/People/martin lealnclk).

Katie Lopez, a wonderful El Paso ghost writer for her help with El Paso haunts.

Ron Maddux of the 1st Class Bed & Breakfast Reservation Service in Fredericksburg for his help in obtaining information on the Flagstone Sunday House, Country Cottage Inn, and the Chuck Wagon Inn.

Ernie Moran, Online editor for JustGo!, Virtual Texan, and Travel (www.virtualtexan.com) for his help in obtaining information on Smokey Toes Island Grille, now Jamba Juice, within the historic Jett Building.

Jeanine Plumer, friend, historian, the renowned guide for Austin Promenade Tours, and author of *Weird Texas*. Austin Promenade Tours offers ghost tours of Austin, and Weird Austin publishes a quarterly magazine on everything weird in the area (www.promenadetours.com and www.weirdaustin.com) (512-498-4686 and e-mail: plumer@io.com).

John Roberts for permission to use his photographs of the Jett Building and Jamba Juice in Fort Worth (http://home.flash.net/~jtrobert/jett.htm)

Carol Rust, a gifted writer for the *Houston Chronicle* (carol_rust@hotmail.com), for her story about the Grove House in Jefferson, as well as information about the Excelsior and Fort McKavett. Her article about the Grove and other haunted spots can be found in the September-October 2000 issue of *Texas Journey*.

Jo Anne Shaw, a native of El Paso and the planning director and originator of the Haunted El Paso Ghost Tours, and director of tour planning for the El Paso/Juarez Trolley and Tours (Phone: 915-877-3002 and Fax: 915-877-9040) for her help with several haunted locations in El Paso. Jo Ann will be conducting the first international ghost tour beginning in October.

Raymond Terry for providing historical information and photographs of the Rice Hotel/Sambuca.

To Edward Weissbard, El Paso Ghost Research (e-mail: elpasogr@hotmail.com), for his help obtaining information regarding haunted locations in El Paso as well as putting us in touch with others familiar with haunted El Paso.

Mitchel Whitington, who kindly provided a recent story and a photograph of Snuffer's (www.whitington.com).

Donna Woods, librarian at the Austin History Center, for her help with background information pertaining to the Carrington Bluffs Inn.

Randy Woods for help with haunted Spring, including Puffabelly's Old Depot Restaurant. For information about The Walking Ghost and History Tours in Old Town Spring, call 281-528-0200. Woods is the president and publisher of Souvenir Tours and *The Spring Souvenir* newspaper (www.oldtownspringonline.com or e-mail rwoods@infohwy.com).

Docia Schultz Williams, the prolific Texas ghost writer and ghost hunter, whose spirited books about haunted Texas provided the backbone for a portion of our initial research. Her works are available through Wordware Publishing's Republic of Texas Press (www.republicoftexaspress.com).

To family members Beverly Kiger, Diana Skripka, Emma Lou Powell, and Lee Benner for their assistance in obtaining information and photographs of the Spaghetti Warehouse and Treebeards in Houston and the Puffabelly's Cafe in Spring.

To our parents who raised us with open minds, instilled in us a desire to learn, take the less beaten path through life, explore, and continually question what we see, as well as seek answers to the unseen universe, our relationship to all things, and our ultimate purpose here. They gave us the world and all its wondrous mysteries to explore and in turn, encouraged us to leave something for the next generation to ponder. Hopefully we have done this and will continue to do so by writing these books.

To the gracious and helpful owners, managers, innkeepers, and hosts of the restaurants, taverns, hotels, and inns across the

Lone Star State listed herein for their help in bringing this book to life and instilling good ol' Texas spirit in each story.

To those who wrote and published the books referenced in each story, which we were able to utilize during the initial selection phase, a profound thanks. Without the basic reference information, our job would have been extremely difficult to complete. Keep writing those great bits of folklore, history, and legend, which contribute to our history and are so much a part of the magic of storytelling. These books educate as well as enthrall children and adults and keep us all coming back for more. And, finally, to the children who love ghost stories, for they are the next generation of storytellers, who will continue the legacy of keeping the spirits alive as an integral part of our heritage.

Introduction

Ghosts "R" us, or should we say "were us." We are all of like energy, separated only by the constructs of time and space. One of us still occupies the physical level of reality while "they" have moved or traveled to another level, one of many energy grids or dimensions that some say exist in this universe or within a kind of cosmic consciousness. Ghosts essentially co-exist with us, perhaps in a parallel universe or environment, one that may be invisible to us most of the time and perhaps vice versa from their perspective. Yet our paths cross more frequently than most are willing to admit. Do they simply walk alongside us, occupying the same space yet existing at a different energy frequency? Although the phenomena of ghosts and hauntings is complex, with classifications such as intelligent spirit, residual energy, spirits, poltergeists, and so on used to differentiate types of occurrences, most ghost hunters will attest to the fact that the interacting ones are habitual creatures who have feelings and emotions and can do pretty much everything we can do, perhaps with greater ease or less apparent effort.

Call them what you will: phantasms, wraiths, phantoms, spooks, specters, supernatural beings, manifestation, haunting, paranormal phenomena, haints, shadows, apparitions, poltergeists, spirits, but a rose by any other name . . . still equals a ghost! This, however, does not explain what "they" are and why the phenomena exist. In fact, ghosts walk among us and they are essentially us—or the part of us that is left after the shell, the physical apsect, the body, has proved no longer useful. But as energy, our essence remains, and sometimes this energy, soul, or spirit comes in contact with the physical dimension and our world. Inter-dimensional meetings and crossovers are more frequent than many realize. Why do some people see ghosts more than others? Who knows. Perhaps as some suggest, a few people are more psychic or more in tune than others. The fact is, the living and deceased do make occasional contact and have been doing so for thousands of years. It is a cross-cultural phenomenon and transcends race, color, religion, philosophy, politics, etc. Do we see ghosts because we believe in them, or is it perhaps belief that makes seeing possible. Many a clandestine skeptic at his or her core "wants" to believe and therefore see.

Ghosts can be encountered anywhere at any time by any person. In other words, wherever there is human contact, there is a likelihood for encountering ghosts.

According to renowned paranormal investigator and writer Troy Taylor in his book *The Ghost Hunter's Guidebook* (1999), 90 percent or more of the cases he's involved in have perfectly natural explanations behind the phenomena that is reported. However, he aptly concludes that it is the small percentage of "unexplained" phenomena that keeps all of us coming back for more. Taylor suggests there are several different types of ghosts and related paranormal activity. Two types of activity, however, seem most prominent: the intelligent spirit and the residual haunting. The intelligent spirit is a lost personality that for some reason did not pass over to the other side at the moment of death. It shows intelligence and a consciousness and often interacts with people. Sometimes they manifest themselves as a rush of cold air, a chill, or an overpowering presence. Their physical interactions can be a little more startling through sight, sounds, contact, and even smells. Residual hauntings occur at a specific site and represent an imprint left on the environment, marking an event or series of events that happened in the past. These events were usually traumatic ones, but not always, and are often likened to a video tape playing repeatedly—a moment in time that is on instant and constant replay mode.

Furthermore, Taylor suggests that one part of the human perception uses our five senses while the brain processes the information. The brain only allows us to see what it thinks we can handle. Some individuals are simply on a different "wave-length" and act as "receivers" to an energy field that most of us cannot or will not see. Taylor does not believe that ghosts are seen by people as they really are, and that is why photographs sometimes show balls of light, orbs, and strange mists, which is more in character with how psychical energy is probably manifested. Taylor does believe that when people see ghosts wearing clothing, they are actually witnessing residual impressions because they are not conscious spirits—merely imprints left behind. Conscious spirits will sometimes appear in clothing because people are sensitive enough to see the spirit as it once was. They see the spirit as it still visualizes itself.

L.B. Taylor in *The Ghosts of Virginia* Volume III (1994) suggests that stories of hauntings go back thousands of years. What are ghosts? Taylor suggests that the only real definitive and indisputable answer is, simply, no one knows. Experts attempting to label and explain ghosts for centuries concluded that:

- Ghosts are the disembodied spirits or energy that manifests itself over a period of time, generally in one place.
- Ghosts are the souls of the dead.
- A ghost is the surviving emotional memory of someone who has died traumatically, but is unaware of his or her death.
- A ghost is a person who has died and is stuck in a kind of limbo existence.
- Apparitions are the super-normal manifestations of people, animals, objects, and spirits.
- Most apparitions are of living people or animals who are too distant to be perceived by normal senses.

Some experts believe that a ghost is a manifestation or recordable occurrence of persistent personal energy, or is an indication that some kind of force or energy is being exercised after death, which is in some way connected with a person previously known to have existed on the earth. A number of studies and investigations suggest that spirits appear:

- To communicate with the living in a time of crisis such as sickness or death.

- To provide a warning to the living of some impending tragedy or disaster.
- To comfort those who are grieving or lamenting a serious loss.
- To transmit or communicate to someone in particular valuable personal information.
- To complete a vocation, mission, or duty that was left incomplete while on earth.
- To right a wrong that was done to them, essentially seeking justice for a wrongdoing or transgression.
- To ask the living for help, guidance, or understanding. Sometimes ghosts seek out individuals to help them complete a specific task such as find their missing body and give it a proper burial, or pinpoint the location of an object that must be given to someone in particular.

L. B. Taylor (1994) implies that a majority of ghostly manifestations involve sound and noises, unusual smells or odors, extreme cold, the movement or disappearance of objects, visual images, tactile sensations, and disembodied voices. While the most common perceived image of a ghost is a filmy apparition, in actuality, visual images are seen only in a small percentage of reported cases. Such figures are always clothed and most often appear in period costume.

The term "haunt" comes from the same root as "home" and refers to the occupation of houses by the spirits of deceased people and animals who lived there. Other haunted sites seem to be places merely frequented or liked by the deceased or places where violent death has occurred. Some haunts are continual; others are active only on certain dates that correspond to the deaths or major events in the lives of the dead.

Are ghosts real? That question has remained unanswered through the ages. It is, ultimately, up to each individual to decide. A Gallop poll reported that 14 percent of Americans said they have had a ghostly experience; in Great Britain and other parts of Europe the percentage is much higher. Certainly, most reported supernatural happenings are usually explained by scientific or rational means. But not all! As psychic expert Hans Holzer once said, "There are theories, but no proof, as to why [hauntings] happen. But that the incidence of such happenings exceeds the laws of probability, and that their number establishes that there is something to investigate, is beyond dispute."

Regardless of one's personal feelings, there is, unquestionably, an innate longing in human nature to "pierce the veil" that hides the future after death. Thus, the origin and nature of ghosts have popularly appealed to mankind at all times and in all places and will doubtless continue to do so until the craving to know something of the unseen world is satisfied.

According to Dale Kaczmarek (1999), after being involved with many investigations both into private and public buildings, restaurants, churches, cemeteries, Indian burial grounds, historic locations, battlefields, and murder sites, he has found that no area is totally free of ghostly activity. Most areas seem to begin to produce phenomena after a sudden, violent, emotional, tragic, or traumatic death such as a murder, suicide, or tragic accident like a car or plane crash. The current theory is that because of the way the people met their demise, an energy is released at that location and can be seen, felt, smelled, or sensed in some way by people passing through the area. Other times a location where a person might have spent a great deal of their time such as a house, restaurant, church, or tavern could become haunted by the deceased simply because the ghost might come back to "check in" once in a while to see loved ones or the structure itself.

We may not know why ghosts exist, but we do know they do. This book is not intended to resolve philosophical or metaphysical issues regarding ghosts. Instead, it has as its primary intent to entertain the traveler searching for unusual getaway locations and the seekers of spirits by providing myriad places where ghosts or paranormal phenomena have been reported. Perhaps at one of these destination spots, under the right circumstances, you might feel, hear, or see the otherworldly.

Austin

With a population of almost 500,000 people, a clean environment, numerous lakes and rivers, and beautiful countryside, this Texas city is no longer the best kept secret in the U.S. In 1839 five mounted scouts in search of a new capital city for the Republic of Texas found it on the north bank of the Colorado River. The site was occupied at the time by four families who called their home Waterloo. The present name honors Stephen F. Austin, the "Father of Texas." During September 1839, archives and furniture of the Texas government were transported from Houston to Austin by fifty ox-drawn wagons. Austin is home to The University of Texas at Austin and is nationally recognized for its diverse music community and live music scene. The city is also home to the nation's largest urban bat colony, located under the Congress Avenue bridge.

Bitter End Bistro & Brewery

Address:	311 Colorado Street, Austin, Texas 78701
Phone:	512-478-2337
Fax:	512-478-2462
E-mail:	bitterend@sgrg.com
Contact:	Reed and Betsy Clemons
Dining Hours:	Monday-Thursday: 11:30 A.M.-10:30 P.M.; Friday: 11:30 A.M.-11:00 P.M.; Saturday: 5:00 P.M.-11:00 P.M.; Sunday: 5:00 P.M.-10:30 P.M. /Late Night Hours: Monday-Thursday: 10:30 P.M.-midnight; Friday-Saturday: 11:00 P.M.-1:00 A.M.; Sunday: 10.30 P.M.-midnight

Payment:	American Express, cash, Diners Club, Discover, MasterCard, travelers checks, Visa
References:	15, 16, 19 (see page 243)

History

The Bitter End opened in 1993 as a microbrew pub and fine dining establishment. In 1996 the owners rented the B Side adjacent to the Spaghetti Warehouse. The building containing the Bitter End bar and restaurant was constructed in the late 1800s to serve as a grocery warehouse. Some think that portions of the building were later used as a bordello, for illicit gambling, and even as a possible opium den. The Bitter End serves up nouvelle American cuisine, locally brewed beer, live music on the B Side, and spirits!

Phantoms

Chris, a bartender at the Bitter End for six years and working in the B Side since it opened, normally closes the bar at 2:00 A.M. and performs cleanup in preparation for the next business day. Several nights, while alone, Chris felt someone watching him. Responding to the disconcerting feeling, Chris continually looked around as if expecting to see someone; however no one was ever there—that is, until one evening when, out of the corner of his eye, he saw a dark image standing at the end of the bar. In the wink of an eye the shadow moved away from the bar, through the doorway, and into the back room. Chris quickly followed, rushing from behind the bar and calling out for the person to come out from hiding. Since there was no exit from that portion of the building, he waited, knowing that someone would have to come out sooner or later. No one emerged, and a thorough search produced nothing but a few chills up Chris's neck.

Guests and staff have often reported being treated to other "specialties of the house" in the bar area. A female bartender and manager of the B Side had an otherworldly encounter on one occasion. Familiar with the stories of ghosts, the bartender noticed that a pile of magazines in the corner of the room was soaking wet. She thought that perhaps someone had spilled some drinks or that the air conditioner was leaking. After closer inspection however, she noticed that the dampness was confined to the magazines, and there were no leaks anywhere. Calling out for a friend, the two noticed that the wet area was being caused by a misty cloud, which had mysteriously formed over the magazines, although the space above the cloud and below the ceiling was dry. The strange mist, which was also sighted in 1998, lasted for a few hours then vanished.

The mystery cloud is one of many paranormal events that have some of the bar's staff so spooked they won't go into the B Side alone, especially at night. However, there are others who are aware of a "presence" but do not fear it and instead feel peaceful and comforted. Late one evening after closing, a manager saw a dark, shadowy figure that moved from the left side of the bar toward an alcove where the restrooms are located. Thinking the figure was a customer, the manager followed behind, all the while telling the "patron" that the bar was closed. The figure suddenly disappeared. After a search of the area, the manager was unable to find anyone inside. He was truly baffled, as he realized that to exit, someone would have had to pass by him!

On another occasion a bar employee was napping in a small room at the top of the stairs during off-hours. It was hot and stuffy in the room since the air conditioning was off, but when the employee awoke he was shivering. The room had suddenly turned ice cold. Filled with fear and anxiety, the employee had trouble rising and couldn't move. Goosebumps covered his body. The area the man was in was once the storage area for a general store that had been located in "Guytown," a notorious red-light district in the late nineteenth century, an area filled with gambling establishments and brothels. The employee was finally released from his temporary paralysis and ran out of the building. No one knows the identity of the spirit who frequently makes his or her presence known, but several other employees have also been given the "cold shoulder" in this area.

On numerous occasions small items have been reported missing, only to be found later in the bar area. One day the bar manager noticed a round ball of mist or cloud-like vapor appear in the entryway to the B Side. This strange-looking gray mass emitted a misty liquid and remained in a stationary position above the entryway on the ceiling for two hours before dissipating. A manager walking by a table near where the strange mist had been reported noticed a puddle of water resting in the middle of a table. He wiped it off several times, but the spot kept returning before finally disappearing.

Another manager, closing up one night, finished pushing twenty-five chairs under the bar counter. After inspecting the place one more time, he returned to the bar only to find all of the chairs pulled back out! Then, in front of several people, all the lights simultaneously blew out on one side of the wall. At the same time, one of the red boards that cover the window flew off and landed on the floor. According to employees and patrons alike, occurrences like these are run of the mill at the Bitter End!

Carrington's Bluff

Address:	1900 David Street, Austin, Texas 78705
Phone:	512-479-0638
Fax:	512-476-4769
Toll Free Number:	1-800-871-8908
E-mail:	governorsinn@earthlink.net
Website:	www.governorsinnaustin.com
Contact:	Lisa Wiedemann
Accommodations:	Six guestrooms
Amenities:	Breakfast; private baths; air conditioning; ceiling fans; telephone; spacious porch overlooking Shoal Creek
References:	15

History

The property, an original outlot of the Republic of Texas, dates back to 1856 when L.D. Carrington bought the twenty-two-acre site from David Burnett. Carrington owned a general store, served as a city alderman and county commissioner, and was the commander of the brigade that protected Austin from Indian attacks. His farmhouse and porch faced Shoal Creek where he could keep an eye out for impending attacks. Carrington sold the house and land to Vicar Molesworth and his wife in 1877. The rooms in the main house are named after family members, including Vicar Molesworth (who passed away before ever setting foot in the house), Martha Carrington (Martha Hill Molesworth married a Carrington), Kathleen Molesworth, and L.D. Carrington. Across the street is the Carrington cottage, once the dairy barn. The Molesworths lived in the house from 1877 to 1919. The house sat vacant until G.M. Howell and his wife Eileen occupied it from the 1920s to 1960. Kathleen Molesworth occupied the house until 1974.

Phantoms

Friendly spirits often greet guests and staff of this lovely, cozy inn, as well as the adjacent cottage. To date, the general consensus is that a male spirit is confined to the cottage, while a female spirit watches over the main home. Reports confirm a presence that enjoys watching people, and a number of guests and staff have reported that while strolling through the downstairs dining area and library room, they often feel invisible eyes following their every movement. Guests often respond with an emphatic, "You have ghosts in this house!" Further questioning reveals that guests have things move around, seemingly on their own, hear footsteps, or encounter an actual apparition. In addition, there are the occasional sounds of someone walking downstairs through the dining room and into the library. Staff also report cleaning certain rooms and, upon returning minutes later, finding things moved all around. Sometimes Lisa's two dogs will jump up for no apparent reason and begin growling at an unseen presence.

One strange event at the inn involved the cottage television. It began one midnight in the Cottage Room where the innkeepers resided. As they were sleeping, the television suddenly turned on by itself to Channel 13. The startled innkeepers bolted upright in bed, got their bearings, then quickly got up to turn it off. Thinking it was some kind of strange electrical phenomenon or a cable malfunction, they turned the set off and went back to sleep.

This strange phenomenon continued for fourteen straight days, always at midnight. It was indeed baffling to the innkeepers, as there was no remote control device for the television. A knob had to be physically pulled out to turn on the appliance. No matter what the innkeepers tried, it didn't help; the TV continued to turn itself on. The cable company was called in but had no explanation for the malfunction and said to disconnect the cable box. Even after the innkeepers did this, the set continued to turn on—until the fifteenth day, when the unexplainable activity abruptly ceased. Thinking the event was some kind of weird electrical flaw (even though nothing unusual was ever found), the innkeepers were greatly relieved when the activity stopped. However in less than a month it began again, this time at three A.M. instead of midnight. This event continued for seven straight days, always at 3:00 A.M. Desperate and now convinced that this was the action of a mischievous ghost, they called out in frustration to their mysterious TV watcher: "Do whatever you want during the day, but please leave us alone at night so we can sleep!" From that day forward, there was never a reported incident with the television set.

Another eerie story involved a husband and wife who were visiting the inn and staying in the Martha Hill Carrington room downstairs adjacent to the library. While the husband was taking a shower (the door to their room was opened a crack), his wife was sitting in one of the library chairs talking to innkeeper Lisa Wiedemann. As both women were chatting, they heard the husband talking to someone in the shower. Apparently, while in the shower, the husband was shampooing his hair when he felt someone else massaging the shampoo into his scalp. His eyes were closed, and he naturally assumed that it was his wife. After awhile, the man said that he had had enough shampooing and asked "his wife" to stop so he could rinse his hair. But the shampooing continued, and the man again told "his wife" that he had had enough shampooing. Meanwhile, the innkeeper and the man's wife were listening to him calling out and were confused as to whom he was talking. Suddenly, the man burst out of the room wearing his robe and white as a ghost! He had realized that it couldn't possibly have been his wife with him in the shower, because the door had been latched from the inside. In a hopeful tone, however, he asked his wife if there was any way she could have entered the bathroom. She replied that it could not have been her because she had been in the library the entire time, talking to the innkeeper, Lisa. In fact, the two women told the dazed man they had heard him talking and couldn't figure out who he was talking to. Then the man told them just exactly what had happened, that a ghost had been shampooing his hair! He was extremely shaken and even a bit nauseated over what had transpired. Nothing happened to the couple for the remainder of their stay, but the husband, a vocal skeptic of the paranormal, quickly became a believer and came away with a memory he would never forget.

When visiting the charming Carrington's Bluff, it may happen that you get a free shampoo or some extra added TV time. If so, don't fight it—just relax and enjoy yourself!

The Driskill Hotel

Address:	604 Brazos Street, Austin, Texas 78701
Phone:	512-474-5911
Fax:	512-474-2214
Toll Free Number:	1-800-678-8946
E-mail:	information@driskillhotel.com
Website:	www.driskillhotel.com
Accommodations:	178 guestrooms and suites
Amenities:	The Driskill Grill; the Lobby Bar; Driskill Ballroom; Governor's Board Room; Maximilian Room
Payment:	American Express, Carte Blanche, Diners Club, Discover, MasterCard, Visa, personal checks, gift certificates, travelers checks
References:	8, 15, 16, 23, 36, 37

History

Missouri-born cattle baron "Colonel" (an honorary title) Jesse Lincoln Driskill made a fortune providing beef to the Confederacy during the Civil War. He built the Driskill Hotel in 1886 to serve as the Frontier Palace of the South in the capital city of Texas. Driskill lost the hotel in a poker game in 1887 and died three years later. Constructed in the Richardsonian Romanesque style from local brick and limestone, the hotel is characterized by arched windows, spacious balconies, and exceptional ornamentation. The hotel's most spectacular architectural features are the floor-to-ceiling arched doorways located at the entrance. Busts of Jesse and his two sons are placed high atop each entrance along with stylized heads of Texas longhorn steers.

Phantoms

According to management, the ghosts of the Driskill include: Colonel Jesse Driskill, a small child, Mrs. Bridges, Peter J. Lawless, two brides who died tragic deaths, and a few other phantoms who roam about this famous and historic hotel. Driskill, who was made an honorary colonel by the Confederate army during the Civil War, built the hotel at a cost of almost $400,000—an unheard of price at that time. People told him that he was foolish to spend that much money on a hotel, and he proved them right. He went bankrupt and lost the hotel in a high-stakes poker game. Three years later, in 1890, he passed away. It is said that since he was unable to enjoy his namesake creation, he haunts the hotel to this day. He makes his presence known by smoking his cigars in guests' rooms and playing with their bathroom lights.

A second spirit is simply called "The Small Child." According to Driskill lore, a U.S. senator was once staying at the hotel. While he was attending an event on the mezzanine, his four-year-old daughter was playing with a ball near the grand staircase. The little girl accidentally tripped and fell; she died instantly at the base of the stairs. Some nights guests hear her ghost bouncing the ball down the steps and giggling. If she makes too much noise, she can only be quieted by the front desk staff.

Another spirit is known as "Mrs. Bridges," a woman who worked the front desk for several years in the early part of the century. Though she didn't die in the hotel, Mrs Bridges is often seen there late at night. She is clothed in a Victorian dress and is walking from the vault out into the middle of the lobby, the site of the old front desk. She seems to fuss with the flower arrangements that would have been there in her day.

The spirit of Peter J. Lawless is also reported to roam the Driskill. Lawless lived in the hotel from 1886 until 1916. During these three decades the hotel was closed several times, but Lawless stayed on, often without staff. He had a key to his room and to the front door. He is sometimes seen in spirit on the fifth floor traditional side near the elevator. When the doors open, he checks his pocket watch.

A phantom female also haunts the hotel and is referred to as "Tragic Bride #1." This story goes back about thirty years. The wedding was scheduled to take place in the hotel, and the bride was staying there as well. The bride-to-be was told by her fiancée the night before their wedding that the engagement was off. The devastated girl ran up to her room and took her life by hanging herself. This is one of the Driskill's most active ghosts. She can be seen on the fourth floor traditional side in her wedding dress, walking the hallways. She is most often spotted by guests who are attending a wedding or bachelorette party. It is usually considered good luck for brides to see the ghost before their weddings.

Another spirit has been dubbed Tragic Bride #2. The woman, a Houston socialite, was engaged to be married. When her fiancée called the wedding off, she hurriedly left on a trip to Austin to recuperate. She booked a room at the Driskill for an entire week and went on a shopping spree with her ex-fiancée's credit cards. After "maxing out" all the cards, she returned to her hotel room, where she took her life. She was eventually discovered by a bellman. The woman's ghost is often seen in the hallways, particularly around Halloween, where she is wearing a wedding gown and sporting a handgun. She is also seen in the restrooms on the balcony level. A woman once went into the restroom while her husband waited outside the door. While the woman was in the stall, another woman suddenly stuck her head under the door and leered at her! The woman seated in the stall screamed loudly, and her husband came running into the bathroom. He felt something move past him, but he saw no one. When his wife described the woman she saw to the front desk staff, they immediately recognized the description of Tragic Bride #2.

Although these are the only spirits with actual names, several other entities are believed to haunt the hallways and corridors. The spirits are both helpful and mischievous: Hotel elevators ascend and descend without the help of guests or staff, yet no one ever gets on or off. The elevators have been repeatedly examined by repairmen, but no mechanical malfunction has been found. Housekeepers often report that the elevator doors will open without the buttons being pushed or find that the button to their destination floor has already been pushed by someone unseen. Guests have called the front desk in the middle of the night reporting that someone has pushed them out of bed. Other guests find that their furniture has moved during the night. Singer Annie Lennox, while staying at the Driskill during a concert tour, laid out two dresses on the bed prior to an appearance. After showering she found that one of the dresses had been put away. The lead singer (Johnette Napolitano) of her band wrote a song about Lennox's ghostly experience: "Ghost of a Texas Ladies Man." It is assumed that Lennox had been visited by the ghost of Colonel Driskell himself!

On one occasion a hotel banquet director was standing in front of the mirror by the tower elevators at around six in the morning when he heard laughter and conversation coming from the elevator. He waited for the noisy group to reach him, but when the elevator doors opened it was empty, and a cold wind brushed by him. Confused, the man was about to enter the elevator when he was startled to hear the same voices he had just heard now coming from behind him. Quickly turning around, he was stunned to see an empty corridor, yet he could hear voices continuing down the hall!

A hotel janitor was working in a guestroom on the fourth floor when the lights suddenly switched off and on, followed by water that began running in the bathroom sink. The janitor had experienced a similar incident months earlier while shampooing the rugs on the fifth floor. That time he kept hearing the doors opening and closing. So he attributed this recent incident to the spirits who also enjoyed toying with the ice machine even though it was unplugged. Another time he was greeted by an elderly man dressed in a tuxedo, walking toward room 529. The trouble was, you could see through this guest as he walked right through the door. The janitor followed close behind, opened the door to the room, and as he suspected, it was empty except for the faint smell of cigar smoke.

Jeanine Plumer, a historian and tour guide for Austin Promenade Tours, reports that Colonel Jesse Driskill is sometimes seen wandering through the old portion of the hotel. His spirit often leaves the odor of cigar smoke, and he seems to enjoy toying with bathroom lights. The young daughter of a senator who fell to her death on the grand staircase is said to be responsible for unexplained footsteps and cold spots on the stair and down certain hallways. The ghost of Mrs. Bridges is sighted only at night and only around the front desk, wearing Victorian clothing, and is usually accompanied by the smell of roses.

During 1997 one girl in a group of five, who began their evening in the Driskill lounge, went to the restroom while the others waited. While she was alone in the bathroom stall, an elderly woman peered in on her although the girl never heard the outside door open or close. Once outside, the girl asked her friends about the older woman who peeked in her stall. They all denied seeing anyone enter the bathroom while they were outside.

Peter Lawless, who sold tickets for the railroad in Austin for over thirty years, has only been witnessed on the fifth floor and is dressed in period clothing. He has been spotted outside a room, unlocking the door, and standing in the hallway and in front of the elevator. Housekeepers have a hard time completing their cleaning chores in room 419. After finishing, the maids frequently find footprints on the newly vacuumed floor, disturbed bedcovers, dresser drawers pulled open, and they report being overcome by the feeling of being watched and followed.

The Hideout

Address:	617 Congress Avenue, Austin, Texas 78701
Phone:	512-236-8485
Fax:	512-597-1224
E-mail:	shana@thehideout.org
Website:	thehideout.org
Contact:	Shana Merlin
Open:	daily from 7:00 A.M. to 2:00 A.M.; improv comedy on the weekends
References:	15, 16

History

During Sam Houston's second term as president of the Texas Republic, John Wahrenberger, the owner of the building, overheard a conversation between Houston supporters planning to steal the state land archives and move them to Houston. At that time Austin's possession of the land archives was the only thing that technically allowed Austin to remain the capital. Wahrenberger, a Mirabeau Lamar supporter, alerted city officials and prevented the document removal. Wahrenberger was rewarded by the gift of a city lot that is now 617 Congress. Wahrenberger, around 1849, built the westernmost part of the building (617 Congress), which became the first bakery (Wahrenberger Bakery) in the city and also served as a general store. During 1862 Wahrenberger moved away and gave the property to his sister Mary, who married a man named Lindeman.

From 1862 to 1880 the Kluge Restaurant and Saloon was in operation. The owner, Mr. Kluge, mysteriously drowned in Shoal Creek on September 14, 1880, and is buried at Oakwood Cemetery. From that point, 1883 to 1888, Bennett, Harris, and possibly Isaac Melasky ran a men's clothing store. Mr. and Mrs. Melasky had two infant twins who died in 1870 and are buried in Oakwood Cemetery. From 1893 to 1935 it was Chilton and Jackson Collateral Broker, jewelers and dealers in general merchandise. John A. Jackson took over the business and later became a pawnbroker and agent for the Steamboat Dixie and Lone Star Trailer. Jackson died June 16, 1943. From 1941 to 1951(?) the Rapp Brothers were news dealers, cloth dealers, along with Leutwylers Watch Shop. In 1952 it was Shaw Jewelers and Leutwylers Watch Shop; 1955-1960, Shaw Jewelers. From 1960 to 1973, Blomquist and Clark, men's clothing, and 1965, Blomquist and Clark Shoe Department Store. 615 Congress was a billiard hall in 1893, while 619 Congress was a shoe store in 1893.

Phantoms

As renovation was taking place during conversion to a dinner theater/cafe, several people claim to have experienced the strange and unexplained. Thanks to the diligent research and interviews conducted by our friend Jeanine Plumer, there are indications that the building's past has filtered through to the present. As Plumer suggests, "My experience has been that some haunted places are active during the renovation process, while others surface when things settle down. The age and history of the building and the fact that it was empty for so long makes it a place to watch." Mr. Kluge, who ran a restaurant/saloon in the building for almost twenty years, died suddenly and under questionable circumstances while bathing in Shoal Creek—he drowned in less than three feet of water. A man on horseback walking along the creek saw a dog sitting faithfully next to a pile of clothing. After continuing farther downstream, the man found Mr. Kluge's body floating in the river. The sudden death of Mr. Kluge under dubious circumstances and the fact that the building is possibly the oldest on Congress Avenue may contribute to the haunted nature of this structure.

During the construction and renovation process, a number of electrical and plumbing problems have taken place. Sometimes this is significant in that spirits usually do not like change and tend to show their displeasure by contributing to incidents that appear unexplainable. There were two separate occasions during the installation of modern plumbing, when the bathroom faucets had been turned off and the plumber was checking the pipes, that the water began flowing. The plumber was able to tell while inspecting the pipes that someone had opened the faucets, because water was moving through the pipes. Going back to the source, sure enough, both faucets had been left in the open position. Thinking it was one of the other workers in the building, he questioned them. None of them had been in the area where the faucets were located, so they couldn't have turned them on.

On another occasion, without explanation, all the electricity in the building suddenly went off. Someone other than a worker had tripped the breaker, and no worker was anywhere around that part of the building when it happened. All the men felt a little spooked after this happened, but it didn't end with a single event. Three times the lights went off without explanation during renovation. Finally, there were four electricians closing up the building. Three exited the outside back gate and locked it (as was required to keep curious visitors out) as a fourth electrician inspected the building before leaving to ensure that everything was shut down. As the electrician was exiting the building, he noticed that the back gate was wide open. When he checked later with the other men, they swore that as they left, they had secured the gate—it was tightly locked. Our guess is, after the building opens and has been operating for awhile, a number of other ghost stories will surface—perhaps Mr. Kluge remains behind to ensure another smooth transition in owners since his sudden demise in 1880!

Highlife Cafe

Address:	407 E. Seventh Street, Austin, Texas 78701
Phone:	512-474-5338
Fax:	512-476-4177
Contact:	Mary Hall Rodman, chef/owner
Open:	Sunday through Wednesday from 9:00 A.M. to 12:00 A.M.; and Thursday through Saturday from 9:00 A.M. to 1:00 A.M.
References:	15, 16

History

This rather nondescript building with a blue exterior is home to the Highlife Cafe where even the simplest dishes receive a little twist. Located away from the tourist congestion of 6th Street, chef/owner Mary Hall Rodman has earned a reputation for breakfast dishes that are almost otherworldly, like some of her clientele.

The building at 407 East Seventh Street was constructed in 1872 and designed as a home by Mr. Sheehan, owner of the limestone quarry, at Neuces and 7th Street where the Austin's Womens Club is today. Sheehan sold the building to a man named Reisher in 1875, and it became the offices and a boardinghouse for the New Orleans stagecoach. The stables for the stagecoach horses are where Love Joys is today. In 1886 a single woman with children, named Fanny Davis, purchased the building. She owned and lived at 407 until her death in the 1920s. Little is known about the building and its occupants during this time. It is believed, though, that it was a bordello. A high-dollar bordello. One of the few known facts about Miss Davis is that her son was a bartender on 6th Street for many years. Following Fanny's death it became a residence until the mid-forties.

During the 1940s this area became a predominately African American business district. From 1950 to 1964 the building was known as the California Hotel and was a popular place for visiting African American jazz and Big Band musicians to stay. In 1965 again it became a bordello. Rumor has it that at this time the longest running game of crap in the city's history took place. Apparently is was a mid-level house of ill repute until 1980 when ownership changed and it became an art studio/living quarters for the local punk rock community. This occupancy ended in 1987. The Highlife Cafe opened in July of 1996, an opening that included its spirited tenants.

Phantoms

The current occupants believe Miss Davis may be the frequently sighted apparition and the phantom responsible for the numerous mischievous events that take place regularly inside. For two years prior to this, the current part owner, Scott, maintained an office on the second floor. During his stay he never had anything unusual happen inside. However, less than two months after the Highlife Cafe had their grand opening, Scott was sitting at the bar with his stool turned toward the front of the cafe, when out of the corner of his eye he saw a woman walking up the stairs. She appeared to be wearing a long white dress with long sleeves. Her hair was gathered together on the top of her head in a bun. His first thought was that he knew all of the woman who had offices on the second floor, and none of them looked like the lady who had just ascended the stairwell. He waited to hear the opening or closing of an upstairs door, but no sound came. Now facing the stairs he saw the same woman walk back down the stairs and then back up again. Recently a rash of burglaries had been happening in the area. Scott's immediate concern was that someone who was not supposed to be in the building had somehow gotten in and didn't realize he was watching. Quickly he stood and went up the stairs. He opened the door of every office and checked each room thoroughly but found no one on the second floor. It never occurred to Scott that what he had just seen was a ghost.

Several journalists, who had planned an evening of poker, rented the wine cellar for an evening. They also had invited two strippers to dance. When the women arrived they changed clothing upstairs and then proceeded to the cellar for their performance. Later they walked back up the stairs and left. Not long after their departure, Scott heard one of the men yell up the stairs, "Hey, you can turn the lights back up! What? Turn the lights back up; the dancers are gone!"

Beneath the building there is not only a wine cellar but also a walk-in refrigerator. All of the electrical wiring on the basement level is connected. Because of this connection the cellar lights are never turned off—to do so one would also turn off the refrigerator.

In addition, there is one control panel that regulates the electricity on that level, and that control panel is located on the wall behind the bar. That evening Scott and his bartender were the only employees in the restaurant. Both claimed to have never touched the lights, and both could not recall anyone even going near that side of the bar the whole evening. Scott was sitting at a table, and Wayne was serving drinks on the opposite side of the bar from the control panel. When Scott went to the control panel he found that the switch, in fact, had been lowered. Confused, he descended the stairs to determine what was going on. An enthusiastic cheer greeted him. "Great light show!" He was told that the lights had been blinking on and off to the sound of the music. Not only that, when the strippers walked around the room the lights followed them the whole time. Scott began to suspect something was not right in the building.

On a particularly busy evening after which the cafe finally closed, Scott was standing outside, holding the door and waiting for the remaining staff to leave. Let us return to the busy evening. During that evening, at least three times, Scott had switched the CD player because it began playing the 5th CD, an oboe concerto. The cafe was empty, and before locking the door he remembered that the stereo had not been turned off. So he went back in and turned it off. Satisfied, he closed and locked the door, then walked up the street and had a drink at a local bar. When he said his good-byes and left his friend's bar, Scott impulsively decided to check the Highlife before heading home. When he opened the doors he saw the stereo lights shining in the darkness and heard the sounds of the oboe concerto. The hairs on the back of his neck stood up and reality struck home—the ghosts were at play.

An ex-boyfriend of a long-time employee also had an unusual experience in the building. As Jim was helping to wash dishes at the cafe on a particularly crowded night, he was standing behind the bar washing glasses after everyone had left the building. "Hey, someone is still in the building," Jim exclaimed. "There's a woman sitting on the sofa." He was facing towards the doorway leading into the sitting area. Knowing the building had no patrons, Scott continued counting the money and asked Jim, "Is she still there?"

Realizing the vision had come and gone, Jim remarked that the woman was gone. "What did she look like?" Scott inquired. "She was young, wearing a lengthy dress with long sleeves, and her hair was set on top of her head." "Hasn't anyone told you of our ghost?"

On a Tuesday morning, Lisa opened the door, entered the building, and went behind the bar to begin getting the cafe ready for the 9:00 A.M. opening. Out of the corner of her eye she saw a woman wearing a bright blue dress and sitting at one of the right front tables. Lisa's first thought was that she forgot to lock the door after she came in. As she turned toward the front of the building then back, she noticed the woman was gone. Lisa searched the building for the woman to no avail and went back behind the bar. Again, minutes later, out of the corner of her eye she saw the woman in the blue dress sitting at the same table. This time when she turned and faced the woman directly, Lisa clearly saw the woman sitting at the table. The radiant blue of the dress was what would later stand out in her mind. As she began walking around the bar towards the woman, for an instant Lisa's attention was diverted, and when she glanced back towards the table at the front of the building, the woman was gone.

One evening a fire on the block behind the building caused a power outage in the entire area. Nonetheless, Highlife lit candles and stayed opened until 12:30 A.M. The clientele was small and consisted mostly of regulars. One couple present on this evening were good friends of the owners. The husband happened to be an accomplished piano player and after some coercion agreed to play one song. In the shadowy candlelight and aware that the building was haunted, he chose to play the Alfred Hitchcock theme. Later that evening when the closing process was in full swing, Scott and an employee were taking the trash out the back door. Following this task while standing by the back boor, in the area of the piano both heard the clear striking of middle G on the piano.

The Spaghetti Warehouse

Address:	117 West 4th Street, Austin, Texas 78701
Phone:	512-476-4059
Fax:	512-476-4071
Contact:	Gerardo Baranovicht
Open:	Monday through Sunday from 11:00 A.M. to 2:00 A.M.
References:	15, 16

History

Connected to the Bitter End Bistro but with the entrance on 4th Street rather than Colorado Street, the brick building was constructed in the 1870s and served as a grocery warehouse. There are rumors of tunnels running under the building connecting to parts of old Austin that burned down long ago. The basement area, which serves as storage space, once connected to the underground tunnels, which are now sealed, at least the portion joining the warehouse.

Phantoms

The activity in the restaurant seems to be rather general due to the fact that a majority of the present staff are new to the building, and those who have been there for any length of time have only heard whisperings of haunted activity passed down second-hand over the years. What seems fairly obvious to us is that there must be a connection between the spirits of the Bitter End B Side and the Spaghetti Warehouse. After all, the restaurant bar and the Bitter End are only separated by a brick wall that may or may not have been there originally.

As far as the ghostly stories go, we were only able to come up with the fact that the place is "probably haunted," and that "strange things" continue to take place in parts of the building. One woman responded by saying that the basement is so spooky and has had so many "things" happen over the years, some of the staff refuse to go down there alone. Reported activities consist of cold spots, mysterious shadows that move along the walls before disappearing, the feeling of being watched or followed, strange mists or hazy forms appearing in the basement, and an occasional tap on the shoulder when the person is alone in the bar area.

This is definitely a spot that deserves additional research, and the fact that it adjoins the Bitter End, another notorious local Austin haunt, adds to its potential as a significant location for paranormal activity. When you visit for a bite to eat or have a drink at the bar, keep your senses tuned in to potential paranormal activity. Even if nothing happens, you're sure to have a good time inside this 1870s building that never sleeps.

The Tavern

Address:	922 West 12th Street Austin, Texas 78703
Phone:	512-474-7496
Fax:	512-474-8403
Contact:	Tom Lycan
Open:	Monday through Sunday from 11:00 A.M. to 2:00 A.M.
References:	15, 19

History

As their slogan says, "You're never too far from 12th and Lamar." The structure was built in 1921 by Niles Graham, who wanted to open a pub, but Prohibition got in the way, so it became a grocery store. Graham hired Hugo Kuehne to design the store on a then dirt road on the outskirts of town. The grocery store, modeled after a German public house, operated until the end of World War I. Then, during the Great Depression, the store moved next door, and the original building has operated since as a restaurant and later as a restaurant and bar. Today The Tavern is a local hangout, sports bar, and traditional pub, serving home cooked meals, ice-cold brews, and stories carved in the bar. The upstairs rooms still have the old numbers above the doors from a time when the building served as a brothel (or so the owner claims).

Phantoms

An interview with general manager Tom Lycan suggests that the spirit or spirits of The Tavern are very active. That the building served as a brothel and speakeasy during the 1920s-1930s probably accounts for the frequent sightings inside. According to Lycan, the spirit of a murdered lady of the night named Emily is the most frequent ghost guest at the establishment. She is frequently witnessed walking up or down the stairs, through doorways, and into the kitchen. Her presence has been felt by many staff and patrons, an event that usually triggers a person's hair standing on end or being surrounded by a cold gust of air.

There are constant reports of televisions being turned off by unseen hands. Staff and guests have heard unexplained sounds coming from unoccupied areas of the building during closing. A quick search always finds no one in that particular room. A waiter once witnessed a little girl sitting on a second floor window ledge for a moment before vanishing. Another staff person recalled seeing a woman standing in the dark near the corner of the pool hall. When he went to see who the person was, the image vanished.

The spirits of the woman and little girl may belong to Emily and her daughter. According to lore, Emily, a prostitute, and her daughter were killed by soldiers during the 1940s. Apparently a brawl between several men turned ugly, and the poor woman and child were caught up in the fight and murdered. Psychic activity reportedly began right after the event took place.

The Capital City Ghost Research Society, with renowned ghost hunter Martin Leal leading the way, investigated The Tavern. Leal and company discovered the legend of a prostitute named Emily who was either murdered in this building or died in childbirth, as well as her spirit, which still lingers inside. Employees have heard footsteps on the third floor of the building when no one was up there. They have also witnessed glasses fly off shelves on the first and second floor. After closing, they've heard a game of pool being played upstairs when no one was in the room.

Waitresses have reportedly been pinched or tapped on the shoulder as they passed the stair area while serving food and beverages. Many a night employees have reported the feeling of being watched or felt an icy breeze pass right through them both upstairs and down. Add the fact that some patrons have claimed to have seen a hazy apparition wander around upstairs before suddenly vanishing, and you have a good case for an active haunting.

An employee at the Conoco gas station across the street saw a woman standing at the second-story window of the bar. The woman was described as having short, brown hair and just staring down from an upstairs window when The Tavern was unoccupied. The Tavern's workers have christened the spirit "Emily." Further evidence that the ghost is probably a woman lies in the fact that the televisions frequently change to non-sports channels. Like sports fans loyal to their favorite team, the spirit of Emily is also loyal, in this case, to The Tavern.

Boerne

Known for its magnificent setting in the Texas Hill Country at the southern rim of the Edwards Plateau, Boerne (pronounced bernie) combines the best of the past with the best of the present only minutes from San Antonio. German immigrants first settled Cibolo Creek nearly 150 years ago, and today more than 140 historic structures remain in Boerne. The Guadalupe River lies a few miles from Boerne, along with miles of bicycle trails, scenic vistas, lakes, caves, and the spectacular Guadalupe River State Park.

Country Spirit

Address:	707 South Main Street, Boerne, Texas 78006
Phone:	830-249-3607
Contact:	Sue Martin
Open:	Sunday through Thursday from 11:00 A.M. to 9:00 P.M.; Friday and Saturday from 11:00 A.M. to 10:00 P.M.; Closed Tuesdays.
References:	2, 10, 15, 27, 36, 37

History

The building was one of Boerne's first two-story houses and was known as the Mansion House. It was built in the 1870s by French architect Frank LaMotte. In 1883 the property and house were sold to Matilda E. Worcester for $2,800. The gracious building has been a home for many of Boerne's prominent families including the Rudolph Carstanjens, Charles Gerfers, Henry Grahams, and Gilma Halls. During the early 1900s it served as an annex to the

Phillip Manor Hotel across the street, and a drugstore was located on the ground floor. Augusta Phillip Graham owned the home from 1923 to 1943. The Mansion House was remodeled with respect for its historical architectural integrity by Sue Martin, and it opened as the Country Spirit in the fall of 1984.

Phantoms

The spirits of Augusta Phillip Graham, David, and Fred consider the County Spirit their home. According to psychic investigators, the restaurant is a very active location. One lively spirit belongs to a young boy named David, who prefers to remain in the upstairs men's restroom. Local lore suggests that David was an orphan in his early teens who frequented the Mansion House. The cook gave him handouts, and the boy was allowed to play with the other children of the household. It seems that David was accidentally killed while playing in the driveway during the late 1880s. Since then the orphan boy seems content to remain in the only home he knew while alive.

Since becoming the Country Spirit restaurant, a number of eerie events have been reported in the building. A candle was once seen moving unassisted from one side of a table to the other as stunned guests, who were having dinner, looked on in amazement. A middle-aged man, sitting at the bar in the rear portion of the building, watched in awe and fear as four wine glasses suddenly flew off the shelves, one at a time, and smashed on the floor in front of him, narrowly missing his feet.

There have been other events as well: The beer spigot suddenly turns itself on, as if unseen hands are operating the equipment; spoons have lifted off countertops and flown across the kitchen, hitting the walls or landing on the floor. The lights in the bar will sometimes go out even though no one is anywhere near the switch that turns them off. A number of individuals, enjoying a drink upstairs, have heard partying coming from the unoccupied downstairs area. A quick check of the area reveals a deserted room. Footsteps are sometimes heard in the upstairs portion of the restaurant when it is unoccupied late at night.

Paranormal investigators have encountered the spirit of Augusta Phillip Graham in the women's bathroom, usually as a reflection in the mirror that glares back for an instant before vanishing. Graham has also been spotted standing in the ladies room when women walk in. Upon entering, women often see an "odd-looking" woman standing near the stalls and think nothing of it until the wraith suddenly vanishes as they take a second look. A third spirit, called Fred, has been seen eating at table 13 before dematerializing, or just sitting at the table watching the humans pass by until he's had enough sightseeing and just disappears.

A trip to one of Boerne's first two-story houses, now a wonderful restaurant, will most certainly liven your spirits and perhaps spark some otherworldly entertainment from the three patrons who, although deceased, still have a great time in the restaurant. The name is apropos for a place that is full of country spirits.

Ye Kendall Inn

Address:	128 West Blanco Road, Boerne, Texas 78006
Phone:	830-249-2138
Fax:	830-249-2138
Contact:	Shane & Vicki Schleyer
Website:	www.yekendallinn.com
Accommodations:	17 guestrooms and suites
Amenities:	Private baths; air conditioning; television; continental breakfast; a restaurant on the premises
References:	15, 27, 36, 37

History

Made of twenty-inch-thick limestone walls, Ye Kendall Inn played host to the likes of Jefferson Davis, Robert E. Lee, and Dwight D. Eisenhower. The history of Ye Kendall Inn began April 23, 1859, when John James sold the land to Erastus and Mary Sarah Reed. John F. Stendebach built the center section of the inn as their home, which was first called the Reed house. The Reeds began renting out their spare rooms. Harry W. Chipman leased the property from the Reeds, renting rooms to horsemen and stagecoach travelers.

Colonel Henry C. King and his wife, Jean Adams King, purchased the inn on May 4,1869. While Colonel King served as state senator and covered his district on horseback, Mrs. King ran The King Place. In 1878 C.J. Roundtree and W.L. Wadsworth of Dallas purchased The King Place and renamed it The Boerne Hotel. In 1882 Mr. Edmund King and his wife, Selina L. King, and children came to Boerne from England and leased The Boerne Hotel. King was killed in a hunting accident in back of the hotel on September 26, 1882. The Boerne Hotel served as an authentic stagecoach inn throughout the 1880s.

Dr. H. D. Barnitz bought the hotel in 1909 and changed the name to "Ye Kendall Inn." In 1914 Alfred Giles bought Ye Kendall Inn with plans to add cottages by the creek; this never materialized. Robert L. and Maude M. Hickman owned the inn from 1922 to 1943. After a succession of different owners from 1943 to 1960, the inn was bought by the William Grinnan family and was operated by them as a hotel and restaurant until 1970. The inn was bought and lovingly restored by Ed and Vicki Schleyer in 1982.

Phantoms

Restoring this old building to its former grandeur also resuscitated a dormant spirit or, as many believe, spirits. According to numerous reports of unexplained events that have taken place inside since 1982, the spirits of the Ye Kendall Inn are actively involved in the daily operations—especially greeting guests! Many witnesses have heard heavy footsteps on the upper floor when it is unoccupied. This unnerving event always leaves the staff baffled because no one is ever found in the area when the event is taking place.

A worker once fell as he attempted to install a bathroom fixture. It was as if an invisible hand pushed him off the ladder, causing him to fall through the floor as it gave way to his weight. The claw footed legs kept falling off the old bathtub no matter how many times they were securely fastened. Doors have frequently opened then slammed shut when staff and guests were not in the area, and doors that have been securely locked beforehand will occasionally manage to open on their own.

Staff working in the restaurant have reported that crystal prisms have fallen off the chandelier a number of times as if individually pulled off by an unseen hand and thrown to the floor. The doorknob between the restaurant and the shop will often rattle as if someone is trying to enter, even though a quick inspection reveals that no one is on the other side. Some lights in the building will suddenly dim or turn on and off without human assistance. A guest encountered an elderly woman wearing Victorian clothing, who said her name was Sarah before suddenly vanishing—the first owner's wife was named Sarah Reed.

Other haunted areas include: The Rose Room with its French queen bed, floral accompaniments, fireplace, and 12-foot ceilings where sightings have taken place and items either move or vanish. The Sewing Room located downstairs with an antique sewing machine and dressmaker's form has been witness to visits by Sarah Reed. The Sarah Reed Room, with its floral drapes, oak queen-size bed, 12-foot-high ceiling, and fireplace, is also frequented by the ghost of Sarah Reed, who enjoys looking in on guests as well as rearranging furniture. The Marcella Booth Room, named for the lady born at Ye Kendall Inn at the turn of the century, with its antique swing bed, 12-foot-high ceiling, and fireplace, frequently shows signs of spirited activity. The bed, after being made, exhibits signs of someone having just sat or slept on it by leaving a noticeable impression. The building also has frequent moving cold spots, and in many rooms there is the unsettling feeling that you are not alone—probably because you're not!

According to the owners of Ye Kendall, their spirits are just playful and enjoy lingering in their beautiful stage. At this house of spirits, life and afterlife frequently co-mingle with surprisingly enjoyable results.

Comfort

Comfort was established by German settlers in 1854, who established Camp Comfort there on their way to New Braunfels. The midtown area has been placed on the National Historic Register due to its many vintage structures. Also well known is the 1930 art deco Comfort Theater, currently used for live theater productions.

The Meyer Bed & Breakfast on Cypress Creek

Address:	845 High Street, Comfort, Texas 78013-2354
Phone:	830-249-2138
Toll Free Number:	1-800-364-2138
Website:	www.bbchannel.com/bbc/p211952.asp
Contact:	Shane Schleyer or Kate Barrett, innkeeper
Accommodations:	Nine units; two with kitchenettes
Amenities:	Private baths; full breakfast; swimming pool; cable television, air conditioning
References:	15

The Meyer Bed and Breakfast is located on Cypress Creek, just one block from historic downtown Comfort and within walking distance of the Guadalupe River. Amenities include nine suites and units, all with private baths, air conditioning, cable TV, and antique decor. There is an in-ground swimming pool, or you can fish or picnic on Cypress Creek. The spacious grounds on Cypress Creek make a perfect location for family reunions, weddings, or company picnics.

History

The Stage Stop was managed by Frederick Christian Meyer on the Old Spanish Trail. This building is the oldest in the Meyer Hotel complex, built in 1857. It was the last stop before the stage crossed the Guadalupe River going toward San Antonio. The Maternity House was added in 1872 to accommodate Mrs. Meyer's business as a midwife. She delivered babies for the women of the surrounding ranches in this quaint duplex. The duplex now provides a pair of comfortable two-room suites, each with a full-size bed and private bath. The Cottage was also built in the complex in 1872. One story has it that this cottage was built and used as a room for Mr. Meyer to recover in following his late night encounters with excessive alcoholic consumption.

This romantic cottage overlooks Cypress Creek and is a perfect place for two for a quiet, cozy getaway. The Cottage has a queen-size bed, a sitting room, and a private bath with a claw foot tub. The White House Hotel, built in 1887 when the railroad came to Comfort, houses the kitchen and the dining room on the first floor where a generous country breakfast is served each morning. The second floor has a beautiful room with a queen-size bed and private bath and a two-room suite with a queen-size bed, a full-size bed, a private bath, and a private screened porch overlooking Cypress Creek.

The Stucco Building is the newest of the buildings in the Meyer Hotel complex. Constructed in 1920, the building was operated as the Meyer Hotel by one of the Meyer daughters, Julia Ellenburger, until her death in 1956. Each of the four two-room suites has a full private bath. The old homestead is now the innkeeper's residence. In 1869 Mr. Meyer had a stone house built of locally quarried, hand-faced limestone. In this building Mr. Meyer and his wife, Ernestine Mueller Meyer, reared eight children and took in overnight guests.

The site of the original stage stop dates to 1857, and the Meyer House dates to 1862. Founded by German Freethinkers in 1854, the unincorporated town of Comfort is unique. With a population of only 1,350, it has over one hundred pre-1900 buildings in its National Historic District. Many of these are located in the center of what is considered the most complete nineteenth-century business district in Texas. Antique and craft shops abound and are within an easy stroll of the bed and breakfast. The "Treue Der Union" Monument in Comfort honors the courageous efforts of area men who were considered disloyal and then killed for refusing to join the Confederate army. It is the only monument to the Union that is located south of the Mason-Dixon Line and is one of only six sites around the nation that may fly the American flag at half-mast in perpetuity.

Phantoms

For all its history, the complex of buildings formerly called the Gaust Haus do not disappoint when it comes to ghostly tales. Friendly Kate Barrett and her daughter manage the complex, and during our visit to this treasure, situated along peaceful and serene Cypress Creek, we were able to enjoy the ambiance and stories, which represent only the tip of the paranormal iceberg at this establishment.

The Cottage, built in 1872, where Mr. Meyer would often sleep, was the scene of a sighting involving a little girl with red hair. A guest staying in the queen-size bed awoke one morning to the sight of a young girl with striking red hair looking at him from the foot of the bed. The startled guest couldn't believe what he was seeing and for a moment, thought that another guest's child or one of the staff's children has somehow managed to sneak into his room. Then the reality of the situation dawned on him. His door was locked, and within seconds the smiling child turned and vanished. Interestingly enough, when he described the event to a staff person, the red hair triggered a questioning look from the employee, who went inside the former hotel for a photograph of Julia Ellenburger. That's right! Juila had a striking head of red hair. Was Julia returning to her former home as a child, perhaps visiting the room her father used to occupy after making a few too many toasts?

Another haunted building is the Maternity House, which was added in 1872. Here, Mrs. Meyer performed the services of a midwife and helped deliver a number of Comfort children into this world. The ghost story, however, has little to do with crying babies or an apparition of Mrs. Meyer. The story in this building centers on room A next to the old stage stop building. It was in this room that a guest was reportedly confronted by a ghostly Native American woman, who appeared to her. As the story goes, the two became quite good friends and ended up talking to each other for over an hour. What they talked about and what language they were conversing in remains a mystery. Speculation is that the woman may have been from a local tribe who used to live on the banks of Cypress Creek. Perhaps she used to work in the old hotel or assisted the Meyers in some way. Or perhaps she is buried on the land and just drops in from time to time.

Cypress Creek also plays a part in the tale involving a crying woman who is often heard along the creek. Staff and guests have reported hearing a mournful wailing coming from behind the building complex in the evening. Numerous reports are pretty consistent with regard to the eerie sounds. People will be walking near the creek or resting in their rooms when a loud, soulful cry begins filtering through the woods in back of the house along the creek. Lasting for several minutes, the cries will have no particular source, almost surrounding the individuals until they suddenly cease. Some speculate that the cries might be related to a mother's loss of a child in the creek, possibly a Native American woman who lost her child during childbirth or through an accident.

Moving along to the Meyer Hotel complex built in 1920, the building was operated by Julia Meyer Ellenburger until 1956 when she passed. Some say her spirit never left the place she loved. There are four two-room suites in the building, and the activity seems to be spread evenly throughout the building. On the upper and lower level porches, guests often report being awakened by the sounds of furniture being dragged about or of people shuffling or walking outside their rooms late at night. To date no one has spotted the cause of the disturbances, yet they continue to occur. Sometimes the guests will walk outside to see who is responsible, and the noise will quickly abate—that is, until they go back inside their room. As their door shuts, the noises return. Perhaps they are imprints from the time guests did not have air conditioning and spent much of their time on the outside porches relaxing in long-since-removed furniture.

Four people once rented room 2. The husband and wife occupied the back bedroom, while the sister and mother-in-law occupied the front living space. Early one morning the wife was awakened by the sound of the shower going. She wondered who was up that early in the morning. Separating the two rooms is a door and window. She saw what she thought was her mother-in-law still lying in bed and correctly surmised that her sister was in the shower. It was only then she realized that something was wrong, because she glanced around the other room and saw her mother-in-law looking out the front window. Looking back to the bed, she once again saw an elderly, almost balding woman occupying a portion of the bed. Within seconds the old woman vanished. The guest wasn't frightened, just startled to see the uninvited visitor in their suite. Who was this visitor? No one has been able to establish that fact—yet!

Although the White House Hotel and Old Homestead seem less active than the other buildings, there are still occasional reports of mysterious shadows, cold spots, voices, and unexplained footsteps reported by guests and staff. As time goes by, we're sure we'll be hearing more about the congenial spirits of the Meyer House complex.

Corpus Christi

Spanish explorer Alonzo de Pineda discovered a beautiful, sheltered bay on Corpus Christi Day, in 1519, and so named it. The area was inhabited by Indian tribes, and while the Spanish and later the Mexicans knew of the bay, no settlement was established there until 1839. Colonizer Colonel Henry Lawrence Kinney founded a trading post there, doing business with some of the settlers in the area. The little post remained obscure until 1845, when its real growth began. Today it is one of America's major seaports and an important recreational area as well. It is the home of the Texas State Aquarium and the USS *Lexington* Museum.

Blackbeard's on the Beach

Address:	3117 Surfside Boulevard, Corpus Christi, Texas 78401
Phone:	361-884-1030
Fax:	361-884-1030
Website:	www.caller.com/entertain/rev132.htm/
Contact:	Steve Bonillas
Open:	Sunday through Thursday, 11:00 A.M. to 9:00 P.M.; Friday and Saturday, 11:00 A.M. to 10:00 P.M.; wheelchair accessible; full bar; live music on the patio Tuesday through Saturday
References:	15, 28

History

Blackbeard's is located along North Beach featuring Tex-Mex food, sandwiches, steaks, and seafood specials. It was previously known as the Spanish Kitchen. Steve Bonillas bought Blackbeard's in June 1991. The menu provided by Bonillas describes the building and legend as follows: Back in the summer of 1955 the original building was a weather-beaten old bar. The North Beach area was fun, active, and sometimes a wild place to hang out. On warm nights people crowded to the bar, laughing and talking. During one of those still summer nights before hurricane season, there was an argument over a red-haired woman. It started with angry words but ended with shots being fired. The red-haired woman and a fast-talking New Orleans roughneck sped north on the old causeway, and neither they nor their gold Hudson Hornet were ever seen again. But they left behind a man on the floor and possibly a ghost as well! Over the years strange occurrences have been reported by both customers and employees. Chairs move. Doors slam. Lights blink on and off. Salt shakers jump from table to table. Arguments can be heard long after the last customer has gone. One old-timer used to order two beers every time he came in. He left the second one on the bar for the ghost!

In 1962 flamboyant entrepreneur Colonel Larry Platt built a new little bar and added a dining room. He called it the Spanish

Kitchen, and from the start it was the "in" place to go on North Beach. Popular for good food, fun, and a gathering place for friends and visitors, the Spanish Kitchen tradition continues today as Blackbeard's on the Beach. Is the ghost a Spanish explorer, a forgotten Texas soldier, or victim of foul play—who knows? Some do and some don't believe in ghosts...but at Blackbeard's we still leave a beer on the bar just in case that old spirit is thirsty!

Although the ghost story told on the back of the menu is entertaining, according to Bonillas, it was a fabrication, probably to entice patrons into the bar. The "real" ghost came from the old bar at a time when there were small apartments next to it, occupying the same lots. An oil roughneck in his mid-forties was renting one of the apartments and would visit the Spanish Kitchen every night and have a few brews. The man always carried a hunting rifle and played the same song, "As Time Goes By," repeatedly on the jukebox. One night the man downed his beer, walked out of the bar and into his apartment, where he put a shotgun to his mouth and pulled the trigger. He was said to be despondent over the loss of his girlfriend. The man's spirit never left the bar he enjoyed in life.

Phantoms

A cook came in one morning and heard a noise coming from the dining area. Investigating, the cook was shocked to see the salt and pepper shakers dancing up and down on an empty table, as if an unseen force were toying with them. Within seconds the shakers came to rest on the table, and all the chairs suddenly flew away from the table as if the same force yanked them all back in a fit of anger. Needless to say, the cook vanished quicker than you could say "ghost," according to Bonillas.

After buying the restaurant, Bonillas was alone in the building. As he stood at the front counter making preparations for the day's clientele, the front door suddenly opened then closed, as if an invisible customer had just entered the establishment. Bonillas went to the door, thinking that someone had come to look inside and then turned to leave. When Bonillas opened the door and looked outside, there was no one anywhere around. The wind that day was blowing directly at the front door, making it extremely difficult to open the door, yet it had opened effortlessly. On another occasion some customers were saying they didn't believe in ghosts. Suddenly the ceiling fan above their table began to vibrate violently, and the light globe crashed down onto the table in front of the skeptical patrons.

There was a period of several months when the lights would flicker on and off, even the newly installed ones. This occurred only in the main dining area. No electrician could find the problem, and one day the problems just mysteriously ceased. One summer morning two girls came in to report that the jukebox was on after hours and playing loudly the night before. Bonillas had to show the girls that the place had no jukebox.

Several summers in a row, on July 4th, a major explosion occurred to the electrical line running to Blackbeard's, putting the establishment out of business for several hours. Additionally, several people have reported seeing an apparition floating through the building, although no one could tell if it was a male or female.

Recently a wall-mounted television, securely anchored to the interior cinder block wall, was ripped out of the wall and flew across the room, narrowly missing a boy. The television worked afterward but was never remounted. Instead, another television was anchored in the same manner. It has not been disturbed since it was put into service.

The occasional cold spots, chairs being moved by unseen hands, doors opening and closing on their own, items flying off of tables and falling from the walls, strange voices, and eerie feelings of being watched or followed are part of the ambiance of this haunted establishment. According to Bonillas, a majority of the paranormal events seem to occur during the summer months, so if you prefer not to dine in the company of spirits, try visiting Blackbeard's before or after summer is over.

Dallas

A present-day population of over a million people belies the fact that the first Anglo-American settler built a lone cabin in 1841 in what is now downtown Dallas. Two years later the "town" consisted of two log cabins. By the mid-1870s Dallas had become a thriving business town and market center due to several immigrations of skilled and cultured groups of French, German, Swiss, English, and other Europeans. Today Dallas, second in size to Houston, is regarded as the most metropolitan and cosmopolitan city in Texas. Dallas is the Southwest's largest banking center, the leader in wholesale business, second in the nation for insurance company home offices, third in the nation in "million dollar" companies, and number two in convention sites.

Snuffer's Restaurant

Address:	3526 Greenville Avenue, Dallas, Texas 75206
Phone:	214-826-6850
Fax:	214-824-4087
E-mail:	owners@snuffers.com
Contact:	Pat Snuffer/Steve Cole
Website:	www.snuffers.com
Business Hours:	The restaurant serves until 2:00 A.M., seven days a week.
References:	5, 7, 8, 15, 26, 37

History

Pat Snuffer opened this restaurant on June 28, 1978. Business continued to grow so Snuffer's purchased an adjacent lot containing a gas station and garage, and on March 2, 1987, Snuffer's Patio opened for business. The Patio contained 35 tables and a service bar. The original Snuffer's consisted of a small one-room space that seated 55 customers. The original tables and booths are still used today in the Front Room. The Back Room doubled seating in 1979. It's the burger and cheddar fries that have guaranteed an international reputation.

Phantoms

After additions were made to the original building, an unidentified spirit began appearing. The frequently sighted ghost was witnessed wandering though the hallway that connects the old building to the new one. There were cold spots and drafts of freezing air that would suddenly manifest in areas not susceptible to drafts. Doors would open by themselves, and unexplained footsteps would be heard in portions of the remodeled addition.

Mitchel Whitington of Dallas provided this recent story. Over the years the restaurant has held a secret: It is haunted by at least two spirits. The dark, hazy figure of a man has been spotted in an old hallway joining the original section of the restaurant and a newer addition. The restrooms are located off the hallway, and when Snuffer's closes for the evening and the crew is shutting down, the door to the gentlemen's room has been heard swinging open by itself. Some of the staff feel this is the spirit of a man who was killed in the old part of the building long before Pat Snuffer opened his restaurant. The apparition has even been witnessed stepping a few feet out into the restaurant before vanishing in the hallway.

Another phantom figure occasionally spotted in the restaurant belongs to the lady in black. This mysterious woman of unknown origin usually vanishes as quickly as she appears. Other reported events include unexplainable noises, staff being touched by invisible hands while working alone, and nicely arranged table settings found in disarray. The overhead lights will occasionally swing by themselves as if pushed by an unseen guest.

Pat Snuffer told Catherine Cuellar of *The Dallas Morning News* during an interview that he didn't believe in ghosts before opening Snuffer's in 1978, but by the following January he knew the place was haunted. Manifestations have occurred in the original portion of the restaurant. Snuffer and his staff often get cold chills, hear their names called out, feel a phantom hand on their shoulders, and have had glassware and ashtrays inexplicably move from their original locations in unoccupied rooms. Although the ghosts have never hurt anyone, Snuffer didn't like to talk about ghosts while in the building.

Perhaps when adjacent property was purchased to enlarge the restaurant, the owners bought more than the land. The folks at Snuffer's continue to serve up their delicious burgers, though, without worrying too much about the spirits that share their restaurant. Their presence is only a minor annoyance and makes for great conversation over a plate of cheddar fries.

Sons of Hermann Hall

Address: 3414 Elm Street, Dallas, Texas 75371-2077, P.O. Box 710277, Dallas, Texas 75371-2077
Phone: 214-747-4422
Phone/Fax: 214-341-8978
Website: www.sonsofhermann.com
Contact: Jo Nicodemus
Open: Wednesday-Saturday from 5:00 P.M. and some Sundays (Closed Monday and Tuesdays); the upstairs ballroom has a hardwood dance floor, a full bar, a raised stage and complete professional sound system.
References: 5, 15

History

Hermann Sons was founded in Texas in 1861 by two German immigrants who migrated from New York City. The Grand Lodge or headquarters is located in San Antonio, Texas, and there are 154 local lodges in 139 communities across Texas. The Sons of Hermann Hall in Dallas has a long and colorful history. The two Texas Sons of Hermann lodges in the hall today are Dallas #22 and Columbia #60. Dallas Lodge #22 was chartered in 1890 as Uhland Lodge #22. Columbia Lodge was chartered in 1893. In 1910 the then four Dallas lodges (out of necessity and, more importantly, unity) pooled their resources and built the hall at 3414 Elm. The grand opening was held in April of 1911. The Dallas Sons of Hermann Hall is a Texas Historic Landmark.

Phantoms

The spirits of the building are not afraid to show themselves. Recently a dozen board members were meeting downstairs when they heard children laughing and playing in the back room. After carefully looking around for the playful kids, the group realized they were not of this world. Jo Nicodemus has plenty of stories about the spirited establishment, including the frequent, yet unexplained, footsteps coming from the unoccupied upstairs area, as

well as the sounds of chairs being moved when only a single individual is inside.

During the filming of the television show *Walker, Texas Ranger,* several extras were having a late-night drink in the downstairs bar when a lavishly dressed couple (a man in a top hat and woman in a long dress) walked in from the only unlocked entrance on Elm Street, right through the downstairs corridor. The couple looked like cast members decked out in costumes going to a party. No one saw where they went, and the couple never came back down the hall. After a few minutes a search was carried out, but the couple had vanished. There are many other stories of doors slamming shut unassisted, pictures suddenly falling off the walls, and voices echoing through the building when the hall is locked to guests.

Numerous times members have heard doors open and shut on their own and have listened as furniture is moved around in the unoccupied upstairs ballroom. Upon checking out the eerie noise, the room is always found to be empty. Other times a man's voice is heard harshly scolding children. The man is believed to be the former caretaker Louie Bernardt, who used to shout at the children to stop playing in the building.

One night Ms. Nicodemus was doing some bookkeeping with another member. They were alone in the building. The member suddenly grabbed Ms. Nicodemus's arm. She had a terrified expression on her face and said, "My God, someone just walked past the door!" Both women became very nervous. They knew it had to be a ghost. Ms. Nicodemus says this kind of thing happens quite frequently. She also spoke of a photo someone had taken one evening of the band playing in the haunted ballroom. The developed photograph showed a vague outline of a skeleton with shoulder-length hair, hands, and fingers, standing next to a band member. Unfortunately the person who took the picture never gave it back to Ms. Nicodemus; however, she says that it will be forever etched in her memory! Perhaps the voluminous memories of the past are indelibly imprinted on the fabric of the hall where spirits drink and enjoy music and dancing and reveling in life and the afterlife, separated only by the thin veil of death.

El Paso

For over 400 years El Paso has been a favorite destination for visitors from all over the world. During 1581 the Rodriguez-Chamuscado expedition reached the Pass of the North. In 1598 Don Juan de Onate colonized the area, officially naming it "El Paso del Norte." In 1827 Juan Maria Ponce de Leon built a hacienda in what is now downtown El Paso. By 1849 the first U.S. Army post was founded to protect the settlers from marauding Apaches and Comanches. During 1858 and 1859 El Paso served as a major stop for the famous Butterfield Overland Mail coach. In 1873 El Paso became a U.S. city. During 1881 the Southern Pacific Railroad established the cornerstone of an east/west hookup here. From 1881 to 1887 gunfighters, cattle rustlers, saloons, famous marshals, and Texas Rangers became an integral part of El Paso's history. In 1916 General "Black Jack" Pershing began his expedition to find Pancho Villa in El Paso. It's a Texas city with international and otherworldly roots.

Camino Real Hotel El Paso

Address:	101 South El Paso Street, El Paso, Texas 79901
Phone:	915-534-3000
Fax:	915-534-3024
E-mail:	help@caminoreal.com
Website:	www.caminoreal.com
Accommodations:	17-story hotel with 375 units including 32 suites
Amenities:	Private baths; cable television; two restaurants, lounge; heated outdoor pool; health club
References:	15, 21, 25

History

The hotel's builder, Zach T. White, was drawn to El Paso by its magical name, "Pass of the North." After witnessing the 1892 burning of the Grand Central Hotel, which stood on the site of the present-day Mills Building, White dreamed of an elegant hotel that would be the center of social life and a gathering place for tourists. The local architectural firm of Trost and Trost designed a brick, steel, and terra-cotta building, with interior walls made of gypsum from nearby White Sands National Monument, which was structurally sound and fireproof. The Hotel Paso del Norte opened Thanksgiving Day 1912 with a lavish ball and was hailed as the "Showplace of the West."

The hotel supported its own bakery, ice factory, butcher shop, laundry, and bar stocked with every known liquor. The rooftop ballroom and patio were the scene of many lavish dances. It was also a favored place to gather and watch the progress of the Mexican Revolution and Pancho Villa across the river. The hotel claimed that more head of cattle were bought or sold in its lobby than at any other single location in the world. The hotel remained in the White family until 1970, when TGK Investment Co., Ltd. bought the hotel from Mary and Katherine White, the daughters of Zach T. White. During 1986 a seventeen-story tower was added.

Phantoms

This beautiful old historic landmark boasts an intriguing history, which includes the rumored presence of a female specter, who has been spotted wearing a white dress or gown in the basement of the hotel. The forlorn woman frequently appears, walking through the basement area, and sometimes turns to stare at the cleaning staff before vanishing.

Legend has it that one of the first events held at the hotel was a planned wedding, which was to take place on the tenth floor. The bride was pregnant, the groom didn't show up, and the humiliated and despondent bride leapt from a tenth-floor window to her death. The area where the troubled woman took her life, now an equipment storage area, does not deter the phantom bride from making her presence known to staff, including an engineer who witnessed a spectral woman, dressed for a wedding, manifest then vanish in front of him.

On the mezzanine level where the older part of the hotel joins the newer portion, housekeepers report that while they are cleaning, a door suddenly appears where there is no door. Behind the phantom door they will often hear loud noises as if people are partying. When they go to report the incident, they return with management to find that the door has vanished.

In the older portion of the hotel, the night manager entered on El Paso Street. The area now houses the Dome Bar, which was built in 1986. As the manager entered the door to the bar, he glanced over at a mural, which is a contemporary rendering that includes a group of people standing around a piano. He made his way to the bar and went behind the counter to tally up the night's receipts. As he stood there, he felt a chill engulf him. Distracted, he looked up and over at the mural. As he was transfixed on the mural, he watched a woman glide out of the mural and stand on the floor in front of him. She was dressed in period attire with a flowered hat. The phantom woman looked puzzled as she continuously glanced from side to side with a "where am I" expression on her face. She never looked at the manager, but as he moved in her direction, the woman suddenly floated up and dissolved back into the mural. The confused and frightened manager gathered his receipts and, post haste, left the building to conduct his business elsewhere. Several weeks later another employee reported seeing the same woman step out of the mural and appear in front of him. Not waiting to see if she ever made it back into the painting, he ran out of the building as fast as his feet would carry him.

During remodeling work, workers on the fifth floor often reported feeling "something wicked" stalking them. Although they never saw anything, there was a constant feeling of being watched or followed and of something lurking in the hallways as they passed through. In time none of the workers wanted to work in the area alone. In fact some of the workers reported having their tools stolen from their toolboxes only to appear somewhere else on the fifth floor. Workers frequently called security, thinking an intruder was playing jokes on them. The security men never found anyone besides the workers on the fifth floor during remodeling.

Several flight attendants from Southwest Airlines were checked into fifth-floor rooms but refused to spend the night because their televisions would suddenly turn on and off by themselves, even after being unplugged. A couple of the women reportedly stood helplessly in the hallway as a lady in a bathrobe passed right through them and then vanished.

A suicide occurred one Saturday afternoon when a man jumped from a tenth-floor window of the new tower and hit the roof of the manager's office on the third floor. The body didn't go through the roof, but since that time there have been reports of disturbances coming from the tenth-floor area where the man jumped, and in the manager's office where the body landed. Some items have been knocked off the office walls, while others suddenly disappear from the night manager's desk. Loud, unexplainable banging and thumping noises often come from the tenth floor as well as inside the manager's office. Although this beautiful hotel is filled with modern amenities, its spirited past somehow continues to filter through its rooms and corridors, bewildering as well as delighting staff and guests.

L & J Cafe Inc.

Address:	3622 E. Missouri Avenue, El Paso, Texas 79903
Phone:	915-566-8418
Fax:	915-566-4070
E-mail:	ladcafe@aol.com
Contact:	Leo A. Duran
Business Hours:	Closed on Sunday, it is open Monday through Friday from 10:00 A.M. to 8:00 P.M., and on Saturday from 10:00 A.M. to 6:00 P.M.
References:	15, 21

History

Also known locally as "the old place by the graveyard," the restaurant is situated roughly 50 feet from the old Concordia Cemetery. Three generations of the Flores and Duran families have operated this restaurant. Built in 1904 as a residence, the building also housed an apartment complex. In 1927 Antonio O. Flores decided to start his own business and found the perfect place across the street from the Concordia Cemetery, a landmark since the 1850s. Flores now had a building that could serve customers and also serve as a residence. When he opened his establishment on September 19, 1927, Prohibition was in full swing. Flores operated his unnamed bar, which catered to locals who bought the Flores home brew as well as contraband liquor from across the border. Flores,

with his wife Juanita G., ran a very successful business while raising their children. During Prohibition, Flores, well known and liked, particularly by law enforcement personnel, was continually tipped off prior to a raid.

After Prohibition in 1934 the now legitimized establishment became Tony's Place. The bar/cafe served soldiers from Fort Bliss and locals who came for the great food and to relax. In 1968, after forty-one years of operating Tony's Place, the business passed to Lilia Flores Duran and her husband John G. Duran. The second generation was now in charge of L & J's. On February 24, 1988, current owner and third generation family member Leo A. Duran began running the business with his wife, Frances. The Durans continue the family tradition of great food and friendly service and a place to come and relax. The former attached three-and-a-half-bedroom residence, used by the family for the last time in the early 1990s, now serves as a storage area for their locally grown chilies and as office space.

Phantoms

Situated on fifty-four acres, the historic Concordia Cemetery has about 65,000 plots and at least fifteen separate sections with burials dating as far back as 1850. Directly across the street is the cafe/bar. No wonder the locale lends itself so readily to ghost tales. The cemetery was once part of the Hugh and Juana Stephenson hacienda. Stephenson was from Missouri, and he married Doña Juana Ascarate, a local who subsequently died in 1856 and became the first person buried in the cemetery.

The cemetery is the site of a number of hauntings, with many of the stories circulated by those who have worked at L & J's. Employees have frequently heard wailing and moaning sounds and experienced spectral lights floating through the cemetery late at night. A tour group passing through the old cemetery was pelted by limes, even though there are no lime trees or limes anywhere around. Others have heard the sorrowful sound of a woman wailing and sobbing late at night. Perhaps, as the legend goes, the horrible wailing was caused by a woman who supposedly died in childbirth but was subsequently found to have been buried alive. There has also been a spectral wagon sighted, carrying a casket through the cemetery, followed by a woman in black who suddenly vanishes. There are also those who swear they have seen the ghost of John Wesley Hardin, who was born May 26, 1853, and buried in the cemetery on August 19, 1895. Hardin is often referred to as the "dark angel of Texas." The fact is, on any given night you might see spirits inside L & J's or across the street in the cemetery. It's that haunted!

Leo Duran told us that one time, while living in the building, he was suddenly awakened by the loud sounds of a woman crying, as if in inconsolable pain. It didn't take him long to realize that the sounds were coming from the cemetery. Fearing that a girl was being raped, he called the police, grabbed his gun, and ran across the street. He propped himself up on the six-foot-high fence with gun in hand to see if he could pinpoint where the sounds were coming from. For ten minutes the ghastly wailing continued. When the police arrived they heard the moaning and entered the cemetery. As they did so, the sounds stopped instantly. The cause of the crying was never determined. Duran also told about the spectral fires that have been witnessed from his parking lot by staff and patrons after closing at 2:00 A.M. The fires looked so real that the fire department was summoned by those looking on in disbelief. After arriving and inspecting the cemetery, the firemen found no evidence of a fire.

Inside the building, a former employee, closing the bar and clocking out in the room between the office and cafe, saw a tall, well-dressed man gazing around the restaurant as if inspecting it. Not noticing the woman, the strange gentleman finally vanished. The next day the woman approached Duran with her story. As she was talking she noticed a picture on the back of a menu he was holding, and she pointed to a face, saying, "Who is this man?" Duran replied that the two photos on the back were of his grandfather Antonio and his father, John, then asked why. Visibly shaken, the woman pointed to the photo of Duran's grandfather and said without hesitation that she had witnessed Antonio Flores standing in the restaurant before vanishing.

Another incident involved a coffeemaker in the dining room that would suddenly begin brewing coffee without the assistance of the staff. This inexplicably continued until one day the brand of coffee was changed. From that day the otherworldly coffeemaker stopped brewing voluntarily for the staff and guests.

There have been occasional reports by those wearing aprons in the kitchen that someone invisible has come up from behind and gently tugged on the string to release the apron. When this happens, no one else—human that is—can be found anywhere around. Finally the windows in the bar have been known to suddenly and mysteriously open and close three or four times in succession before stopping. The windows have to be opened by hand, and there is no one in sight when this occurs.

The spirits keep Duran and the staff on their toes, along with the customers who can't seem to get enough of this wonderful, family-owned restaurant across from the old cemetery. It's a must visit gem in El Paso.

La Hacienda Restaurant & Parilla Patio Grill

Address:	1720 W. Paisano Drive, El Paso, Texas 79922
Phone:	915-533-1919
Fax:	915-533-3636
Website:	lahaciendarestaurant.com
Contact:	Chip & Jo Johns
Open:	Sunday through Thursday 11:00 A.M. to 11:00 P.M.; Friday and Saturday from 11:00 A.M. to 1:00 A.M.; Mexican food luncheon buffet is served Monday through Friday from 11:30 A.M. to 2:00 P.M.; Live musicians play six nights a week; bands play on the patio during summer months
References:	15

History

The building housing La Hacienda was constructed by Simeon Hart as a residence and gristmill in 1849 for his bride, Jesusita. The California Column arrived and established the Union army headquarters in the area during 1862. In 1881 the military initially moved their entire base near La Hacienda then shifted locations to the current site of Fort Bliss. The restaurant has been in operation since 1940. An extensive collection of photographs and memorabilia are featured inside including the death mask of Pancho Villa. The 10,000-square-foot building contains the real Rosa's Cantina, from Marty Robbins fame, and the 6,000-square-foot patio. The Hart's Mill Patio has its own bar circled with handmade chairs depicting the "star of Texas" and is surrounded with flowering plants and trees. A number of monuments outside of the building commemorate Don Juan de Onate's 1598 crossing, the first real colonization of the United States as well as the beginning of the first highway in the United States, called the Camino Real, which stretched from Mexico City through Hart's Mill and on to Santa Fe, New Mexico.

Phantoms

During the early 1900s General John J. "Blackjack" Pershing went on his quest to capture Pancho Villa. One of the rumored ghosts who haunt the building is, you guessed it, none other than Pancho Villa. He is occasionally sighted in his namesake room. There are also reports of the famous Spanish explorer Don Juan de Onate visiting the patio area of the restaurant. Onate reportedly crossed the Rio Grande in 1598 near the spot of La Hacienda with 600 companions.

Two additional spirits haunt this quaint building. One spirit called John, a man in his twenties, has been frequently sighted by staff and guests. Psychics spending time inside picked up on his energy and found themselves hard put to exit the building. Every time one of the psychics tried to leave, "something" kept pulling and tugging at her hair and clothing. The ghostly tug-of-war was eventually won by the psychic, who decided never to return. A second spirit belongs to a woman who is frequently spotted sitting on a barstool in the basement bar, smoking a cigarette and laughing at people who see her.

It is also said that on certain nights the apparition of a woman can be seen walking near the restaurant, weeping loudly and asking for her children, who have drowned in the river. Other reported events inside include staff who have witnessed plates and utensils suddenly move or fly off tables on their own; disembodied footsteps that make their way through unoccupied parts of the building; ghostly voices that call out to staff persons; cold spots that suddenly materialize in the dining area; and doors that open by themselves.

Some guests have reported feeling breezes that feel as if a woman's skirt has brushed up against them. Staff have sometimes opened in the morning and found pictures on the wall tilted in odd directions. Chairs that have been carefully placed around tables after closing will be found moved into aisle spots the next day. Place mats that were put in certain spots the prior evening have been found relocated the next day.

La Hacienda stands on the shores of the mighty Rio Grande, a proud monument to Native Americans, the Spanish, the military, founding fathers, travelers, cowboys, ladies of the night, travelers, guests, and ghosts.

Fort McKavett

The park is located twenty-three miles west of Menard. It was originally called Camp San Saba because it overlooks the headwaters of the San Saba River Valley.

Fort McKavett State Historical Park

Address:	P.O. Box 867, Fort McKavett, Texas 76841
Phone:	915-396-2358
Fax:	915-396-2818
E-mail:	mckavett@airmail.net
Contact:	Kurt Kemp
Open:	8:00 A.M. to 5:00 P.M. daily-facilities include picnic tables, grills, and drinking water. The park offers a Texas State Park Store.
References:	15, 18

History

The fort was established by five companies of the Eighth Infantry in March of 1852 to protect frontier settlers and travelers on Upper El Paso Road. The camp was later renamed for Captain Henry McKavett, killed at the battle of Monterey on September 21, 1846. The fort was abandoned March 1859 and reoccupied April 1868. When the U.S. Army returned to Fort McKavett in April of 1868, none but the commanding officer's quarters were habitable. The task of reconstruction fell to the Fourth Cavalry, along with reinforcements from three companies of the 38th Infantry, all of whom were African Americans.

Apparently a settlement known as "Scabtown" arose on the opposite banks of the San Saba River and with it, discipline problems. Colonel Ranald S. Mackenzie took command of the 38th Infantry in 1869. By September of that year, the 38th and the 41st were combined to form the 24th Infantry of the United States Army. This company, along with the 25th Infantry and the 9th and 10th Cavalries, comprised the renowned buffalo soldiers, the African American troops of fame and legend. Fort McKavett was not the object of hostile attacks in the late 1860s and the 1870s. Rather, the troops there provided support for other campaigns throughout neighboring territories. By the late 1870s Indian wars in Texas were over, and Fort McKavett began closing down operations in 1882. By midyear 1883 the post was officially closed. Buildings had been turned over to local civilians. Those buildings that were occupied and cared for throughout the years still stand in good repair. The nearby Scabtown all but disappeared, except for the cemetery and a few other buildings.

Phantoms

While Carol Rust was working on a story entitled "Holding Down the Fort" for the *Houston Chronicle*, she had an encounter with its ghosts. The following are excerpts from Rust's article:

"If you know the fort, it is an 'L-shaped' design leading from the infirmary at one end of the 'L' to the 'war office,' I guess you'd call it, at the other end. I was standing right by the fort in the outside corner of the L with the wind blowing through my hair when I heard heavy footsteps, like those made with boots, walking slowly and (in my imagination's eye) pensively from one end of the 'L' to the other, complete with Doppler effect. I could just picture a man bent slightly forward, walking and thinking with his arms clasped behind his back."

Continuing, Rust said, "All of eight people live at Fort McKavett, a dot on the map where the trading post is the hottest spot in town and the ruins of an old army post play host to ghosts." According to Rust, today the trading post is a no-frills establishment and the only place within thirty miles to buy gas or toilet paper, get a hunting license or fresh deer sausage, or choose from a sparse stock of groceries. A visitor walks alone through white stone doorways absent of doors, into rooms with no ceilings, and stands in front of perfectly cut stone fireplaces that haven't been used for nearly a century. The perpetually blowing winter wind rumbling past his ears may sound faintly like a parade drum in the distance, but there's only prairie grass rustling on the former parade grounds.

Standing there, where the absence of urban noise is almost deafening, it's easy to understand the isolation that haunted soldiers stationed at the fort established as an Indian outpost in 1851. It was an isolation that gnawed so deeply that scores of soldiers deserted despite penalties that ranged from death to branding: A "D" was burned onto the soldier's hip, then he was kicked out into the heart of rattlesnake and Comanche country, bereft of weapons or provisions. Still, plenty of men risked the consequences and abandoned the fort at the first chance that presented itself, some for the bright lights of San Antonio to the southeast, others to El Paso to the west, and some just as far away as they could get. It's not that this part of West Texas is unattractive, although it's just two hours from Fort Clark near the border town of Del Rio, which prompted the famous quote from U.S. Gen. Philip H. Sheridan in

1855: "If I owned Texas and Hell, I would rent out Texas and live in Hell."

The fort was a tiny dot of civilization between the larger and more well known Fort Stockton to the south and Fort Davis to the west. It was at least 100 miles west of aspiring settlers and was never great for morale. During the fort's first year of existence, during which soldiers built their own sleeping quarters, it wasn't much different than it is today. The rooms had no floors, doors, or windows. The soldiers either used the weapons they showed up with or were issued inferior firepower ranging from muskets to rifles. Uniforms were mismatched, as the men were clothed with whatever was on hand. The army quartermaster rode out only three times a year to pay the troops. There was nothing to do except work, which might explain why the fort's thirty-acre garden was the most successful in the state, and the lime quarry a few hundred feet from the post hospital was more than self-sufficient in providing sanitary products for outhouses and for preserving bodies for burial at the fort. Stuck far out on the blustery frontier as it was, the fort was frequently overlooked or forgotten altogether when the army's budget was being allocated.

The army provided soldiers a paltry whiskey ration, along with pork and flour, but it was rarely enough to drown their loneliness. And so Scabtown sprang up across the San Saba River. Graphically named for the symptoms that sometimes appeared on soldiers after a visit, it was a parasitic, plank-board population of prostitutes, bordellos, and dust. For soldiers who couldn't afford the trip, either financially or morally, there was hunting, (more) gardening, foot races, and target practice. Not surprisingly, Scabtown prospered.

The fort was shut down in 1859 but reopened two years later when the Civil War began. It was abandoned for a second time in 1883. Soldiers might have been happy to vacate the fort, but the ready-made living quarters were quickly filled up by civilians, keeping most of the buildings in good repair into the twentieth century through constant use. But the businesses that stayed on after the soldiers left eventually closed, and families moved away one by one. In 1911 a fire destroyed part of the fort where a few people still lived.

Kraft, twenty-two, the on-site fort staff member, says people carefully avoided the stone building behind the post hospital that once housed the morgue. It was called the dead house, and nobody ever went in there. There are numerous stories of ghosts including the sound of heavy, measured footsteps down the covered walkway from the infirmary to the morgue, sometimes several times a week. "The fort is definitely haunted," she says, "but it's not an evil presence." Actually, there may be more than one ghost that calls Fort McKavett home.

Around the turn of the century, legend has it that a family traveling westward stopped at the fort and stayed the night, nursing a young daughter who had become increasingly ill on the trip. She died during the night, and the family went on with their journey without her. A few years later a family living at the fort heard a knock on their door in the middle of the night. They opened the door to find a young girl dressed in clothing that had been fashionable several years earlier. The girl said, "Follow me!" and darted off into the darkness. Family members followed the girl, in part to learn what the child was doing out so late, then watched her melt into the outside wall of another bunkhouse. They could find no trace of the girl inside, nor could other fort inhabitants and visitors who reported similar sightings. Kraft says she's heard the mother calling and the girl laughing and running away. "The mother never catches up with her," she says. However, the footsteps that Kraft and Ed Quiroz (a history major at Angelo State University in San Angelo, and who specializes in Fort McKavett's past) hear today are somewhat different. And they aren't the only ones to hear them.

Bischofhausen, now an Irving businessman who misses his West Texas home, says he heard them one day when he knew he was alone at the park. They stopped when he looked outside then resumed when he went back into his office. "And you'd hear doors open and slam that were locked tight," he said. During that time he was living in a home on the park premises where Kraft lives today, doing a similar 24-hour-a-day maintenance and overseeing job for the Texas Parks and Wildlife Department. Texas Rural Communities, a private agency, now operates Fort McKavett and four other infrequently visited historical sites in the state for the park department.

One twilight Bischofhausen said he heard distant shouting, "like a first sergeant talking to his troops," he recalls. "He was really laying down the rules." Knowing there was no one at the park, Bischofhausen called his wife, Kathy, to see if she heard it, too. "Yeah, maybe we're both crazy," she replied. As they walked toward the parade ground, where the sound seemed to be coming from, the tirade grew louder. But it stopped when they reached the ground and started again when they were back at home. "The thing is, I don't really believe in ghosts," Bischofhausen said. "But you can't deny what you hear."

The spirits are still very active at the fort. One can hear disembodied footsteps, orders being given by ghostly soldiers, apparitions floating through unoccupied buildings, ghostly lights, cold spots in the heat of the day, and the feeling of being watched or followed by unseen eyes. No one is immune from the paranormal here—neither the rangers nor the visitors.

Fort Worth

Most Fort Worth natives will tell you that the West begins in their city. During January 1849 United States Army General William Jenkins Worth, hero of the Mexican War, proposed a line of ten forts to mark the western Texas frontier from Eagle Pass to the confluence of the West Fork and Clear Fork of the Trinity River. Upon General Worth's death General William S. Harney assumed command and ordered Major Ripley S. Arnold to find a new fort site near the West Fork and Clear Fork. On June 6, 1849, Arnold established a camp on the bank of the Trinity River, naming the post Camp Worth in honor of General Worth. In August 1849 Arnold moved the camp to the north-facing bluff which overlooked the mouth of the Clear Fork.

The United States War Department officially named the post Fort Worth on November 14, 1849. When a new line of forts was built further west, the army evacuated Fort Worth on September 17, 1853, and settlers took uncontested possession of the site. John Peter Smith opened a school with twelve students in 1854; Henry Daggett and Archibald Leonard started department stores; Julian Field ran a general store and flour mill in 1856; and the Butterfield Overland Mail and the Southern Pacific Stage Line used the town as a terminus on the way to California.

During the 1860s Fort Worth suffered a population drop to 175. During 1873 the city was incorporated, and by 1874 the first westbound stage arrived. During 1878 the Yuma Stage Line made Fort Worth the eastern terminus to Yuma, Arizona, and the Texas and Pacific Railway designated Fort Worth as the eastern terminus for the route to San Diego, California. By the 1890s Fort Worth was known as the Queen City of the Prairie, and beef became a major business with the Texas Dressed Beef and Packing Company, the Union Stockyards Company, and the Fort Worth Stockyards Company all operating. In 1909 a devastating fire motivated the construction of a dam on the West Fork, and the city limits were expanded to 16.83 square miles. By the 1950s the city limits expanded to 272 square miles. Although the population has grown from under 7,000 in 1880 to 500,000 in 1990, Fort Worth has retained its western flavor and is still known as the city "Where the West Begins."

Jamba Juice/The Jett Building

Address:	400 Main Street, Fort Worth, Texas 76102 (located in the Jett Building at Sundance Square)
Phone:	817-870-1001
Fax:	817-870-1878
Contact:	Leasing Representative, Sundance Square
Business Hours:	Monday through Thursday from 7:00 A.M. to 9:00 P.M.; Friday from 7:00 A.M. to midnight; Saturday from 8:00 A.M. to midnight; Sunday from 10:00 A.M. to 8:00 P.M.
References:	9, 15, 23, 29

History

Constructed about 1902, the Jett Building originally served as the Northern Texas Traction Company Office as their main terminal and ticket office. They operated the first "inter-city" rail line service between Fort Worth and Dallas, which ran from 1902 to 1934. After the N.T.T. Co. left, the old office building and terminal became a candy factory. By the mid-thirties it housed a title company, and by the mid-forties the U.S. Sandwich Shop became the only other long-term tenant. The building sat vacant for several years during the late 1970s. In 1985 Sundance Square hired artist Richard Haas to design the Chisholm Trail mural facade for the

south and west sides of the building, now a Fort Worth landmark in its own right. The building's storefront was also rebuilt at this time. The building has been home to Fort Worth Books & Video, Deep Ellum Cafe, Leatherwood's, Smokey Toe's Island Grille, Mi Cocina, Pangburn's Chocolates, and now Jamba Juice.

Phantoms

Four restaurants once operated during a six-year period, all leaving the building, although one former owner was more emphatic as to the cause, "It was the ghosts!" Most people who owned or worked in the former establishments claimed that there was something unusual and often unnerving about the place, especially in the upstairs portion of the building above the functioning businesses. These noisy spirits loved to make life unpredictable for the numerous owners and their wary guests.

During Halloween a lone bartender, while closing the bar, witnessed the figure of a phantom woman standing in the mirror. The managers of another restaurant, Mi Cocina's, also had tales to tell about their spectral guests. While in the process of relocating their business, the spirits won out. Numerous employees quit after seeing apparitions or having intense paranormal experiences. Speculation still prevails as to the identities of the myriad souls still calling the building their afterlife home. Some think that one of the spirits may belong to a child who rolls a ball around one of the rooms late at night. Others suggest that murder is another reason for the hauntings. Rumors persist of the murder of two women on the third floor during the 1940s to 1950s. No names are given, and the story is a shadowy tale with blurry details that continues to fuel the phantom flame associated with the building.

As different owners come and go, one thing remains constant here—the spirits and the paraormal events that accompany them: numerous cold spots; the feeling of being watched or followed; the sounds of a woman walking in high-heels across the unoccupied upstairs floors; hair-raising chills that greet people in the basement level area beneath the main dining room; lights that flick on and off or dim without human assistance; the lever-operated frozen drink machines that are turned on by invisible hands; the pleading, desperate cries of someone seeking help; a photograph once taken of the boarded-up building revealing unboarded windows on the third floor with a lone figure standing in one window; and an invisible woman's hysterical laughter emanating from the powder room. These are but a few of the reminders of the afterlife in this haunted building.

Among the employees, a common topic of conversation is quite naturally the restless spirits. There seemed to be enough unexplainable things happening inside that daily "activity" reports were frequent. On one Super Bowl Sunday, before the establishment opened, a party was arranged in the building for the employees to kick back, get acquainted, and have some fun. During party preparations, an owner was moving items from the basement to the third floor, with the only access to the upper floors by means of an old, curved wooden stairway. While attempting to locate a light switch, the man stopped and looked around the basement, sure that "someone else" was watching him. Finding the switch and flipping it on, the man was so convinced he was not alone, that he scrambled back upstairs, reluctant to return alone to the large, spooky basement. After telling one of the employees of his encounter, he was told matter-of-factly that things like that were common, considering the building had a reputation for being haunted. The following evening the same man heard footsteps coming from the upstairs area. Thinking it was just another employee working late, he went up to check. To his amazement, there was no one else in the building!

On another occasion a woman who wanted to live on the third floor approached the owner about the possibility and was allowed to spend some time in the building by herself to see if it would work. She enjoyed her personal tour of the building and loved the endless possibilities that fixing up the third floor presented. Most of all, the woman was thoroughly delighted with the spectacular view of Main Street from the third floor windows, which were adjacent to the employees locker. It was a short time later when she was talking to the owner that she was astonished to find out there was no view of Main Street from the third floor! The owner assured the woman that the windows had long since been boarded up. Not believing the man, she insisted upon seeing for herself. With the owner by her side, the woman made her way back up to the third floor. When they reached the spot where she had looked out earlier over downtown Fort Worth, there were now only boarded up windows! A time warp? Ghosts? No one ever knew for sure.

Will Jamba Juice, the current owner, be immune to the spirited activity? Only time will tell. On your next visit to Fort Worth, try some delicious juice and keep a keen eye out for one of the resident spirits.

Miss Molly's Hotel

Address:	109 1/2 W. Exchange Avenue, Fort Worth, Texas 76106-8508
Phone:	817-626-1522
Fax:	817-625-2723
Toll-free:	1-800-99MOLLY
E-mail:	missmollys@travelbase.com
Website:	www.resobase.com/destinations/ft-worth/miss-mollys
Contact:	Mark and Alice Hancock
Accommodations:	Eight guestrooms.
Amenities:	Complimentary breakfast; bar; adjacent restaurant
References:	9, 15, 29, 31, 37

History

When the railroad came to Fort Worth, the city became a major shipping point for livestock. Some prominent Fort Worth citizens built large holding pens, forming the stockyards that brought fame and fortune to their city. In 1902 two large packing companies located their plants in the stockyards area, and Fort Worth soon became the second largest livestock market in America. Within ten years, sixteen million cattle passed through the stockyards, and the city acquired the nickname "Cowtown."

While it was a livestock town, numerous brothels catered to the needs of the cattlemen. The building now called Miss Molly's, once part of the original red light district, is now a respectable inn

located a short distance from where the world's first paying rodeo was held in 1918. The building opened in 1910 as a boardinghouse for salesmen, cattle buyers, and visitors. During the 1920s the place was managed by one Amelia Elmer, who called her establishment "The Palace Rooms." Following The Palace Rooms, the establishment became known as "The Oasis." In the 1940s the big packing companies moved into the stockyard area and brought in numerous workers, servicemen, and cowboys looking for a good time. That was when "Miss Josie" King took over the building and converted it to a bordello called the "Gayette Hotel."

As one story goes, a young man who frequented the Gayette always requested the same young lady who occupied room #9. He became so enamored of her that he even proposed marriage, but the young woman did not return his love. Having had enough of the situation, she packed her things and left Miss Josie's with no message or forwarding address for her young admirer, who was crushed. The madam took pity on the love-struck youth, saying she had another woman who would make him forget the girl of his dreams. With nothing to lose, he went to the girl's room and knocked. As the door swung open, the boy faced the mirror image of his mother in her youth! Stunned, the lad fled the building, never to return.

After Miss Josie's closed down, it became an art gallery with the rooms used by artists as studios. Today the building has been renovated and is a beautiful inn called Miss Molly's, Molly being a name often given the leading cow on a cattle drive. Fort Worth is a city rich in western tradition and home to numerous ghostly residents, including the haunted Miss Molly's.

Phantoms

Good golly, Miss Molly, according to management and staff, you surely are haunted! Guests report that while spending the night they are awakened by a mysterious form, which literally materializes before their eyes as they lie in bed. According to one account, an attractive young woman with blonde hair suddenly materialized in the Cowboy Room as a local journalist awoke from a deep sleep. He knew instantly that the female was an apparition, and after a few seconds the "stunning" blonde vanished. The journalist was saddened because he knew he would never be able to conjure up such a beautiful image again, and he even stayed awake for a while, hoping the woman would return.

The Cattlemen's Room became the focal point for a paranormal event when a visiting Englishman awoke to see an elderly lady standing at the foot of his bed, staring through him. She was wearing period clothing and sporting a sunbonnet. After hearing the report of the incident, the staff surmised that the woman might be Amelia Eimer, who ran the place in the 1920s.

Another time several females visited Miss Molly's to take a tour of the former bordello. One of the women was said to be very "sensitive" and upon entering the kitchen, immediately sensed a female spirit adjacent to Miss Josie King's former room. Could it have been the spirit of the former owner?

Other reported events include hearing unexplained footsteps; seeing items moved by an unseen force; lights that have a mind of their own, dimming or turning off and on by themselves; an occasional door that opens and shuts without human assistance; and cold spots that suddenly manifest in front of startled witnesses, who report that someone unseen is brushing passed them.

A visit to Miss Molly's is a real treat, with a few tricks from their friendly spirits included at no extra charge.

The Texas White House Bed & Breakfast

Address:	1417 Eighth Avenue, Fort Worth, Texas 76104
Phone:	817-923-3597
Fax:	817-923-0410
Toll Free Number:	1-800-279-6491
E-mail:	txwhitehou@aol.com
Website:	www.texaswhitehouse.com
Contact:	Jamie and Grover McMains
Accommodations:	Three guestrooms
Amenities:	Private baths; full gourmet breakfast; early coffee service; afternoon snacks; free soft drinks
References:	15

History

This house was built in 1910 by a Mr. Bishop for his son, but records indicate that his son never lived there. Instead it was sold to the William B. Newkirk family. At the time the Newkirks had three young boys; a fourth, Robert Newkirk, was born in the house. The Newkirk family lived in the house until 1967. During that time the four boys finished high school and three attended college before the Depression of 1932 took a severe toll on the family. The three boys dropped out of college to help with the family business and expenses. Then World War II took all of them into various branches of the military. Fortunately, all four returned and finished college, two becoming accountants, one a set designer for Hollywood movies, and one a lawyer. All four married and raised children who in time married and raised children, all of whom came to this home regularly. The father, William Newkirk, died in the home in 1957 at the age of ninety-seven. The home continued to be Mrs. Newkirk's residence until she died in the house in 1966. Following Mrs. Newkirk's death, the family sold the home to be used for small businesses, ultimately becoming a bed and breakfast.

Phantoms

Multiple occurrences of a similar nature have happened in the home since it became The Texas White House. All have occurred in a room now known as "Lone Star," the original master bedroom of Mr. and Mrs. Newkirk. On one occasion when two women were in bed, both women felt a third party lie down beside them in the bed. The feeling was described as someone lying against each of their backs. The women lay there without moving long enough that the presence finally moved off the bed. When the women turned to see who had just vacated the space between them, they were startled to see nothing. Furthermore, one of the women reported that within about three seconds of her trying to see who had intruded on their sleep time, the cell phone she had plugged in on the other side of the room began flashing and ringing. It stopped after about five seconds, with a check of who might be on the other end failing to produce a voice.

Considering the fact that the Newkirk family occupied this house for so many years, it is easy to speculate that the spirits of this place are probably family members trying to get used to their house being turned into a bed and breakfast!

Fredericksburg

With a present-day population of almost 200,00 people, Fredericksburg was first settled by immigrant families who came from Germany in 1846, led by John O. Meusebach. Although the original settlement was on the Comanche frontier, The Meusebach-Comanche Treaty of the following year established lasting peace. Numerous older buildings retain traditional German styles with several units comprising a National Historic District. German is still spoken occasionally, and old customs are regularly observed. The town is the birthplace of Fleet Adm. Chester W. Nimitz, Commander in Chief of the Pacific Fleet during World War II.

Chuckwagon Inn B & B

Reservation contact:	Ron Maddux-1st Class Bed & Breakfast Reservation Service
Address of Service:	909-911 East Main Street, P.O. Box 631, Fredericksburg, Texas 78624
Phone:	830-997-0443
Fax:	830-997-0040
Toll Free Number:	1-888-991-6749
E-mail:	stay@fredericksburg-lodging.com
Website:	www.fredericksburg-lodging.com
Innkeepers:	Sam and Becky Higgins
Accommodations:	Three guestrooms, two of which are located in a converted barn
Amenities:	Full breakfast; barbecue grill; television; the bunkhouse features a kitchenette with a microwave,

refrigerator, coffeemaker and dishes; king-size bed; claw foot bathtub with shower.

References: 15

History

This rustic inn is named after a boyhood friend of the owners, who lived in the Texas Hill Country and was a colorful cowboy character. The old stone house was built in the German tradition in 1854 and functioned as a dairy farm around 1901. The original house now serves as the dining room for the current house. The 100-year-old barn has been recently restored and converted into two guestrooms in the former loft area and a sitting room and small cantina downstairs where guests can relax and imbibe.

According to the family who sold the place to Sam and Becky Higgins, the cabin was constructed in the 1850s. The wood-framed, board-and-batten house material came from a building that was skidded next to the log cabin to form a "dog trot" type residence. This building's history is connected to the Edmondson and Bollinger families, who moved into the Locker area of San Saba in the early 1800s.

On the morning of November 10, 1925, Fred Bollinger was found shot in the chest and dying in the cabin on this ranch. He was taken to Brownwood, Texas, where he died thirty-seven days later. Will Edmonson was convicted of the killing. He owned the land adjacent to Bollinger's ranch. According to accounts from relatives, the shooting was the result of an ongoing dispute concerning hogs. Will had a reputation for being mean and ornery. He had run several people off from the area. He went to trial for Bollinger's killing, was convicted, and according to legend, served time, was released, and came home.

Upon returning from Brownwood, Edmondson and his son-in-law got into a dispute on the Mesquite Cemetery road behind Edmondson's ranch. He pulled a knife on his son-in-law, and the young man shot and killed Edmondson. The sheriff came and questioned the relatives to determine if everyone agreed with this version of the story. They did, so it went down as a justifiable homicide.

Phantoms

Two spirits are believed to make their home in this rustic, yet charming inn. The female spirit rumored to inhabit the house may be a former owner named Mrs. Mueller, while the other ghost is a feisty male spirit who seems to enjoy keeping guests company in the converted barn. Mrs. Mueller, who owned the Mueller Dairy with her husband, died in the 1950s in what is now the Chuck Wagon Room. In fact Mr. Mueller unexpectedly dropped by one day after the place was bought by the Higgins couple and made a strange request: He asked if he could spend some time in the bedroom where his wife had passed away. The request was granted, and from that time on, the new owners had a name for all the strange things that went on in the house and particularly in the bedroom. It was decided that it had to be Mrs. Mueller. She truly loved her house and the farm she helped run for so many years. Mrs. Mueller was apparently very young and had several children when she died suddenly from a massive heart attack—which may help account for her presence in her former home.

The lone guestroom in the house has had many unexplained events since the present owners bought the place. Mrs. Mueller's spirit loves toying with the lights as if letting the owners and guests know that she is still around and cares about what happens to her place. Numerous times the chandelier lights will brighten or dim to an otherworldly rhythm. One bulb will brighten then dim, followed by the other bulbs, even though they are all on the same switch. Light bulbs in the house often would go crazy; when the Higginses first moved in, that they had to call an electrician to check on the problem. He declared that it was NOT the wiring!

On one occasion, two dining room lamplight bulbs suddenly exploded for no apparent reason. One night after moving in, Becky Higgins was in the house alone, reading in the upstairs bedroom. Only a shade covered the window. As she was reading by a lamp with three bulbs, each bulb dimmed by itself, one after the other. Shortly after the dimming of the third bulb, the window shade suddenly rolled itself up!

On yet another occasion, while Becky was folding clothes, she placed her favorite kitchen towel off to the side. After completing her folding, she turned to where she had placed the kitchen towel, but it had disappeared. She looked everywhere to no avail. Then, two weeks later, the towel reappeared in the same place where Becky had originally placed it. She says that hide-and-seek is one of Mrs. Mueller's trademark games. She'll take just about anything when she's in the mood and hide it for a period of time before returning it.

A guest once staying in the house had a curious encounter as well. While packing the last of her things, with her husband already loading up their car, the woman suddenly became aware of someone standing behind her. She turned, expecting to see her husband standing there. To her dismay, there was no one anywhere around. She called out, but there was no answer. Shrugging off the strange feeling, she continued packing and wrapping up her favorite piece of jewelry—a bracelet. She packed it away with her other things and left the room.

Later that afternoon, when Becky was cleaning the room, she noticed a bracelet sitting on a barrel that served as a nightstand. She immediately phoned the guest who had occupied the room. Becky explained what she had found in the room. The woman was stunned—she had noticed her bracelet missing when she had unpacked. She swore that she had wrapped the bracelet up and packed it away before leaving and furthermore, knew that she hadn't had the bracelet anywhere near the barrel! She then told Becky about the feeling of being watched in the room just before leaving. Becky knew it was just Mrs. Mueller playing her special game of hide and seek!

An old hat rack, brought into the recently converted 1890s dairy barn—now Crazy Sam's BBQ—seems to have a will of its own. Loaded to the hilt with various hats and caps, one hat in particular—a Tom Landry golf hat—repeatedly falls to the floor between sundown and sunup. The hat always falls in the same location, as if it were grabbed from the rack and gently laid on the floor.

It has been noted that nothing unusual happened in the barn until Sam Higgins bought an old log cabin from Colorado and transported the pieces to Fredericksburg. The log cabin was meticulously disassembled piece by piece, labeled and numbered, and is stored next to the barn, where it awaits resurrection. Perhaps an untimely death is associated with this structure and it awakened a spirit when it was relocated. People staying in the barn have reported seeing four wet footprints suddenly materialize, although there has been no sign of water anywhere else around. The wet prints simply appear, as if someone walked out of another dimension, took a few steps, and disappeared.

On another occasion a husband and wife were staying in a loft room. While the husband was asleep, the wife decided to take a bath. She left her underthings on the floor, intending to pick them up the next morning. The woman then enjoyed a leisurely, warm bath. Early the next morning she woke up and went into the bathroom. She was about to pick up her personal belongings, when she noticed that someone had beaten her to the punch. Her items were already neatly hanging over the bathtub. Thinking this was very odd, she awakened her husband to question him. The startled man insisted that he had not even awakened during the night, let alone hung up any underwear! This "unmentionable" mystery was never solved.

The Country Cottage Inn

Reservation contact:	Ron Maddux-1st Class Bed & Breakfast Reservation Service
Address of Service:	909-911 East Main Street, P.O. Box 631, Fredericksburg, Texas 78624
Phone:	830-997-0443
Fax:	830-997-0040
Toll Free Number:	1-888-991-6749
E-mail:	stay@fredericksburg-lodging.com
Website:	www.fredericksburg-lodging.com
Owner:	Susan Muncey
Accommodations:	Four suites that may be opened to each other for groups up to 10 people.
Amenities:	Private baths, some with Jacuzzis; cable television; shared phone line; continental breakfast; central heat and air.
References:	15, 30

History

The building was constructed in 1850 by German immigrant and town blacksmith Friedrich Kiehne (pronounced KEE nee) for his wife, Maria. It was the first stone building and one of the first two-story dwellings in the small community. The Kiehnes came to Fredericksburg from Everode, Germany. A blacksmith by trade, Kiehne made most of the window hardware used in the construction of the house, which has been carefully restored. A recorded Texas historic landmark and listed on the National Register of Historic Places, the historic house is located a short distance from the former Nimitz Hotel and other fine shops and restaurants.

Phantoms

At the Country Cottage Inn, the spirits are provided at no additional charge! Unexplained events that have taken place over the years include disembodied voices or whispering sounds coming from unoccupied guestrooms while staff are cleaning or guests are spending the night. Objects have levitated in front of startled witnesses only to be placed gently on tables or countertops a few seconds later. Cold spots are frequently felt in the upstairs bedrooms, kitchen, and stairway areas. Mysterious footsteps are oftentimes heard pacing back and forth upstairs while guests or a staff person is downstairs. A wooden figure was mysteriously lifted off a mantel by unseen hands and placed on the floor several feet away. Locked doors, particularly the back door leading into the kitchen area, sometimes open and suddenly close as if someone walked in or out of the building. Guests have reported the odd sensation of being watched or followed even though they are alone, and the shadowy figure of former owner Mr. Kiehne has been occasionally sighted checking up on guests in their rooms before vanishing.

A former cleaning lady formally declared the building haunted. On one occasion, while about to clean an upstairs locked bedroom, she heard a voice bellow out from inside asking her to enter. An immediate inspection of the room revealed that she was alone. The same woman often reports feeling intense cold spots that suddenly engulf her then dissipate within seconds.

A strange occurrence took place with another former housekeeper. As the woman was cleaning the curtains in one of the guestrooms, a photograph materialized from somewhere above the curtain rod and landed at her feet. After looking up for a moment to see if something else might float down, she bent over and picked up the picture. Bearing no image, the only information on the photograph was a scripted warning that the place is haunted. How it materialized and where it had come from still remains a mystery.

A female staff person heard shuffling followed by heavy footsteps making their way across the upstairs floor. Thinking that another staff member had come in, she called upstairs. The noises ceased for a moment, but no one responded. Within moments the woman heard the footsteps again. She then decided to check on the activity. As she reached the top of the stairs, she was engulfed in a feeling of intense cold. The noises ceased when she called out, and the cold dissipated. Gathering her composure, the woman quickly went to inspect the rooms, only to find that she was alone in the house!

On another occasion a housekeeper was working during the evening. Entering the kitchen downstairs, the back door, which led into the kitchen, suddenly opened on its own accord, even though it had been securely locked earlier. This happened to another staff person as well, in an upstairs bedroom: A door, which was locked, suddenly flew open, then slammed shut all by itself! And the doors in the place aren't the only things that open by themselves. Recently, Connie, a staff member, reported that cabinets downstairs are repeatedly opened by invisible hands after she has carefully shut them. She says that the shutter-like doors are not easily opened and "click" into place when closed; yet many times the cabinets somehow open themselves back up! Connie tells of another occasion when she heard the locked back door unexpectedly open; she then heard footsteps pacing back and forth upstairs. Having heard the rumors about the spirits of the inn before taking the job, Connie admitted to being a bit apprehensive but says she has never been frightened. According to her, the overall feeling is one of relaxation and comfort, as the friendly spirits of the Country Cottage Inn seem to thoroughly enjoy their guests.

Flagstone Sunday House

Reservation contact:	Ron Maddux-1st Class Bed & Breakfast Reservation Service
Address of Service:	909-911 East Main Street, P.O. Box 631, Fredericksburg, Texas 78624
Phone:	830-997-0443
Fax:	830-997-0040
Toll Free Number:	1-888-991-6749
E-mail:	stay@fredericksburg-lodging.com
Website:	www.fredericksburg-lodging.com
Accommodations:	One guestroom upstairs with a king-size bed; a queen-size sofa sleeper downstairs. Can accommodate up to six people.
Amenities:	Full kitchen; full bath; air conditioning; flagstone patio
References:	15

History

A "Sunday house" was used by the local farmers who lived on their country ranches but built small structures in which they could stay when coming into town to attend church services, social events, or pick up supplies on the weekends. The lot (#369) on which the house was eventually built was first issued in 1846 to Mariaelisa Dattner, a widow with two children, Lisa and August. One portion of the lot was sold by Henry Keese to H.C. Keese et al. on February 24, 1904, while another portion was sold to John Kneese, who was married to Henry Keese's daughter Carolina Keese on February 24, 1904. John Kneese and Carolina Keese were married in 1892, and their first child, Adolph, was born in 1893. Henry Keese conveyed several lots to his children for the purpose of building their own Sunday houses.

Speculation has it that the Flagstone Sunday House (so named for the flagstones in the backyard) was built sometime during 1904. The house was originally built with an open porch that was enclosed after it had been sold by the Kneese heirs. It had one room downstairs and one room upstairs with an internal stairway. Adolph Kneese, son of John Kneese, sold this house to Mrs. Ella Fries on October 21, 1944, and Damon Fries sold it to Guy Jackson on February 1, 1971.

Phantoms

Fortunately, since being turned into an inn, a guest register has been left in the downstairs main room for comments, some of which reference encounters with the otherworldly occupant or occupants. One group of guests fondly named one spirit "William" and provided a drawing of the spirit.

A number of references in the guest registers discuss the spirit(s) as follows: "We really enjoyed our visit. We saw the ghost upstairs and named him William. Don't be afraid of the ghost!" "Heard noises and saw the ghost." "The television sometimes comes on by itself... We checked it out and there is nothing wrong with it." "There are not one [but] two ghosts, one white man and one Indian, both friendly!" "Heard ghost say [a] bad word during the night in a very distinctive voice... Not only heard, but also felt it—We believe!!!" "Didn't know about the ghost's existence until reading this book just before leaving the next day!" "The ghost drank our coffee; he was very accommodating and turned the lights on in the evening." "The ghost scared my wife to death!" "We played cards with the ghosts, and they cheat!" "There are three distinct entities occupying the house."

A current housekeeper says she does not enjoy going into the house alone. She continually hears the sound of people walking around inside and other eerie noises. A check of the house always finds the place unoccupied. The housekeeper's husband also had an encounter with the unknown. While alone in the house, the husband was moving the television set when he heard some shuffling noises coming from the upstairs room and kitchen area as if people were walking around. He reluctantly checked but never found anyone up there. Then, returning to the kitchen, he noticed a small closet door wide open. He distinctly remembered that it was shut when he entered. He shut the closet door and returned to the dining room. He noticed that the light had been turned on. After quickly completing his work, the man left, vowing never to return.

A guest spending the night in the place complained that the water in the shower would turn on by itself. The owner immediately made a thorough inspection of the shower, faucets, and pipes, finding that everything was in perfect working order. The guest later remarked that it must have been the ghost taking a shower!

Galveston Island

Located about fifty miles from Houston and with a population of almost 60,000 inhabitants, Galveston Island has been occupied since the early 1500s, serving as a home to Akokisa Indians; Cabeza de Vaca; pirate Jean Lafitte; and Jane Long, who became "The Mother of Texas," giving birth to the first Anglo-Saxon native Texan, Mary Jane Long. It has been known as "Little Ellis Island," "the Wall Street of the Southwest," the richest city in Texas, and the site of the worst natural disaster in U.S. history. The island was named for Bernardo de Galvez, who never set foot on the island.

In 1836 Michel B. Menard, a native of Canada, purchased the land for $50,000 from the Austin Colony to establish the city of Galveston, which he did with the financial backing of nine other men. Several prefabricated houses arrived from Maine in 1837, one belonging to Augustus Allen, which was sold to Michel Menard in 1839 and still stands. The Strand became the "Wall Street of the Southwest" for the largest and most important wholesale houses west of the Mississippi River.

The *Galveston News*, founded in 1842, is the oldest daily newspaper in the state. A bridge to the mainland was finished in 1860. The bridge opened the opportunity for railroad expansion. Galveston's prosperity came to an abrupt halt on September 8, 1900, when the deadliest natural disaster in United States history hit the island killing over 6,000 people. The dead were uncovered at a rate of seventy per day for at least a month after the storm. To prevent such a natural disaster from devastating the island in such magnitude again, the city built a seawall seven miles long and 17 feet high and began a tremendous grade raising project, which began in 1902, was completed in 1910, and included 500 city blocks. Galveston has over 550 designated historical landmarks on the National Register of Historic Places and over 1,500 historic homes.

The Queen Anne Bed and Breakfast

Address:	1915 Sealy Avenue, Galveston, Texas 77550
Phone:	409-763-7088
Toll Free Number:	1-800-472-0930
E-mail:	quccnanne@ev1.net
Website:	www.welcome.to/queenanne
Contact:	Ron and Jackie Metzger
Accommodations:	Four guestrooms
Amenities:	Full gourmet breakfast; private baths; climate control; reserved for retreats, formal receptions, showers, teas, and club meetings.
References:	6, 15

History

The house was built in 1905 by prominent businessman James J. Davis for $4,780. He and wife Emma had three daughters and a son when architect George B. Stowe was hired to design the Davis' new family home. In 1922, at the age of fifty-five, James Davis died after suffering a stroke, and two years later his wife sold the house to the First Methodist Church, which was located across the street. The church was moved to 53rd Street in 1964 and renamed Moody Memorial First United Methodist Church. The original sanctuary on Sealy Avenue was demolished.

The First Methodist Church used the Davis property as an elder's home for the next twenty-one years. In 1946 the church sold the property to one of its members, A. B. Graves. Within months Mr. Graves resold the house to Emma "Effie" Tucker, another member of the First Methodist Church. A widow with five children, Mrs. Tucker was an educator by profession. She is best known as the founder and director of the First Methodist's day school. Effie Tucker lived in the house until her death in 1988. She was 100 years old. The house stood vacant until 1990 when it was purchased and restored to its present beauty by two gentlemen from Houston, Earl French and John McWilliams. Jackie and Ron purchased the property in October 1998 and have operated the inn since its renovation in 1992.

Phantoms

Former owners claim that at least one spirit frequents this historic inn. On a number of occasions people working upstairs have heard someone walk downstairs, open and close a door, and continue walking. Upon inspection, there is never anyone seen where the footsteps emanated. One former owner was dumbfounded when he found an early photo in a closet. The photograph of a former occupant had an uncanny resemblance to the former owner—so much so, that some family members and friends swore the two could have been twins.

On another occasion, as people were in the dining room, a brass ring that was securely fitted to the top of a candleholder suddenly shot up off the top of the holder and landed on the table. The ring would have had to be physically lifted off to have been released, yet some invisible hand had effortlessly lifted and tossed it on the table.

There is also a lumbering, heavy rocking chair in one of the rooms that frequently will begin rocking back and forth as if someone unseen came into the room, sat down, and decided to relax. A cleaning lady also reported a number of times, while changing the guest sheets, that a tall, thin man would walk out of one room, down the hall, then disappear into another guestroom. No one knows who the phantom is, but since the ghost is friendly, everyone seems to let him do his thing while they do theirs. The spirit is very friendly and mindful of the guests and staff.

According to Jackie Metzger, "My dad is living here now since my mom died. Early one morning he was sitting outside smoking a cigarette. His nose was dripping and he was in need of a tissue. He said out loud to himself that he should go inside and get a tissue. At that exact moment a tissue dropped right into his lap. He used the tissue and left it on the table. When we returned it was gone."

Metzger was on a porch situated off one of the guestrooms upstairs, which is accessed through a walk-through window. There is a screen door on the window with a hook latch. While she was outside wiping off the table and chairs, the door closed and latched. The latch is not easy to hook and takes some effort. Metzger had to call to someone to unlock the door.

The owners say that you can hear footsteps across the entry floor from their quarters below during the early morning hours. One night soon after they bought the house, the Metzgers had gone upstairs to turn back the air conditioner and turn off the lights. The attic door was firmly closed, and everything looked fine. During the night Jackie heard the footsteps, and the next morning when she went upstairs, the attic door was open and a round reddish spot about the size of a dinner plate was on the carpet at the top of the stairs. It took the housekeeper, Metzger, and a carpet cleaning company to finally get the stain out, and no one had any idea what it was.

Before retiring to bed one night, Metzger was pulling down the kitchen window shade, when a cookbook that had been resting on a shelf in an easel suddenly landed on the floor. While she was picking up the cookbook, the window shade went back up. On other occasions Metzger's husband saw a shadowy form go from their closet, through the wall, and into the room next door. A vase sitting in the middle of a table landed on the floor. During a storm late one night Metzger recalled seeing a shadow hover above her left shoulder while working on the computer. Each time she looked up, it was gone.

Metzger concludes by stating, "Our experiences have been few and have not felt threatening. The house feels happy, and we are glad to be here." We are sure you will enjoy your stay at this fabulous haunted inn where the spirits never sleep.

Gonzales

Founded in 1825, the city earned its page in history as the place where they fired the first shot of the Texas Revolution. Named after Don Rafael Gonzales, the governor of the Mexican province of Coahuila and Texas, the 1825 settlement had Indian troubles, and to help scare them off, the Mexican government loaned the settlers a small brass cannon. When the Mexicans felt the first stirrings of the Texan revolt in 1835, they tried to get the cannon back. Texan volunteers fired on them October 2, 1835, under a flag saying "Come and Take It." The Texas Revolution had begun, and Gonzales had earned its title as the "Lexington of Texas." After a short fight the Mexicans retreated, with one casualty, against no loss on the side of the Texans.

The following February thirty-two men from Gonzales broke through the Mexican lines to enter the Alamo. General Sam Houston arrived in Gonzales on March 11, 1836, and it was here that he heard the news of the fall of the Alamo. Threatened by Santa Anna's superior force, Houston ordered a scorched-earth retreat, burning Gonzales.

This has always been cattle country, and the first brand was recorded here in 1829. Cattle is still of major importance to the local economy, but now it has been joined by the production of eggs, broilers, and turkeys, usually ranking number one or two in the state.

St. James Inn

Address:	723 St. James Street, Gonzales, Texas 78629
Phone:	830-672-7066
E-mail:	email@stjamesinn.com
Website:	www.stjamesinn.com
Contact:	Ann and Rew Covert
Accommodations:	Six guestrooms
Amenities:	Private baths; American breakfast with dessert; picnic baskets and dinners by reservation.
References:	14, 15

History

The St. James Inn occupies a home built in 1914 by a descendant of a family that was involved in Texas history right at the beginning. Walter Kokernot, who built the house, was the grandson of a merchant seaman who came over from Holland and was the captain of three ships of the Texas navy for which he was granted several leagues of land. He turned the grant into the Big Hill Ranch and made his fortune with cattle on the Chisholm Trail.

Phantoms

A beautiful house restored to its former glory by Ann and Rew Covert, the St. James Inn offers comfortable quarters with a style seldom seen today, along with some invisible guests. Ann and Rew both have heard footsteps upstairs several times and have gone to investigate, looking in every nook and cranny, not finding anyone. It is commonly held that Walter Kokernot still wanders through "his" house, checking on guests and overseeing everything.

One of the Kokernot children was Josephene, who used one of the front bedrooms now serving guests, while two sons used the back bedrooms. On one occasion a guest awakened in the night to find a man asking, "What are you doing in my daughter's room?" When asked the following morning what he said, the guest stated he said nothing and then spent the remainder of the night on a couch in the hall.

Another couple who slept in Josephene's room had the wife awakened to find a woman talking to her. She described how the woman was dressed in old-style clothes with a high collar and buttons like girls once wore. Strangely her husband did not wake up at all. "Walter," as the ghost is called, evidently likes to have a hand in every activity. Rew said that one time he was working on the house, and nothing would go right. He kept dropping things or would drive a nail in the wall and it wouldn't hold, or nothing would work. Finally out of frustration Rew said, "Walter, if you will just leave me alone and let me do this, I promise that everything's going to work out all right. You'll like it when I get through. Now leave me alone." Then everything went right, leaving Rew to believe he really was talking to Walter.

A guest sleeping in Walter's bedroom woke up in the middle of the night to feel someone looking at her, like out of the mirror, and she felt a presence in the room. She sat up in bed, turned the light on, and "poof" it disappeared. On the third floor is an area with small doors into the attic called the children's playroom. When certain guests stay in there they are asked, "Did the gnomes come out and tickle your toes last night from the little bitty doors that go out into the attic?" The guests reply, "I don't know who was there, but somebody was up there."

Ann says they have gotten used to Walter and his daughter roaming the house, but when she hears footsteps upstairs and she is alone, she does not go up to investigate. Both Ann and Rew agree that the ghostly visitors do not mean any harm, but they do add to the excitement of this lovely home.

From time to time, while on the first floor, the Coverts hear footsteps upstairs. A door will slam on the second floor for no reason. There is no wind blowing on the second floor, so they can assume that someone is coming and going. One guest related that when he stepped out on the second floor balcony he glanced to his right to see the silhouette of a man and a women dressed in cowboy and cowgirl outfits with boots and hat. Another guest once asked where the cat was. Anne Covert said they didn't have a cat, but the man insisted that he had felt one in the hallway a few hours earlier, as well as seeing the phantom feline racing across the room.

The spirits are not covert at this beautiful inn, so come prepared to be entertained by the friendly former owner Walter Kokernot and his daughter, who seem to enjoy company.

Helotes

Helotes is on State Highway 16 roughly sixteen miles northwest of downtown San Antonio in northwestern Bexar County. Originally an Indian trail carved around the hill, valleys, and caves of the area, the Scenic Loop was often the setting for fierce battles involving nomadic Indian tribes battling over land rights during the untamed Texas of long ago. The "Treaty Tree," a majestic oak located in the meadow adjacent to the inn and said to posses a "peaceful energy," was used by these Indians to come together on a neutral "spiritually healing" ground. It was here that treaties and alliances were negotiated and signed.

The Grey Moss Inn

Address: 19010 Scenic Loop Road, P.O. Box 734, Helotes, Texas 78023
Phone: 210-695-8301
Fax: 210-695-3237
E-mail: nell-jane@juno.com
website: www.grey-moss-inn.com
Contact: Lou & Nell Baeten
Business Hours: Open seven days a week from 5:00 P.M.
References: 15, 30, 36, 37

History

In 1821 Polish mercenary Juan Menchaca settled the area with his Aztec wife and built a house and cultivated a cornfield at the site, which means "green roasting ear of corn" in Spanish. In the years that followed, stagecoaches from San Antonio traveling through the area often faced bandits, who hid their gold (rumored to be still buried) in the caves situated near the Loop. The bandits were pursued by sharp shooting Texas Ranger Captain Jack Hays, who was the law in the area until relocating to California. By 1872 the railroad passed through neighboring Leon Springs, as the Scenic Loop was still used by wagons and stagecoaches journeying to Helotes. Robert E. Lee was a frequent visitor to the area, as was Pancho Villa. A post office opened at Helotes in 1873, and by 1885 the community had a hotel, a school, a general store, a blacksmith, and a population of fifty.

Mary Howell founded the inn during 1929. Howell sold homemade candy from her front porch and often cooked dinner for her neighbors. The inn is the oldest continuously operating restaurant in Central Texas. Water is drawn from fresh spring wells, and their famous pies are made "from scratch" daily. Lou and Nell Baeten continue the tradition Mary Howell began at the Grey Moss Inn, although some say that Howell never left.

Phantoms

Many people are convinced that Mary Howell's spirit remains at the place she started in 1929. She is considered the most dominant force, frequently checking in on the owners and guests and ensuring that the quality of food meets her high standards—she is not displeased. There is oftentimes a strong whiff of the rose cologne drifting through the kitchen and in the dining room located near the kitchen door. The rose cologne, a favorite of Mary's in life, is also her favored afterlife scent. Mary and the other spirits are said to be responsible for the numerous unexplained events that have taken place to this day.

One time a large coffeemaker blew apart in the kitchen when no one was around. The alarm system is frequently activated by an unknown source. Tray jacks will mysteriously topple over along with ice buckets, and dishes will occasionally break on their own.

A couple celebrating their wedding anniversary had a wine bucket brought to the table. While they were waiting for their glasses to be refilled, the bucket fell over on its own—perhaps an omen of things to come. It turned out that within six months after the incident, the couple divorced—-coincidence?

Mary's spirit is also blamed for the computer problems that regularly occur. According to Nell, a new system was recently installed, and "things" happen to it that a computer expert tells her should never happen. In the middle of a crowded Saturday night, always on Friday or Saturday, the computer system will "crash," and everyone has to go back to hand writing the guest checks for the customers. It makes it very difficult for staff when they have to hand write the checks for large parties of thirty to forty guests. What is strange is that the credit card machine is never affected by the computer shutdown.

Nell saw Mary for the first time recently as she was arranging tables in the Main Dining Room, the oldest part of the restaurant. Looking up after feeling as if she were being watched, Nell noticed Mary standing in the distance watching her work, much like a supervisor would watch an employee. Within seconds the apparition vanished.

The Garden Room contains another spirit, who is more rambunctious than Mary. After putting out all the candles, the owner locked up for the evening. When she arrived the next morning, the owner noticed that a fire had started in the Garden Room after she left for the evening. What was strange, however, was that the fire only affected one table, which was situated underneath a giant hex sign that stands for justice. The place mats, napkins, candle, the plate beneath the candle, and tablecloth were scorched. The only area not affected by the fire was directly beneath the hex sign, which included an untouched basket of sugar packets on the table. The fire alarm never sounded, and there was no smell of smoke in the building. Also, the Formica tabletop was not harmed, but the woven straw back of one of the chairs adjacent to the table had burned away. A psychic said an angry male spirit was responsible for the event and that his favorite area was the Garden Room.

Other events have taken place over the years at the Grey Moss Inn: An employee reported that the adding machine would perform unassisted calculations. A staff person with her hands full had the entry gates open for her, courtesy of the spirited clientele. There are frequent manifestations of Mary in front of staff and guests. A shadow is frequently sighted by a window and moves across the wall before disappearing. An apparition materialized into a large black form, then walked through a wall. A mysterious area of water will sometimes literally ooze up in the patio area of the restaurant then suddenly stop. A tremendous clashing of cymbals has come from the inn, setting off the alarm system. However, upon inspecting, the police never find anything amiss. Unexplained footsteps can be heard walking around unoccupied areas of the building. Lights turn on or off by themselves, and doors open and close unassisted. The Grey Moss Inn has great food, plenty of atmosphere, and a spirit or two to add to the ambiance.

Hillsboro

With a current population of under 10,000 inhabitants, the town has been the county seat since 1853. Both the county and city are named for George Washington Hill, one of the numerous Tennessee-born people who came to Texas during the fight for independence. Hill served as the secretary of war under Sam Houston during his second term as president.

The Tarlton House of 1895

Address:	211 N. Pleasant Street, Hillsboro, Texas 76645
Phone:	254-582-7216
Fax:	254-582-3776
Toll Free Number:	800-823-7216
E-mail:	tarlton@hotmail.com
Contacts:	Pat and Bill Lovelace
Accommodations:	Eight guestrooms
Amenities:	Private baths; seven guestrooms have king-size beds; individually air conditioned and heated.
References:	15

History

Greene Duke Tarlton came to Hillsboro with his family around 1890, when the county was the second largest cotton producing area in Texas. Tarlton invested his money in land and cotton and built the three-story Victorian Tarlton house in 1895. At the time it was the largest house in Hillsboro at 7,000 square feet. He used cypress wood for the structure and foundation of the house. Seven coal fireplaces are surrounded with Italian tile, each one different.

The five stained glass windows still in place are original to the house and have over 120 pieces of beveled leaded glass making up the oversized front door and transom. The house once had a dumb waiter that went to the second floor and a speaking tube to the third. The grounds once included eight acres of land with stables, carriage houses, and outbuildings for the staff.

Mr. Tarlton had five children, only one of which was born in the house. The first Mrs. Tarlton died in 1907. When he married the second Mrs. Tarlton, she and the children did not get along. Tarlton built another house next door and lived there with his wife, while the governess and children lived in the first house. In 1929 when the stock market crashed, Tarlton lost all of his money. Two years later an obituary read that Tarlton and his second wife died the same day: Mrs. Tarlton of natural causes, while Mr. Tarlton, at age seventy-four, apparently went to the third floor (then the attic) and hanged himself.

Phantoms

The present owners are positive that it's Mr. Tarlton who still walks the halls of his former home. The Morris family, who lived in the house in the 1970s, had several ghostly encounters. Two members of their family wrote that they heard voices or felt as if someone "invisible" sat on the bed or tugged at the covers in their room.

A former employee of the Rhoads family, who turned Tarlton House into an inn, claimed that while making up a bed in the Tower, she saw Mr. Tarlton bending over and smiling at her! The woman also claims that her young son used to talk about playing with the deceased Tarlton children.

On one occasion current owner Pat Lovelace felt the bed sink as if someone had sat down on it. There is also a small door that leads to an area in the attic, which today houses a hot water heater. Several times while Lovelace was in that part of the house, the door would open by itself. Unexplained footsteps and cold spots are but a few of the strange events that often occur at this historic inn.

A stay in the Tarlton House may actually put you in touch with the original owner, who still enjoys making the guests feel right at home—even though his best intentions come from "the other side."

Houston

Named after Sam Houston, general of the Texas army that won independence from Mexico and president of the Republic of Texas, Houston is the largest city in Texas and fourth largest in the nation. This unique city has experienced phenomenal growth since it was a small riverboat landing established on Buffalo Bayou by the Allen brothers in August 1836. Today the metropolis is the industrial and financial hub for much of the state and is one of the nation's largest seaports and the headquarters of the Lyndon B. Johnson Space Center.

The Ale House

Address:	2425 West Alabama Street, Houston, Texas 77098
Phone:	713-521-2333
Fax:	713-521-2333
Contact:	Angela Jenkins
Open:	Monday-Saturday: 11:00 A.M.-2:00 A.M.; Sunday: 12:00 P.M.-2:00 A.M.; Happy hours Monday-Friday: 4:00 P.M.-7:00 P.M.
References:	3, 6, 15, 23, 28, 37

History

It was originally built as a farmhouse; two Englishmen opened the Ale House in 1981. It was their third English-style pub in Houston, following the prior successes of Rudyard's and Richmond Arms (which is still owned by the Brits). Beer (33 on draft and 70-90 bottled) is the main spirit served at this establishment. The first floor of this three-story turn-of-the-century building is devoted to food, beer, darts, and socializing. The second level is for patrons desiring live entertainment.

Phantoms

The Ale House was built in the English Manor style. It once operated as a "speakeasy" on the second floor, where customers came and went by means of a fire escape. It is known locally as a haunted establishment, and current manager Angela Jenkins has heard enough stories from trustworthy individuals to be convinced that her establishment is "very active." Some people attribute the activity to the woman who died on the third floor when the place was a speakeasy during Prohibition; while others say the spirit of a young servant girl from the turn of the century, who was left to die by her owners, now roams the house. As one staff person remarked, "If your beer glass suddenly turns up empty, don't ask questions, just order another." A third spirit may belong to an irate sea captain who likes tossing lighted candles and smashing glasses.

Given the numerous reported paranormal events that have taken place over the years, there is every reason to believe there is more than one ghostly presence in the building.

Bar glasses fly from the racks; candles mysteriously launch themselves at waitresses from their window ledges; lights flicker on after they've been turned off. A lit candle mysteriously appeared in a window; candles placed on tables appear to light themselves. A candle once floated from a tabletop, sailed through the air, and landed on a second table a few feet away. One summer as a customer was seated at a second-floor table he became engulfed in a blast of frigid air followed by the materialization of a young woman walking from the stairway landing to the bar, where she slowly vaporized.

There is an intense feeling of a strong presence on the third floor of the building. One owner set a chair out on the third-story porch during business hours so that the spirited female ghost would not bother her customers. No one is sure whether this act of consideration actually deterred the ghostly activity. Today the third floor bedroom assumes the atmosphere of a English pub, complete with a bar and dart boards. Employees have complained that after locking up at night, the upstairs lights will suddenly turn on by themselves. There have also been reports of the musical equipment managing to end up in an entirely different area than their original location. Staff, particularly females, have reported feeling extremely depressed when they are alone in the building, particularly near the stairway.

A waitress was closing for the evening and was taking the afternoon's receipts to the second-floor office, carefully locking the gate behind her, when she saw that the chairs in the middle of the floor had been yanked back from tables and scattered throughout the room. She couldn't really dwell on the incident because she had accounting to take care of. As she began going over the receipts, she heard loud noises coming from the adjacent room and quickly went to inspect. When she entered, all the chairs were lined up in a row, front to back, on the dance floor.

During a radio interview with the manager of the Ale House, a mysterious voice could be heard in the background saying, "Let me out! Let me out." Another time an unplugged air conditioner turned on. A night manager remarked that doors will open after being locked, lights will turn on by themselves, glasses will fly off racks or shelves for no reason, keys and other objects end up missing or moved to a different location, and on the third floor, the lights above all three dart boards will suddenly turn on and all three boards will be rotated about fifteen degrees from their normal positions.

One psychic felt two distinct spirits in the building: one being a shy female spirit who stays close to the third floor, while the second floor has a rather seedy male spirit who likes to pinch the ladies sitting at the bar or visit women in the second-floor ladies room. More recently management has reported waitresses, who lock the basement door and go upstairs to count the days earnings, find that the chairs, which were neatly placed upon first leaving, are now in disarray. While busy counting the money, they will hear noises coming from the adjacent room. When they go to inspect the room, all the chairs are once again neatly lined up in a row. Finally, disembodied voices are often heard coming from the unoccupied second floor.

One afternoon an employee, working near a supply closet on the second floor, struck up a conversation with his boss, or so he thought. When he finally looked up, there was no one in the room, and he found out that his boss was never on the second floor. Others have heard a female voice mumbling near the second-floor supply closet and restroom area. A majority of the time the words are garbled and almost impossible to decipher.

At the Ale House whether you lift your glass in toast, play darts, or simply visit the restroom, there's a chance that someone else is watching you or participating—someone you probably can't see!

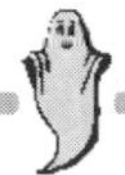

La Carafe

Address:	813 Congress Street, Houston, Texas 77002
Phone:	713-229-9399
Contact:	Carolyn Wengler and Garth Daniels
Hours:	Weekdays: 12:00 P.M. to 2:00 A.M.; Weekends: 1:00 P.M. to 2:00 A.M.; Happy hour: Daily: 4:00 P.M. to 7:00 P.M.
References:	6, 15, 36, 37

History

The Kennedy Bakery, constructed in 1860, perhaps Houston's most beloved historic building, is the oldest commercial structure in the city. From the time Irish immigrant John Kennedy first built his bakery, it functioned as a trading post, apothecary, loan office, and a Confederate arsenal. Settlers often referred to his Indian trading partners as "Kennedy's Indians." During the Civil War the bakery was contracted to turn out hardtack biscuits for Confederate troops. John Kennedy, who owned a large number of slaves and several thousand acres of land in surrounding counties, was also known for running cotton through the Federal blockade.

Phantoms

The spirits of La Carafe occasionally get a little feisty. Given the history of the building, the ghosts could be anyone from just about any time period. Who they are is unclear; however, what is invisibly clear is they do exit and are blamed for the dozens of unexplained events that occur with regularity.

As bartender/manager Tyler Peck came to work early one day, he was about to enter the building when he happened to glance up at a second floor window where the La Carafe's offices are situated. To his amazement, a strange-looking woman was standing in the window looking out toward the street. Since it was early in the morning and he was the first to arrive, he opened the door and tentatively walked up the stairs to the second floor area where the woman was standing. There was no woman or anyone else for that matter at the window, in the room, or in the building; the woman had simply vanished!

On another occasion a staff person named Tobe was closing up around 2:30 A.M. After inspecting the place for stragglers, he locked the front door and began strolling across the street. A gut feeling made him turn around and look back toward the building. Just then, as he looked toward the window near the entrance door he has just secured, his hair stood on end and he got the chills. There in the window was a large, muscular black man gazing at him. Thinking that he left someone stranded inside, he ran back, unlocked the door, and searched the place from top to bottom for the gentleman, but the establishment was empty. Management believes that this spirit belongs to Carl Prescott, who used to manage La Carafe; he died around 1990.

Bartender Gavin Connor came in one Sunday morning and began sweeping the upstairs area, which was standard operating procedure. After completing the upstairs, he did the same to the downstairs area. When he was finished he went back upstairs to make coffee. As he was about to go behind the upstairs bar to get some water for the coffeemaker, he noticed that a box had been placed in his path. It had not been there when he swept a few minutes before. He immediately suspected it was one of the resident spirits playing a prank on him, since he was the only one in the building at the time, at least the only one in the flesh.

A local told us that one time, as he and a friend were standing outside the bar waiting for it to open, they saw a woman in a white dress sitting down at a table in front of the westernmost upstairs bar windows. As they watched the woman, she slowly vanished.

A former bartender heard her named called out several times while she was closing. When she told the manager he just shrugged his shoulders and said it was the ghost. Another time she reportedly heard footsteps crossing the floor in the unoccupied upstairs bar area. As usual, every time something like this happened, someone would quickly run to see who it was and find an empty room.

Other events that have been reported include exploding glasses and bottles and a painting that has flown off the wall. Strange shadows appear on the walls; cold spots frequently appear out of nowhere; the feeling of being watched by invisible eyes is sometimes overwhelming; and disembodied footsteps have been heard walking through unoccupied areas of the building. Visitors are only allowed upstairs at certain times. Also, due to safety codes, the upstairs area only holds eleven people at a time, not including the ghosts!

Sambuca

Address:	909 Texas Avenue, Houston, Texas 77002
Phone:	713-224-5299
Fax:	713-224-5290
Contact:	Courtland Duffield
Open:	every day from 1:00 P.M. to 2:00 A.M.; wheelchair accessible
References:	15, 37

History

Sambuca, a jazz nightclub, nestled inside the historic Rice Hotel, is located where the Supper Club once functioned. The last president of the Republic, Anson Jones, spent his last night in the old Capitol Hotel; and in 1963 President John. F. Kennedy spent his last night at the Rice Hotel before going on to Dallas. The Rice is probably the most recognized historic building in Houston.

The Rice Hotel is built on the site of the old capitol of the Republic of Texas, which housed the Texas Congress from April 1837 until September 1839. John K. and Augustus Allen retained ownership of the building after the legislature moved to Austin. It was sold in 1857 to R.S. Blount. The original building was razed in 1881 by Colonel A. Groesbeck, who subsequently erected the elaborate five-story Capitol Hotel. William Marsh Rice, the founder of Rice University, purchased the building in 1883 and added a five-story annex and renamed it the Rice Hotel. Rice University sold the building in 1911 to Jesse Jones, who then demolished the building and built a seventeen-story structure on the site. The Rice Hotel remained a Houston landmark until 1975 when the building closed. The hotel has been converted into 350 housing units and a commercial development center.

Phantoms

Although Sambuca, within the modernized Rice Hotel complex, is relatively new and stories of ghosts are limited to a few strange events, we expect that with a little more operating time under its belt, encounters with the spirits will become commonplace. Stories about the haunted Rice have circulated for years, including the room John F. Kennedy occupied the night before he was killed in Dallas. A force in that room (now an unrented loft) that frightened staff and guests was said to belong to the restless spirit of JFK! Balls of light, banging doors, a shaking bed, and intense cold spots would force guests to leave the room within a few hours after checking in. They were not welcome in that room, as the rumors went.

Over the years the ghost stories seemed to come from every floor, including the Crystal Ballroom and dining area. Phantom apparitions were frequently reported by staff and guests in a number of rooms in the hotel. There were colds spots that followed guests and housekeeping as they walked down the hallways or were entering rooms. Beds that were made would either be found with impressions in them or they would be in disarray after the cleaning person left the room for a moment. Doors would open then slam shut when no one was around, and disembodied voices would sometimes call people's names.

Ghostly dancers have been sighted in the ballroom. Otherworldly guests have vanished in the lobby as they were checking in. The main elevator is said to stop on the fourth floor, no matter what button is pushed. People continue to feel an icy wind enter the elevator when the door opens and then closes, as if someone invisible has joined them or just left; and closet doors in some guestrooms open and slam shut unassisted in the middle of the night.

Sambuca has already reported unexplainable noises, mysterious cold drafts of air, and unaccountable shadows, so we recommend when visiting this trendy nightspot that you keep an eye out and ear peeled for anything out of the ordinary. It's logical to assume that the spirits of the former Rice Hotel have finally made their way to Sambuca.

The Spaghetti Warehouse

Address:	901 Commerce Street, Houston, Texas 77002
Phone:	713-229-9715
Fax:	713-227-3220
E-mail:	swh_comment@meatballs.com
Contacts:	Sandra McMasters
Open:	Sunday through Thursday from 11:00 A.M. to 10:00 P.M., and Fridays and Saturdays from 11:00 A.M. to 11:00 P.M.
References:	6, 15, 37

History

The Spaghetti Warehouse was founded in 1972 by Robert Hawk. The first restaurant was built in the old warehouse district of downtown Dallas, using a former warehouse building dating back to the late 1800s as its headquarters. The menu items were from authentic Italian recipes handed down through many generations of the Petta family. Victor Petta Jr., who was the original executive chef of the Spaghetti Warehouse, was also the inventor of the patented system for cooking spaghetti. The restaurant is decorated in a nostalgic theme using genuine antiques, stained glass, tiffany type lights, and usually an authentic trolley car forming a dining room within a dining room. In September 1985 the company went public, with stock currently traded on the New York Stock Exchange.

Phantoms

The bayou behind the building once provided a transportation route for ships bringing supplies to this former warehouse from Galveston. Several of these ships, including one believed to have belonged to General Santa Anna, now lie at the bottom of the bayou. It is rumored that during the late 1880s a number of former workers died in the warehouse while unloading various items, some of which were labeled dangerous. One story suggests that a former owner of the building, when it was a pharmaceutical warehouse, died when the elevator cable snapped. Could he be one of the restless spirits?

Staff have reported materialization of a woman, the feeling of being watched, cold spots, items being moved around by invisible hands, shadowy figures appearing on the walls, ghostly footsteps, and disembodied voices that call out people's names. Although no one ever gets used to sharing a place with ghosts, guests seem to enjoy coming to the Spaghetti Warehouse for the chance to dine with an otherworldly patron.

When one waitress heard her name whispered from behind, she turned instantly and was shocked that no one was there. A contractor, while working on the top floor, took some measurements for the work he was preparing to do. As he was measuring, the man swore, someone kept changing the figures on his notepad, forcing him to re-measure a number of times. Finally, after completing his last entries, he saw something misty pass by him, followed by the chairs in the room being moved by unseen hands. The man ran out deciding the job wasn't worth working with a ghost. Sometimes on the hottest days, when the air conditioner is broken, there are certain parts of the building where the temperature is at least 30-40 degrees cooler than anywhere else, and no one can account for it.

A waitress was napping upstairs one time when she heard footsteps walking around. Scared half to death because she knew she was alone, she waited in the darkness until the footsteps got closer. She was ready to let out a scream, then the footsteps halted abruptly. Jumping up and turning on the light, she realized she was alone. Needless to say she no longer napped alone in that area.

While in the top-floor kitchen area during remodeling, a busboy was cleaning up when the plates began jumping off the shelves and began smashing to the floor. The frightened busboy, in a state of panic, ran out of the building and retrieved his father to come back and stay with him while he completed his shift. From that day on the boy refused to work alone upstairs. Two staff persons, working late one night, saw a lady wearing a white dress pass right by them without noticing them. As the two men watched in startled silence, the feminine form just vanished.

During a KTRK Halloween special for the Debra Duncan show, manager Sandra McMasters reported that a lady had died in the elevator years ago and her spirit is often sighted near it. McMasters also stated that unexplained voices are often heard in the restaurant before opening or after closing. The heavy, metal kitchen mats are often found moved to other parts of the restaurant after closing. Once, McMasters walked from the kitchen into a dining area and witnessed four or five ghostly figures get up from a table and slowly vanish. She could see their hair and translucent bodies as they got up. Lone Star Spirit paranormal investigators reported strong energy readings in the entryway, the back portion of the large party room, and in the back stairwell near the elevator shaft, and they recorded ecotplasmic orbs and other anomalies. Furniture is often found moved around. Robert Anderson, a long-time employee, has heard his name called out by an invisible someone and has witnessed a number of unexplained events.

According to Discover Houston (ghost walk) Tours during Halloween, "Sam Houston, the Republic of Texas's first president, and Charlotte Marie Baldwin Allen, wife of Augustus Allen, one of the Allen brothers who founded Houston, will let their presence be known, along with possibly other spirits." Ticket sales begin in the lobby of the Spaghetti Warehouse, and guides depart from the restaurant every hour (713-222-9255).

A visit to this historic building usually proves to be an interesting excursion into the unknown. At the very least, even if the spirits aren't willing, you'll leave a satisfied customer after sampling the bill of fare—good Italian food!

Treebeards

Address:	315 Travis Street on Market Square, Houston, Texas 77002
Phone:	713-228-2622
Fax:	713-225-3708
Contact:	Dan Tidwell and Jamie Mize
Open:	Monday through Friday from 11:00 A.M. to 2:00 P.M. and on Friday from 5:00 P.M. to 9:00 P.M.; Closed on Saturday and Sunday; delivery, take out, catering, children welcome, outdoor seating, smoking section, wheelchair access
References:	15

History

The building at 315-317 Travis was constructed around 1870. Facing Market Square, this two-story painted brick building occupies a fifty-foot-wide lot. Noteworthy features include a nicely detailed cornice of brick corbeling and six rectangular double-hung windows, which are evenly spaced across the second floor. This building is one of the few that are still remaining in original family hands. Previously in the Baker family, it was the property of Rebecca Baker when she married Mr. Joseph F. Meyer Sr. This century's tenants have included a seed store, a tailor shop run by Rex Braun, who eventually became a state representative, a toy store, and several lounges. A restaurant called Treebeard's operated in the left half and also leased the second floor. A tailor shop existed in the right half of the building, but the owner of thirty-five years, Mr. Danowitz, died. Treebeard's obtained the lease to the right half of the building where they expanded their business.

Phantoms

The only story to date was provided by an employee named Anh Tran, who used to work for the owners. According to Tran, when he would open up the restaurant he would often hear someone walking around upstairs even though the place was unoccupied. After checking to see who might have come in before him, he

never found anyone there. Several other employees have heard the sounds of phantom footsteps in unoccupied areas of the restaurant, as well as soft voices speaking inaudibly, just out of earshot.

There are a few cold spots that suddenly manifest, and then there's that uneasy feeling that someone or something is watching or following you when you are alone. The current owners think it might be the former owner Mr. Danowitz, who occupied a part of the building while running his tailor shop until he died. While enjoying the savory chicken-and-sausage gumbo, shrimp étouffé, jalapeño cornbread, red beans and rice, mustard greens, or other Cajun specialties, be sure to keep your senses sharp just in case Mr. Danowitz decides to pay a visit during business hours.

Jefferson

Early settlers were already well established when the town was laid out in 1842. Discovery of nearby iron ore brought smelters and plow works, while plentiful pine and cypress stimulated the lumber industry. The city boasted one of Texas's first breweries and shortly after the Civil War, reached a peak population of 30,000 with as many as fifteen steamboats at a time lining the docks and scores of wagon trains passing through on the way west. Jefferson, confident in the longevity of the steamboat, refused Jay Gould's offer for a railroad. Gould angrily predicted a quick demise for the city and bypassed the town. Jefferson was a bustling inland port in the 1890s then became a ghost town overnight when the riverboat traffic ceased. Current statistics place the population at 2,205 inhabitants.

Excelsior House

Address:	211 W. Austin, Jefferson, Texas 75657
Phone:	903-665-2513
Fax:	903-665-9389
E-mail:	excelsior@jeffersontx.com
Website:	www.jeffersontx.com/excelsior
Contact:	Jessie Allen Wise Garden Club
Accommodations:	15 guestrooms and suites
Amenities:	Private baths; generous plantation breakfast; air conditioning; television; tours
References:	5, 23, 31, 37

History

The Excelsior is the state's second-oldest hotel after the Menger in San Antonio. Captain William Perry built a small hotel not far from the waterfront about 1858, which was known as the Irving House. Today this structure forms the northwest portion of the Excelsior House. A southwest wing was constructed during the 1860s to 1870s. After Captain Perry passed away, the hotel changed hands numerous times and was variously called the Exchange Hotel and Commercial Hotel. In 1887 Mrs. Kate Wood bought the property and renamed the place the Excelsior House.

The hotel gained notoriety during its heyday as the focal point for celebrations similar to the Mardi Gras held in New Orleans. Mrs. Wood and her daughter, Mrs. Amelia Wood McNeeley, operated the Excelsior until 1902. From 1902 until her death in 1920, Amelia Wood McNeeley ran the hotel. The hotel passed to the George S. Neidermeir family, who ran the establishment until 1954, when Mrs. James Peters bought it. Mrs. Peters began restoration of the 100-year-old structure and continued until August of 1961, when the Jessie Allen Wise Garden Club purchased the hotel and continued the renovation process.

Phantoms

Over the years numerous ghost stories that have surfaced point to more than one spirit inhabiting this historic treasure. Some reported events include a woman who spent the night and said the covers were suddenly yanked off her bed, even though there was no one else in the room with her. The woman then watched as the covers were literally tossed across the room, landing close to the fireplace. After hearing a tap on her bedroom door, she rushed over to answer it. When she opened the door, no one was there.

Steven Spielberg is said to have had an encounter with the spirits of the Excelsior. While filming the *Sugarland Express*, Spielberg and his crew checked into the hotel. He was unlucky enough to wind up in a haunted room. Before completing his night's stay, Spielberg woke up the crew, proclaimed that the Excelsior was the spookiest place he had ever visited, and directed them to a nearby, spirit-free motel. For the man who would go on to make *Poltergeist* and *Casper*, the real thing was apparently too much to take.

Several staff persons refused to go upstairs alone in the east wing, because a "headless man" was often sighted wandering in the Jay Gould room. A visitor from Dallas, who considered himself something of a psychic/paranormal investigator, spent the night in the north wing of the Excelsior. Upon checking out, the man complained of heavy breathing coming from an unseen presence who kept him awake most of the night.

A retired ABC newsman and his wife spent the night in the Gould Room. After having dinner at the Galley Restaurant, the two bedded down for the night. The newsman awoke and went to the bathroom and was about to go back to sleep, when he noticed the door beginning to open slowly. He got up and firmly latched it shut. Later, when he had to use the bathroom again, he couldn't turn the knob. It was as if someone was holding it from the other side. Finally the knob turned easily. Glancing around, he looked in awe as a woman dressed in black and wearing a black veil stood across the room. The apparition quickly vanished but not before leaving a scent of perfume that permeated the room. Not wanting to wake his wife for fear she would be frightened and want to leave, he finally drifted back to sleep. However he was awakened a short time later by the odor of cigar smoke and what sounded like someone in the room shuffling through newspaper pages. This was followed by a knocking sound, which came from near the headboard. All night long the man was kept awake by strange noises or vivid dreams. The staff was not surprised when told of his strange encounters in the room, saying that guests often reported "unusual" things in "that" room. Another guest reported seeing a woman in black in the rocking chair, holding a baby. After the figure vanished, the chair continued to move on its own before coming to a complete stop.

A real estate attorney, who frequented Jefferson and stayed at the Excelsior at least three times a month, would request room 201, his "home away from home." Then suddenly the man stopped staying at the hotel. The concerned staff decided to make inquiries and find out if something happened to their "regular" guest. His associate informed management that, at around 1:00 A.M. during his friend's last stay, he was awakened by a young women in a black dress, who was sitting in the rocker next to his bed. The women spoke to him, referring to him by name and asking him if everything was all right. This lawyer had made comments prior to this event concerning his suspicion that a "presence" was in the west wing of the hotel. After the inquiry the man began returning to the Excelsior under the condition that they book his room downstairs in the historic wing. He refused to stay in room 201, and he will never go upstairs into the west wing of the Excelsior again!

A reservationist encountered this same young women in the black dress while working at the reservation counter. She chanced to look up and caught a glimpse of a woman walking out of the manager's office, immediately to her left, and crossing the hall into the night clerk's room. Since no one was supposed to be in the manager's office, she immediately walked across to the night clerk's room. Before she went in, she caught a glimpse of this same woman turning left toward the restroom of the clerk's room. Two steps later she entered the room, and there was no one there.

The woman in black had simply vanished, which is just what the reservationist did (from the room) after realizing what she saw was a ghost.

Two housekeeping ladies saw the lady in the black dress enter room 201. While cleaning a room down the hall, one housekeeper saw someone enter room 201. She thought it was her co-worker, so she called to her for assistance in completing some chores. Immediately the other housekeeper came out of the room directly across the hall from her and asked what she wanted. After explaining what she saw, both housekeepers walked down the hall to room 201 and opened the door. There was no one inside. The housekeeping crew often requests that the manager open the room doors in the west wing of the hotel before they begin their day's work.

Richard Stewart, co-author of *Transparent Tales: An Attic Full of Texas Ghosts with Allan Turner,* decided to spend a night in The Haunted Chamber. During the night, the quiet was shattered when a window shade flapped open on its own. After he enjoyed a brief rest on one of the big beds, three wooden slats fell out, making a horrendous commotion. As Stewart lay on the bed in the room, he saw the figure of a woman in a full, old-time, deep maroon dress quickly glide out of the bathroom toward the door before disappearing. He didn't notice a head on the woman.

A visit to the historic Excelsior may provide you with more than just a nostalgic trip through the past. It may in fact put you in touch with it, by introducing you to some of its spirited guests.

The Grove

Address:	405 West Moseley, Jefferson, Texas 75657
Phone:	903-835-6043
Contact:	Patrick Hopkins, Route 1, Box 260C, Hughes Springs, Texas 75656
Business Hours:	By appointment only for special events
References:	4, 10, 15, 18, 23, 31

History

The Grove, also called the Amos Morrill house after its first owner, is no longer a restaurant. However, by contacting the owner, Patrick Hopkins, you can still visit this historic building and arrange special events and functions. The land was originally part of the Stephen Smith land grant given to Daniel and Lucy Alley, one of the co-founders of Jefferson. Then the property passed to Amos Morrill, the first federal judge of Texas and lawyer. Harriet Potter, the widow of slain secretary of the Republic of Texas navy Robert Potter, then owned the land for a while. Caleb Ragin and his wife, Sarah Wilson Ragin, bought the land, and the house was built after that date, some say around 1861. Sarah was the daughter of former Arkansas representative Colonel John Wilson, who had to "Go to Texas," as many who had problems with the law did, after killing the Arkansas Speaker of the House over hunting rights in the state of Arkansas. The house was then bought back by W. Frank Stilley and his wife, Minerva Fox, from Marshall. They had two sons named John R. and Frank. Mrs. Stilley's will was made out to her sons, with her husband as executor.

During Reconstruction, a northern carpetbagger arrived in Jefferson with four freed slaves and quickly made enemies by saying that ex-slaves wouldn't be free until Jefferson burnt. Shortly after the speech, much of the town burned to the ground, and the locals threatened the man. The occupying Union troops placed this gentleman and four of his black aides in protective custody in the city jail at the east end of Moseley. The Yankee captain lived in the end house on the west end of Moseley. Several months later a group of two hundred men surrounded the jail, disarmed the

Union troops, entered the jail, took the carpetbagger out, and shot him. The brutal act was completed when they took the four black men and either shot or hanged them along Moseley Street.

The Union forces with reinforcements built a stockade two hundred yards south of The Grove, where they imprisoned and tried suspects. A map drawn up by the military court listed one of the witness sites as Mr. Stilley's House. Apparently Mrs. Stilley died around 1879. A family named Burks bought the house for $175, but six months later wanted their money back. The house then went to bridge builder D.C. Rock, his wife, and a live-in employee named O'Toole.

Finally, in 1885, Mr. Charlie Young bought the place with his wife, Daphine, and raised two daughters and a son. Young lived in the house until his death in 1938, while his widow lived there until her death in 1955. Their oldest daughter, Louise, born in 1887, spent her long life in the house, dying unmarried in 1983. According to those who knew Louise, she was constantly frightened of something, since she had every interior door and window fitted with strong locks on them and installed strong lights to keep the yard lit. Worried about someone getting in, she called the police on a regular basis, complaining about prowlers; or was it the spirits!

Current owner and well-known chef, Patrick Hopkins, while looking for a place to open his own restaurant, chanced to drive by the house during 1989. He and his sister, Mary Hopkins Callas, immediately bought it, renovated it, and made it into a fine dining establishment, naming it "The Grove" after the numerous pecan trees in the area. When Hopkins went to sign the papers to close the deal, he learned that the family selling the house was Mr. and Mrs. Grove—coincidence? Hopkins also found out the place was haunted, a fact that didn't concern him.

Phantoms

The Groves told Hopkins that a number of eerie events took place while undergoing renovations that were never completed. Mrs. Grove reportedly brought a Bible to bed with the intention of praying for her and her husband, but she fell asleep. She awakened to a black swirling mass engulfing the bedroom. There were also unexplained voices, disembodied footsteps, sounds of objects being moved by unseen hands, and the apparitions.

According to Hopkins, one of the contractors he hired to renovate the building quit almost immediately, while another kept reporting having horrible nightmares that woke him up at 3:00 A.M. Hopkins and his family also had their share of run-ins with the spirits: Disembodied footsteps coming from the back to the front suddenly stop. Mirrors fall off walls and end up several feet from where they should have landed naturally, and leave objects untouched that should have been crushed. When the place was closed, a loud, mournful wail was heard coming from the upstairs area in rooms that weren't used by the restaurant. Items have been taken from shelves only to reappear in other parts of the house. An unexplained moisture has appeared on a mirror frame and in other spots around the house. A peculiar odor of old sweat, like a person who has been working a long time and hasn't taken a bath, has manifested in one of the rooms. There is the constant feeling of being watched, and people report seeing misty forms materialize, then suddenly disappear. Legend has it that the property lies in an area where several murders occurred, and several unmarked graves reportedly lie under or near the house.

A physic from Dallas once viewed a young, dark-haired, bearded man in a waistcoat walking through the house before disappearing. Shortly before Hopkins was told about the encounter, his niece was having her "Sweet Sixteen" birthday party at The Grove. After the party and while walking down Moseley Street, his niece and seven other girls reportedly saw a black man lying in the road. As they approached to see if he needed help, the man inexplicably vanished! What no one knew at the time was that a carpetbagger and his black servants were viciously killed on Moseley Street, and as a black man was being hanged on the back porch of the house, he died cursing the place.

One evening a waitress innocently walked out of the kitchen into the hallway and was attacked by a black and white dog, which knocked her to the ground. After quickly regaining her composure, she retreated into the kitchen, screaming for help. Hopkins ran in and proceeded to search the building and yard. There was no dog anywhere around. It simply had vanished.

Hopkins was in the house around 4:45 P.M. with his sister shortly before opening. His sister was wearing a white blouse and black slacks. As Hopkins passed through the hall, he noticed the old trunk given to Louise Young by her father in 1906 needed dusting. As Hopkins was busy dusting the trunk, he heard footsteps coming from the kitchen and thought it was his sister. The footsteps abruptly stopped in the Blue Room and crossed the hall. Glancing up, Hopkins saw a woman wearing a long, white dress with puff sleeves approaching him. The woman pulled her skirt aside, exposing high buttoned shoes, and passed Hopkins as she entered the ladies room, which had once served as an old bedroom. Realizing it wasn't his sister, he quickly followed the strange-looking woman into the powder room. There was no one there, but Hopkins recalled how real the woman looked.

During a Candlelight Tour, a couple from the Dallas area took a picture of the Christmas lights on the neighbor's house to the east of The Grove. Their photo showed the Christmas lights in the foreground. In the background was a lady in a high-collared, puff sleeved white dress surrounded by a ring of smoke.

A neighbor lady living a block behind the Grove said that her sister was standing on the porch one night around 9:00 P.M. when she called to the woman to look at the glowing white figure across the street on the east side of the Grove. The lady said she and her sister had witnessed this event several nights in a row before the ghostly woman stopped appearing.

While rehearsing a production of *Angel Street*, a murder mystery done in period dress, the light technician was on the front porch looking through the window, doing some light cues. Suddenly she felt someone staring at her so she quickly glanced in that direction. Standing on the east side of the house by the porch was a lady in white who began walking behind the east side of the house. Chasing the eerie-looking woman, the girl turned the corner of the house, and the woman had vanished. Ironically, there used to be a door on that side of the house leading into the Blue Room. Perhaps the spectral woman used a door from long ago to elude the living! During the same rehearsal, the actress portraying the heroine came down the stairs. When she reached the bottom step she glanced to her right and saw a person in costume she was not familiar with, standing in the corner. When she began to ask the lady something, the woman disappeared.

Carol Rust, while working on an article for the *Texas Journey* magazine, had a strange encounter with the Grove spirits. She set up an appointment with the owner, Patrick Hopkins. When she arrived Patrick's car was there, but there was no sign of him. Making her way to the front door, Rust, thinking Hopkins was inside, tried the door. With little effort the door opened, and she called inside before entering. She immediately sensed "something" in the house with her, yet a quick inspection revealed her solitary condition. She called out to Hopkins, but there was no response. So Rust walked to the back of the building and left her purse on the kitchen table while taking a few photographs of the inside.

Making her way upstairs, the sound of someone else taking a step behind her echoed up the staircase with each step she took. By the fifth step she whirled around to see who was following her. At that moment she glimpsed a short, medium-built, well-dressed mulatto or dark-complected man, with noticeable facial hair, following close behind. In that instant, as she focused on the shape, it disappeared—Rust was alone. Deciding, and wisely so, not to go any further unescorted, she went back to the kitchen to retrieve her purse. Before her was a partially emptied purse, with its contents, not strewn about, but neatly placed on the table as if someone had quickly gone through her purse and pulled out a few items to look at. As fast as she could, Rust gathered her camera, purse, and courage and walked out the front door to an awaiting Patrick Hopkins. Hopkins immediately asked how Rust got in, since he didn't have the opportunity to unlock the door. After Rust explained what had happened and what she saw, Hopkins stated that the man she witnessed was none other than Mr. C. J. "Charlie" Young, a prior owner who lived in the house with his wife, "Miss Daphine," in 1885.

During dinner, every time a particular waitress walked down the hallway, she felt as if some force was passing right through her. Another waitress, Phyllis Duree, witnessed wet footprints appearing in the middle of the hallway even though it wasn't raining outside and there were no plumbing leaks. Stranger yet was that the prints had no beginning or end, they were just there.

One day Hopkins encountered a man who dropped by to tell him what a great job he did on restoring the house. The man was surprised that Hopkins didn't recognize him, since he said he had seen Hopkins four years earlier. The man explained that he dropped by and peeked through the window after he knew the prior owners had left. He was surprised to see that the house was filled with antiques and even more shocked when a man he swore was Hopkins, sporting a much longer beard, came to the window holding a pistol. Hopkins had to explain that he did not own the building four years ago, and in fact the house was "vacant!"

Hopkins shared a story from a few years back involving a woman named Sharon who worked as a reporter for the *Marshall Messenger.* As it turned out, Sharon's daughters were later employed at the Grove. Anyway, Sharon was working on a feature for Halloween and learned the Grove Restaurant was haunted, so a meeting was arranged. The day they were to meet, business was slow, and Hopkins and a waiter named Mark were working the restaurant. Prior to Sharon's arrival for the scheduled interview, Hopkins had to run out to a local store. Upon returning, Hopkins parked his car and took the brick sidewalk diagonally across the gardens to the back of the house. As he was about to open the back door, he heard a loud "thump" followed by a crash and a man's distinctive laughter. Hopkins recalled thinking that it reminded him of someone who clumsily dropped something then uneasily laughed at the mistake. Rushing inside, Hopkins looked to the left into the office area expecting to see Mark standing over something he had just dropped. Instead, there was no one in the area where the crashing sound and laughter occurred. He then proceeded into the kitchen and found Mark, where they both acknowledged the eerie sound coming from an unoccupied area of the house.

Before they could digest what just occurred, Sharon and her daughter Candace arrived for the interview. Almost immediately both women sensed what most people do when they walk through the front door, that someone was watching them. Hopkins shared a number of stories with the women, then Sharon and Candace got up to leave. When the women were escorted to their car, Sharon unlocked the doors with her auto-lock device. As Candace was about to open one of the doors, they suddenly and mysteriously locked on their own. Startled, Sharon pulled out her auto-lock device and reopened the doors. Once again, the doors magically locked. This scenario played out over and over again for at least six more times. Finally, the women were on their way, and Hopkins went back to his business to see that everything was ready for dinner. Making room by room inspections, Hopkins entered the ladies powder room, and there in the middle of the room was a small, wooden shelf that had fallen to the floor. Strangely, a china basket was smashed, but a china crockery set was untouched. Perhaps this was the sound Hopkins heard outside the building, followed by a man's mischievous laughter.

Although known by several names, including The Grove, the name most often associated with this historic gem and probably the most apropos is "haunted."

Maison-Bayou Waterfront Bed & Breakfast Inn

Address:	300 Bayou Street, Jefferson, Texas 75657
Phone:	903-665-7600
Fax:	240-218-8135
E-mail:	cabins@maisonbayou.com
Website:	www.maisonbayou.com
Contact:	Jan & Pete Hochendel
Accommodations:	12 units including cabins, poolside cabanas, riverfront railcars, and replica floating paddle wheeler
Amenities:	Private baths; heat and air conditioning; full breakfast; free canoe & peddle boat for guests; lagoon-styled swimming pool with waterfalls.
References:	15

History

Maison-Bayou is an authentic re-creation of an 1850s Creole plantation, complete with slave quarters and sugarcane! The antebellum family history of owners Pete and Jan Hochendel was the inspiration for this unique setting. After G. Michel Hochendel first immigrated from Strausbourg, France, to New Orleans in the 1830s, he worked for a customs house, was a cabinetmaker, and had a beer house in the Vieux, or French Quarter. After General Butler commandeered the family home during the Northern occupation in 1863, the Hochendel family moved to Baton Rouge and bought a plantation there.

Maison-Bayou is situated on fifty-five wooded acres, right on Big Cypress Bayou and directly across the Polk Street Bridge from the historic downtown district.

Arrowheads were unearthed while clearing wooded areas, indicating the use of the land by Caddo Indians. Then there is the famous legend of Diamond Bessie, who died an untimely and violent death, presumably murdered by her companion Abe Rothschild, who was found not guilty. To this day the murder of Bessie Moore is an unsolved case, and if "Hell hath no fury like that of a woman scorned," then perhaps the mysterious, sometimes angry energy that is part of this setting belongs to Bessie, who is still seeking justice after all these years!

Phantoms

In 1991 construction was begun on the overseer's house, the Hochendels' home while running Maison-Bayou. It was during this time that their first encounter with a spirited energy occurred. Gary Fort, their plumber, while working on repairs under the house, came flying out, saying he felt as if someone had slapped him upside the head, and refused to continue working until the owners could find out the cause. So the Hochendels called their electrician to check the wiring for a short. There was nothing found that would have accounted for what happened to the plumber. The next call was to their utility company, SWEPCO. They suspected DC voltage at play caused by an old telephone line buried from the flood of 1945. Southwestern Bell Telephone came to the property to run some tests but found no evidence of DC voltage in the ground. SWEPCO came back and found AC voltage active in the ground. The existence of AC voltage is next to impossible, since this type of voltage normally dissipates when it strikes the ground. Further tests revealed a ground voltage reading that varied between 3 and 18 AC volts. Even though, to alleviate the problem, SWEPCO shut off the power from the electric meter to the house, the AC ground voltage remained—shocking news. After SWEPCO shut the electrical power off for more than a one-mile radius from the power substation, there was still AC voltage in the ground. Finally, after having the anomalous situation studied by MIT, they concluded that there was no scientific explanation for this kind of situation. Was Diamond Bessie's spirit responsible for the strange energy exerted on the landscape?

One day two employees were sent into the pond located behind the overseer's house to attend to some work. After a few minutes they both began to fumble with their tools and complained of feeling a prickly, tingling sensation while in the water, then feeling tingling weakness in their arms and legs upon standing on land. Another project came to a halt, and this time someone verbalized what most had been thinking; perhaps it was Diamond Bessie's revenge! Cypress Pond lies between the overseer's house and the bank, which is adjacent to the site of the Diamond Bessie murder, and there is a possibility that somehow the two are connected. As the Hochendels contemplated the strange events that had taken place since they began construction, one fact stood out; only the males have been affected by the energy at the place.

In the construction and furnishing of the overseer's house and cabins for the inn, some of the materials used originated from the early 1800s including natural rough sawn pine walls, heart pine flooring, antique bed frames, rocking chairs, and armoires. These materials seem to bring with them more than just pleasing aesthetic; it seems that they also brought a spirit or two to complement Diamond Bessie!

Recently the Hochendels had a young couple in their mid-twenties staying in cabin 2 for the weekend. While visiting with them during breakfast on the Saturday morning, the Hochendels learned that the couple had experienced something unexplainable. During the middle of the night the wife awoke, reached to put her arm around her husband, but didn't feel him beside her. Listening for a moment, she heard the creaking of the rocking chair on the old pine floor. Since her husband's back had been bothering him for some time, it wasn't unusual for him to have difficulty sleeping through the night. At home he often alternated between sleeping in the bed and their recliner, so for him to be in the antique wooden rocking chair was not unusual; that is, until the next morning when the wife asked how he slept. His response was, "Great." It was the first time in weeks he had actually slept like a rock and didn't wake the entire night. The stunned wife then explained what had happened. Retracing the events, the couple noticed that the rocking chair was sitting atop a rug, not on the bare wood floor. Why had she experienced him out of bed, and who was in the rocking chair? Neither could come up with an explanation, but the next night she never let him out of her arms until daybreak!

During a different weekend, just two units down, in cabin 4, a mother, father, and their eleven-year-old daughter spent the night. The cabin is built in an architectural style known as the "Dog-Trot," where two units share a full-length front and back porch but are separated by a six-foot breezeway. There are no front facing windows, only side and back windows on the cabin. After the family spent the day exploring the natural setting provided by fifty-five wooded acres, they returned to their cabin to relax. In the interest of wanting to create an experience that allows guests to enjoy some of the simple pleasures of the past, there are no televisions in the Plantation Cabins. Instead, there are checkers, dominoes, cards, and even cassette players with tapes of programs recorded from the Golden Age of Radio! When everyone grew tired, the lights were turned off, and the cabin became enveloped in a darkness that can only be found in a country-type setting, devoid of street lamps and city lights.

About half past midnight the daughter's soft voice awakened her mother. Thinking her daughter was talking in her sleep, the mother quickly dozed back to sleep. An hour or so later the mother again was awakened by her daughter's voice, this time mixed with conversation and laughter. Not wanting to awaken her sleeping husband, the woman whispered to her daughter, asking what was she doing. The daughter replied that she was talking to the lights at the foot of her bed. Sitting up in bed to look, the mother saw a faint light at the foot of the bed but dismissed it as nothing more than an outside light shining through the window. She urged her daughter to go back to sleep.

The mother ended up asking the owners to turn off the yard light by their cabin, because it kept her daughter awake during the previous night. The Hochendels were befuddled because they knew that there wasn't any yard light in the cabin area. When they pointed this out, the husband interjected that maybe it was one of the other cabin guests coming in for the evening with the headlights of their vehicle shining in the window. Again, the Hochendels thought about it and pointed out that since the side window of their cabin faced the woods with no road or path, there was no way for a vehicle to have come around to the side of their cabin and shine the headlights in the window.

During all this conversation we noticed that the daughter was just sitting quietly, sort of smiling to herself. When she was asked her opinion, the girl said matter-of-factly that it was a "friendly something," like the hovering light of Tinkerbell, who visited her. She continued saying that she had been asleep and dreaming of a little girl who was asking her to play. Something made her wake up from her dream, and that's when she sat up and saw the light at the foot of her bed. When asked by her father if she was afraid, and why didn't she wake them up, like when they were are home and she has a nightmare, she responded that there was nothing to be afraid of. That it wasn't a dream or a nightmare. Her mother asked why she was talking and laughing at the light during the night, and her daughter responded that though there were no voices or words from the light, for some reason she just knew it was listening to her. When asked what type of things she was telling the light, she said, in typical preteen fashion, "Oh, nothing really—just stuff, you know!"

At Maison-Bayou you can select your choice of accommodations and what adventures you wish to include in your daily regimen, but come nightfall, you cannot select the invisible companionship you or your children may encounter, since the friendly spirits of this inn do all the selecting.

The New Jefferson Hotel

Address:	124 West Austin, Jefferson, Texas 75657
Phone:	903-665-2631
Toll Free Number:	1-800-226-9026
E-mail:	jeffersonhotel@jeffersontx.com
Website:	http://jeffersontx.com/jeffersonhotel
Contact:	Ron & Linda Meissner
Accommodations:	24 renovated rooms
Amenities:	Private baths; one suite has a Jacuzzi, and one has a fireplace
References:	10, 15, 23, 31, 37

History

The Jefferson Hotel was constructed in 1851 as a cotton warehouse. The rear of the hotel was once used as the front entrance of the structure. The iron doorframes are still visible where large arched doors of the 1870s era hotel faced Dallas Street. Today the front is located on West Austin Street. The cotton warehouse closed down when the steamboat port closed. The building has since been used for many purposes including a school for girls—actually it was a bordello. A Chinese laundry was downstairs in the back of the building. It was a hotel in the 1920s where gambling parties were held in a back room. The hotel has changed ownership a number of times since the 1940s.

Phantoms

The spirits of the Jefferson Hotel are well known and plentiful. At least ten out of the twenty-four rooms at this hotel including the famous room 19 are home to spirits. Reports include moving cold spots, unexplainable noises, disembodied footsteps, doors that open and close by themselves, knocks on the wall coming from unoccupied rooms, shadowy apparitions, newly cleaned rooms with imprints on the sheets, rooms where there will be a sudden 20-30 degree drop in temperature within seconds, being touched by something no one can see, hearing an unseen someone

breathing, and smelling a cologne or after-shave which instantly materializes in a particular room.

Several spirits have been witnessed: a petite blond with very long hair, wearing white with high neck and long sleeves like a Victorian nightgown; a small woman with dark hair worn piled on top of her head and wearing a long, dark skirt. (She is believed to be Mrs. Schluter, the lady who owned the hotel in the late 1800s and early 1900s. Mrs. Schluter's funeral was held in the hotel.) A man was seen upstairs in room 5 by a little boy who told his parents the man kept waking him up, and another man was sighted at the end of the hall downstairs. He was described as being very tall and wearing a long, tan-colored coat with tall boots and a hat. This male manifestation was sighted by the back door (later found to be locked) by an elderly lady at 5:00 A.M. When she saw him she asked who he was, since she thought she was the only guest in the hotel. The man proceeded to casually walk right through the door in room 20.

A guest once described hearing strange clicking and popping sounds and something knocking on the walls in back of the headboard of his bed. He reported that the noises were coming from behind a very thick wall. An investigation of his problem indicated that his room faced the outside, and there was no physical way someone could be outside making the noises.

A female guest rolled over in bed to face a lady with long wavy hair standing next to her. When she turned away to wake up her husband, the woman vanished. Room 19, located at the end of an upstairs hallway, has its share of tales including guests who are frequently awakened by someone invisible sitting on the bed next to them. Other guests have reported seeing a wispy, shadowed figure hovering in the corner of the room, or they complain that someone they can't see has touched them.

A member of the Texas chapter of the Travelers Protection Association, a Hurst based charity, loves coming to the hotel for their annual meeting because of its reputation. While she was staying in one of the rooms during a prior conference, she was awakened at 3:00 A.M. by someone passing in front of her door. When she went to see who it was, she could hear footsteps walking down the hallway to the sound of shoes hitting a hardwood floor but couldn't see a living soul. To her amazement, the hallway was carpeted.

A lady who stayed in the hotel and knew nothing of the stories stayed downstairs in room 21 with her adult daughter. She awoke at 2:45 A.M. to a cold chill on her neck and pulled the sheet up closer. Within seconds the sheet was gently pulled back down and the chill again blew down her neck. Thinking it might be her daughter playing, the woman rolled over and discovered that she was sound asleep in the other bed. Rolling back over, she immediately felt someone rubbing her hair from the back, followed by a male voice that said, "You have very pretty long hair." The woman screamed, hollered, woke up her daughter, and the two found no one else in the room. The strange thing was, the woman did not have long hair!

A former night clerk reported that one night when the upstairs area was unoccupied, she heard all the doors open and close and the sound of numerous people walking around, talking and making a loud commotion. She was afraid to go upstairs until the noises eventually ceased.

Other paranormal rooms include room 20 where the water in the bathroom sink will suddenly come on full force in the middle of the night; room 5 where guests oftentimes hear knocking on the walls from an adjacent room, which is unoccupied; room 11 where strange sounds are heard coming from inside and behind the walls; the front desk where repeated knocking is heard for several minutes when no one is anywhere around; and the hallway near room 6 where there are strange cold spots. An extremely strong feeling of an unseen presence has caused people to either turn around, expecting to see someone standing behind them, or to leave the area in fear.

In room 2 a police officer working security had a door mysteriously slam shut behind him. When he opened the door no once was there; however, when he tried to shut the door upon leaving, he pulled against it as hard as he could but couldn't shut it—it was as if an unseen force was fighting with him for control of the door. Finally after shutting the door, he heard a loud bang, as if someone had thrown something against the door from the inside. Room 12 is where a smoky, wispy image of a female entity came to visit a couple, who later came back to the hotel and to the same room because the experience was so wonderful.

Lamache's Italian Restaurant, occupying the eastern portion of the hotel's ground floor, is not exempt from paranormal activity. Pots and pans have inexplicably flown off the shelves in front of startled clean-up personnel, and cold spots, strange voices, and unexplained footsteps are also trademarks of the restaurant. Almost everyone at the hotel has had some kind of paranormal experience. No one tries to explain anything that happens any more; they just accept the fact that the place is haunted by several spirits, and they try to co-exist with their otherworldly friends. Guests have enjoyed their visits and the fact that they are in a haunted hotel. Some return over and over just for the chance to meet the spirits of the Jefferson Hotel. A lady's face has been photographed in the bathroom mirror in room 19. Her mouth is open slightly, and she is looking upwards. She has shown up in more than one mirror. A man was shaving in room 7, and this face came up behind him in that mirror to his right. Ghostly activity goes in spurts; you may have no incidents for two or three weeks, then it gets very active.

The New Jefferson Hotel is old hat when it comes to the spirited, yet friendly occupants keep the place lively all year round.

Marathon

Marathon is a gentrified home base for exploring Big Bend National Park, rock hunting, or simply getting away from it all and relaxing. At an altitude of over 4,000 feet and a population of less than 1,000, the West Texas Chihuahuan Desert region has been inhabited for centuries prior to arrival of white men. Fort Pena was established in the area in 1879 to guard the frontier against Indian uprisings. The town developed in 1882 with the arrival of the Texas and New Orleans Railroad. The name was suggested by a sea captain who said the area reminded him of Marathon, Greece.

The Gage Hotel

Address:	102 Highway 90 West, P.O. Box 46, Marathon, Texas 79842
Phone:	915-386-4205
Fax:	915-386-4510
Toll Free Number:	1-800-884-GAGE
E-mail:	welcome@gagehotel.com
Website:	www.gagehotel.com
Contact:	Brock Walden
Accommodations:	37 guestrooms
Amenities:	29 private, 8 shared baths; pool; Cafe Cenizo; White Buffalo Cantina
References:	15, 29, 31, 37

History

Alfred S. Gage left his native Vermont in 1878 at age eighteen to make his fortune in the open spaces of far West Texas. Finding work as a cowhand, he and his brothers later founded the Alpine Cattle Company south of Marathon. By 1920 Gage was a prosperous banker and rancher. Needing a headquarters for his extensive operations, he had the hotel built. Opening in 1927, the brick hotel became a gathering place for many ranchers and miners of the area and was considered the most elegant building in Texas west of the Pecos. Gage, however, was unable to enjoy the success of his hotel, passing away in 1928. After decades of neglect the hotel was

purchased by J.P. and Mary Jon Bryan of Houston. Restoration was begun as well as an expansion of the facilities. The Los Portales rooms were opened in 1992, and Cafe Cenizo opened in 1996.

Phantoms

The ghosts of the Gage are locally well known with the following unexplainable events reported: disembodied footsteps walking down unoccupied corridors; strange music emerging from room 10 when the room is unoccupied; guests in the room hearing ethereal music, people being tapped gently on the arm; people hearing the whisperings of a woman reciting poetry.

A former employee, cleaning up late at night, was frightened by an unseen force while he was working down in the basement of the hotel. Apparently the staff person felt a presence in the room with him and was actually tapped on the shoulder. As he turned in the direction of what he thought was another employee summoning him, he was confronted by the spirit of Alfred Gage, who calmly asked the person to leave his hotel. Not heeding the warning, the person had a second encounter with Gage, who once again asked him to leave—which he did, for good.

A former manager confided that he had heard footsteps walking down a hallway, but he couldn't see a body. A young man employed as a dishwasher used to work late, doing extra chores like cleaning floors, polishing ashtrays and brass, and cleaning the fireplaces. Suddenly he stopped working overtime and didn't seem his cheerful self. The manager finally had a talk with the man, who broke down and said that one evening when he was in the basement level working very late, he suddenly felt a presence in the room with him. As a hand was placed on his shoulder, the man whirled around and was confronted by the figure of Alfred Gage, whom he recognized from the portrait in the hotel. Gage's apparition looked straight at the startled worker and said, "I do not want you in my hotel any longer."

In room 10 there are a couple of old violins hanging on the wall as part of the decor. People have reportedly heard music playing in that room. It's hard to recognize the tune, but it's definitely music, and it's only heard in that room. Also, several guests who have occupied room 10 have reported being awakened by a gentle tap on the arm, followed by the soft voice of a woman reciting poetry. A gentleman staying in room 25 in the new Los Portales unit was awakened by someone tugging on his arm. He then witnessed the figure of a young woman standing by his bed. She appeared to be in her early thirties and was rather misty in appearance. As the startled man stared at her, she slowly faded away.

A young woman also appeared to a maintenance man as he stood by a Coke machine in the Los Portales area at around 10:00 P.M. The woman was young—in her thirties—with short brown hair and wearing a white blouse and a dark blue skirt that was street length. The misty-looking woman walked by him, then proceeded toward the courtyard where the swimming pool is located. As she neared the swimming pool, she slowly dissolved into the darkness.

A night auditor heard someone moving from chair to chair in the lobby. The old leather chairs would make a lot of noise when people sat in them. The woman said it happened all the time, and there were others who heard the noises. No one was ever able to see who was responsible for the commotion. There's no way to gauge how many spirits call the hotel home, but one thing seems certain; Alfred S. Gage is one of them, the once proud owner who still enjoys the place he built!

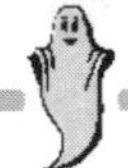

Captain Shepard's Inn

Address:	c/o The Gage Hotel, P.O. Box 46, Marathon, Texas 79842
Toll Free Number:	1-800-884-4243
Contact:	Russ Tidwell
Accommodations:	Five large guestrooms; the original 1890s Carriage House has been converted into a two bedroom bunkhouse with a porch, kitchenette, fireplace, and living area.
Amenities:	Private baths; access to private porches; breakfast included; two sitting rooms; a dining room; a three minute walk to the Gage Hotel where guests may use the pool and other hotel facilities.
References:	15

History

A former sea captain, Albion Shepard, came to the area as a surveyor for the Southern Pacific Railroad in 1881. By 1882 he was assigned to name the water stops between Del Rio and El Paso. The high semi-arid grasslands and rock mountains reminded him of Marathon, Greece, so the name Marathon, Texas, came into being. Shepard became the owner of a large ranch north of the townsite, which today is part of the Iron Mountain Ranch. Shepard helped lay out the town lots in 1885, established the first post office, and served as the first postmaster. He was a rancher running as many as 25,000 sheep, kept by herders with no fences. By 1889 Shepard had built a large two-story adobe home with carriage house 100 yards north of the railroad. The house, occupied continuously since its completion, is now the Captain Shepard's Inn, opening in March 1995 and operated by the Gage Hotel.

Phantoms

This location, although having very little paranormal information at present, will most certainly produce evidence of additional activity in the future. The only stories manifesting from this inn involve a housekeeper named Leasa, who went to open up an old trunk to get a blanket out. As she was removing the blanket, a gust of cold wind came from nowhere and hit her in the face. The startled woman looked around to see if someone had left a window or fan on, but could not find the cause.

Another housekeeper, who also works at the Gage, is convinced that room 2 at the inn is haunted. She refuses to work there unless someone is with her. The housekeeper remarked that the door is always opening and closing by itself, and unexplained shadows have been frequently spotted roaming the building when no guests are staying there.

Could the spirit of Captain Albion Shepard be wandering his former residence? Perhaps one day a guest will see more than a shadow and will provide more evidence as to the identity of the inn's ghost.

Marfa

Marfa sits on a high desert plateau at 4,830 feet. Even in the heat of the Texas summer, the midday temperature rarely rises over 90 degrees while nighttime temperatures sometimes dip into the 60s. Named in 1883 by the wife of a railroad executive for a character in Dostoyevsky's *The Brothers Karamazov*, the town originated as a water stop on the Galveston, Harrisburg and San Antonio Railroad. Marfa's historic ties to the ranching industry are in evidence today. Cowboy culture is a way of life in West Texas and for many Marfans who own or work on large ranches in and around Presidio County. The city is best known for the Marfa mystery lights, which are unexplained light sources that appear almost nightly. They were first reported by early settlers in 1883 and are best seen from the viewing area located approximately nine miles east of town on Highway 90.

The Arcon Inn Bed and Breakfast

Address:	215 North Austin Street, P.O. Box 448, Marfa, Texas 79843
Phone:	915-729-4826
Fax:	915-729-3391
E-mail:	arconinn@iglobal.net
Website:	www.marfalights.com/arcon.html
Contact:	Mona Garcia
Accommodations:	Five lovely rooms on the second floor of the inn
Amenities:	Complimentary breakfast; Spanish tapas and dinners are served to houseguests upon request.
References:	15

History

The Arcon Inn is a gorgeous turn-of-the-century, two-story Gothic Victorian adobe home, located just a few blocks from the Marfa courthouse, on North Austin Street. The house was built from 1886 to 1909 by a doctor who came to Marfa from the Midwest. Emmeline, one of the doctor's nine children born at the house on Austin Street, died instantly from a horseback riding accident at about age fourteen.

Phantoms

Many years after Emmeline's death and after the family had moved away from the area, a pretty young girl enrolled at the local school in the early spring. She was dressed in old-fashioned clothing: a long white dress with lace trim, white stockings, and little white button shoes. She had long blond hair with a blue ribbon tied around her head. She enrolled with the name of Emmeline. She gave her address as 215 North Austin Street, just one block west of the Presidio County courthouse square. She attended school for a few days before becoming absent. Her teacher was concerned and spoke to the principal, who said with great surprise that the teacher must be mistaken because no one had lived in the house at 215 North Austin Street for many years! Old-timers who were kids in school and remember Emmeline's short attendance there have passed this story down to their grandchildren.

Emmeline has been sighted over the years in the north bedroom window on the second floor of the house, gazing out towards the dome of the beautiful and historic 1886 Presidio County courthouse. From various accounts by management, staff, and guests, she is always seen wearing a white dress, with pale blonde hair, and a blue ribbon tied around her head. Emmeline is a very affectionate and benign spirit who loves to play tricks on visitors.

There have also been accounts of cold breezes that instantly chill people to the bone before quickly dissipating, along with the occasional door that opens by itself in the house. Perhaps Emmeline during her brief stay at the house became so attached that she decided to remain behind and see what she missed in life. One visit to this beautiful inn and you'll see immediately why young Emmeline loves the place. She may even pay you a visit during your stay.

Repeat guests asked management if the pretty young girl with long blonde hair, blue ribbon, lovely white dress, and cute little button up boots had been back to visit Marfa! Stunned, Mona Garcia asked them where on the property they had seen the little girl. The guests said she visited them upstairs at the door of the Lima Room (Emmeline's former room) and said that she smiled at them and then closed the door. They assumed that the girl was a guest! No one was staying in that room on the date the guests first saw Emmeline, who has also appeared to locals, standing and looking out from two upstairs windows.

Playful Emmeline is an added bonus for those visiting this beautiful inn; even if she doesn't show herself.

New Braunfels

New Braunfels, with a population of 27,300, is nestled in the heart of the Texas Hill Country, conveniently located between San Antonio and Austin. Founded by Prince Carl of Solms Braunfels in 1845, the town prospered from the region's plentiful water and rich soil, which soon produced a healthy agricultural economy. The city's German heritage and the region's natural beauty currently fuel a thriving tourism industry. At the heart of the city is the spring-fed Comal River, a playground for inner tube riders and swimmers. The scenic Gaudalupe River Road traverses the Hill Country above New Braunfels.

The Hotel Faust

Address:	240 South Seguin Street, New Braunfels, Texas 78130
Phone:	830-625-7791
Fax:	830-620-1530
E-mail:	Innkeeper@fausthotel.com
Website:	www.fausthotel.com
Contact:	Bob and Judy Abbey
Accommodations:	62 guestrooms
Amenities:	Private baths; cable television; conference facilities; air conditioning, ceiling fans, telephones; full service dining facilities, ballroom, meeting rooms, brewpub and bar
References:	15, 30

History

During the 1920s some of New Braunfels' leading citizens decided it was time to construct a modern hotel for tourists and salesmen and provide meeting rooms, banquets, and dinner-dances. Walter Faust (son of Joseph Faust, who had served as a state senator, mayor of New Braunfels, and a regent of the University of Texas),

vice-president of the local chamber of commerce and president of the First National Bank, helped raise funds for the hotel, which opened as the Travelers Hotel on October 12, 1929. The building was constructed on the original site of the Fausts' old homestead, which was moved to the other side of Seguin Street.

Faust became the first owner of the hotel, and he and his wife lived in a suite there until his death in 1933. Three years later the hotel was renamed in his honor. For a time it was owned by the Krueger family. Krueger was a former congressman and ambassador to Mexico. Forced to close in 1975, it was eventually purchased and extensively restored while retaining its early charm and character.

Phantoms

The fact that the Faust Hotel is haunted is no mystery to those in New Braunfels or those who work at the hotel or come for a visit. Paranormal encounters are commonplace yet benign: A bartender, before locking up, always checked the liquor supply and, as is standard procedure, placed the partially filled bottles in front of the filled ones. On more than one occasion he opened the next day to find that the bottles had somehow been reversed. A night clerk was standing at the front desk when the door started swinging back and forth on its own. The water faucet in room 411 sometimes turns itself on. A couple staying in room 415 checked out in the middle of the night because their luggage began moving on its own. The handles on the luggage were in the upright position as if being carried by unseen hands.

In a suite that was once Walter Faust's room, things often get moved around on their own. Additionally, Faust has been seen standing at the foot of the brass bed staring at the guests. Fans have begun spinning even though they were turned off; guests have been locked out of their rooms, unable to enter even with the passkey; and the large hotel front doors have been known to open and close by themselves in the middle of the night.

The roaming phantom child is believed to be Christine Faust, the daughter of Sarah and James Faust, who lived in the original house that once stood on the property. Born in 1837, Christine was an ancestor of Walter Faust. The child's picture hangs in the third floor hallway, just outside room 306, and she is dressed in a checked gingham dress, holding a white cat.

Christine has been spotted several times by staff and guests, playing in the hallways before vanishing. A man whose picture with that of his wife hangs in the hotel was sighted entering the elevator. When all the lights went out during an unusually violent thunderstorm, the night clerk went down to the basement to inspect the breakers. As he stood next to the fuse box, he heard someone laughing in the darkness. As he retreated in fear, running into the lobby, he noticed that the only light in the hotel that was on was above the picture of Walter Faust, even though the outlet had no electricity passing through it.

Christine also enjoys tapping staff on the shoulder while they are cleaning the rooms, appearing as a girl of about four or five years old before vanishing, and running down hallways before passing right through a wall in front of startled guests. Christine has been heard playing games in the hallways, and her feline friend has also been sighted and felt brushing up against people throughout the building.

Some say that a third spirit, a phantom bellman, dressed in period clothing, always appearing friendly and helpful, roams the hotel, particularly in the area of the elevator where there is no bellman or elevator operator. The elder operator is usually sighted wearing a plaid jacket before disappearing. Two more spirits may include a mother and child. While a painting contractor was repainting the doorframe to room 326, a corner room, he saw the transparent bluish figure of a young woman holding a baby on her hip and wearing an old-fashioned robe.

Another time a maintenance man while working on the fourth floor encountered what appeared to be a normal-looking man. He was described as in his early seventies, wearing metal rimmed glasses and wearing a well-tailored gray suit. The odd thing about the man is that he walked from room to room, opening and closing each door, while occasionally turning to see if the maintenance man was still looking on. Troubled by the man's eccentric behavior and dress, he went down to the manager and told him what was happening. The manager said there was no one up there but him, and all of the rooms were locked. On a hunch, the manager showed a picture of Walter Faust to the maintenance man, who immediately identified the stranger. Trouble was, the manager had to explain, Faust died in 1933.

Walter Faust, Christine, and the other ghost guests who are frequently sighted in the hotel are playful and watchful, not harmful. The spirits are an added bonus when you come to visit this historic hotel, and with the original owner seemingly always nearby, any questions you may have will most likely dissolve away!

Karbach Haus Inn

Address:	487 West San Antonio Street, New Braunfels, Texas 78130
Phone:	830-625-2131
Fax:	830-629-1126
Toll Free Number:	1-800-972-5941
E-mail:	khausbnb@aol.com
Contact:	Kathy Karbach Kinney and Ben Jack Kinney
Accommodations:	Six guestrooms
Amenities:	Private baths; in-room TV/VCR; VCR library; Jacuzzi; fireplace; sun parlor; swimming pool
References:	15, 30

History

George and Hulda Eiband in 1890 bought the land on which the house rests. The Eibands were very wealthy due to George's successful dry goods businesses in New Braunfels and Galveston. During 1906 the couple contemplated building a house on their land and went about constructing an over 5,000-square-foot, two-story beige brick building. The Eibands evidently lived a long and happy life, with George passing away in 1935, followed by his wife a year later at age seventy-two.

The property was passed on to the nephews of George's brother, E.A. Eiband, and they sold the house to Dr. Hylmar Emil Karbach Sr. and his wife, Katherine Elizabeth Taylor Karbach, in 1938. With four children, the Karbachs enlarged the house. Dr. Karbach died in 1959, his wife Katherine died in 1985, and the children inherited the property. In 1986 eldest daughter, Kathleen, and her husband, Ben Jack Kinney, bought the house from the other family members and restored it, converting four of the six rooms into an inn.

Phantoms

A house with so many memories has to have ghosts, right? Indeed. The happy spirits of the former occupants, especially the children, can be heard, seen, and felt inside. Guests staying in the upstairs rooms often report hearing the sounds of children playing and laughing late at night. Guests are always quick to point to the playroom at the front of the house as the origin of the carefree, disembodied sounds. Besides the children of the Karbach family, the grandchildren were also frequent visitors in the house. En masse, the children often slept and played in the playroom, laughing and telling stories to one another, including an occasional ghost story. One spectral child is rumored to be twelve-year-old Roy, son of Kathy and Ben Jack, who was killed in a playground accident in Virginia yet seems to have returned to the only home he really knew.

Another phantom guest may be Katherine Elizabeth Taylor Karbach. Frugal in life, always trying to save money for the family, including keeping the electric bills low, she may be responsible for the numerous times the lights are found turned off when no one is using them. Even though the current owners or guests forget to turn off a light or two in the house, it's really no problem, because Katherine's ghost makes sure there is no waste of electricity. Unfortunately, there are times at night when the light issue causes problems, because people are left wandering around in the dark. Her spirit is also blamed for a porch rocking chair (her favorite chair) that occasionally moves back and forth by itself, as if someone is relaxing in it! Hulda Eiband, the original first lady of the house, is also considered a prime phantom suspect, along with Katherine Karbach's younger sister, Martha Jo, who is said to frequent her old room.

Some time back Kathy Karbach Kinney was trying to find her mother's recipe for egg custard. She and her husband were having guests over who mentioned how much they liked custard. Thinking that this would be a great change for the breakfast menu, Kathy searched and searched, going through cookbook after cookbook trying to find the recipe to no avail. Having temporarily given up the ghost with regard to finding the recipe, she began ironing in the upstairs playroom, a room that is not rented out and where their grandchildren stay when they visit. Lots of things are stored in that room due to the immense shelf space. After plugging in the iron and while waiting for it to get hot, Kathy decided to straighten some books on the shelf next to the ironing board. On top of the books was one of her mother's tattered old cookbooks, and inside in her handwriting was the recipe she was looking for. Kathy had no idea why the cookbook was with all the Dr. Seuss and Mother

Goose children's books. Perhaps her mother, sensing her daughter's anxiety, decided to help her out from beyond the grave.

The Prince Solms Inn

Address:	295 East San Antonio Street, New Braunfels, Texas 78130
Phone:	830-625-9169
Fax:	830-625-2220
Toll Free Number:	1-800-625-9169
E-mail:	prince@princesolmsinn.com
Website:	www.princesolmsinn.com
Contact:	Bob and Pat Brent
Accommodations:	10 guestrooms and one cottage
Amenities:	Private baths; full country breakfast; the cellar of the inn is Wolfgang's Pub & Stuff; complimentary wine and cheese at 5:30 P.M.
References:	15, 30

History

The Prince Solms Inn is a bewitching two-story brick building that was built by German craftsmen in 1898 and has always been an inn. The Prince Solms lies within a cluster of historic buildings that were built around 1845.

Phantoms

The basement level houses Wolfgang's Keller, a fine restaurant featuring Continental cuisine in a relaxing atmosphere. Some believe that the spirit of a young woman who may have waited on customers and tended bar still haunts the basement area and restaurant. In fact, a few staff and patrons reportedly witnessed the young woman walking through the area before vanishing.

Another explanation for the phantom female—or perhaps this is another spirit entirely—concerns a young woman who was supposedly spurned on her wedding day and returns perhaps hoping her former partner will finally go through with the ceremony. She is frequently sighted standing at the top of the stairs or walking down the stairs, perhaps repeatedly reliving that sorrowful day.

Another spirit is said to belong to an elderly man who is rumored to have lived in the building when it served as a boardinghouse. The gentleman spirit is thought to be a former Union soldier who moved to this area, where people were more sympathetic to the Union, after the war for health reasons. The man apparently died in the Huntsman Room where his manifestation occasionally greets unsuspecting guests and staff.

Early one cool fall morning Bob Brent was sitting in the courtyard enjoying his coffee. The church bells had just finished the 6:00 A.M. chimes, and it was still dark out. Suddenly, a strange fragrance engulfed him, like perfume or cologne. Looking around for a guest who might have awakened early, he saw there was no one up but him. As Bob sat there the fragrance became stronger. He stood up in an attempt to follow the fragrance, and it dissipated as he moved away from the table. Quickly returning to the table, Bob sat down and said aloud, "What do I smell, perfume or what?" A quiet female voice said, "Don't be afraid; I enjoy my coffee with you each morning." After a few seconds of regaining his composure, Bob decided to play along. He was sure someone was going to step up to him and say, "Smile, you're on Candid Camera."

Deciding to respond to the voice that came from the chair next to him, Bob said, "Who are you and why are you here?" To his surprise the voice said, "I'm Emilie Eggling, and I built the hotel in 1898. Our family owned it for fifty-two years. My relatives operated the hotel until they sold it to outsiders. I was not pleased. I had such pride in my little hotel and wanted it to remain with my family." Then she said, to Bob's surprise, "There have been many owners but only two that I approved of. One family was the Dillons, who also took pride in and excellent care of my hotel. Then on New Years Eve of 1991 you purchased it. I had my reservations about you, Bob Brent, but after nine years of watching you and your wife Pat pour out love for this place and the care you have given the property, as well as the many guests, I feel the property is finally in good hands. I know you have two sons and five grandchildren. There is one, only one, of your grandchildren who will eventually take over my little hotel and maintain it like I did. I know which one it will be, and in fifteen years you will also know."

Bob immediately asked, "Will it be Adam, Alex, Andrew, Katelyn, or Kelsey?" He received no answer, and the fragrance faded. He sat alone at the table drinking his coffee. Other guests have reported smelling perfume, always when they were alone in the courtyard.

Beverly Talbot, the seventy-one-year-old manager for the Brents, was alone one winter evening at the inn when she saw an opaque figure walk into Sophie's Suite. Beverly followed the figure into the room but saw no one there. Her wits still about her, she called out, "OK, I know you are here, and I'm not afraid of you." At that moment she said a serene feeling passed over her. She then asked the spirit to watch over her as she walked to her car late at night. She said, "If you will do that, we will be friends."

Beverly insists that since that encounter she has felt a comforting presence beside her as she leaves each night.

Numerous guests have asked the Brents if there are ghosts in the inn. When the Brents respond, "Why do you ask," they always reply that they felt a presence, saw a misty figure, or felt the bed move on its own. The spirits are not threatening, but they project a sense of calm and peace as if they are watching over the house and the people in it. There is no place like Solms; The Prince Solms Inn that is!

Palestine

During the 1840s it was discovered that the seat of Anderson County, a village called Houston (not the major city of Harris County), was two miles off center. Because of that oversight, the town of Palestine was created as county seat. More than 1,600 historic landmarks are found here with a self-guided walking tour.

The Wiffletree Inn

Address:	1001 North Sycamore, Palestine, Texas 75801
Phone:	903-723-6793
Fax:	903-723-4025
Toll Free Number:	1-800-354-2018
E-mail:	the_frisches@hotmail.com
Contact:	Derick, Jan, or Steve Frisch
Accommodations:	Four guestrooms
Amenities:	Two rooms with private baths, two with shared baths; weddings and receptions
Texas References:	11, 15, 37

History

Built in 1911 the Wiffletree Inn is an outstanding example of the Craftsman Era in home design and has been designated as a Palestine Historic Property.

Phantoms

Indications are that two spirits occupy this historic treasure. The female has been dubbed Lyla Belle, the niece of a former occupant who lived in the house. A second nameless spirit may be an older man who passed away in one of the bedrooms. Both spirits have been occasionally sighted and their otherworldly existence verified by paranormal investigators who have spent time in the structure.

During renovation in late fall, Steve Frisch began tearing out the upstairs walls to convert the closets into bathrooms. During the course of the project, the phone lines upstairs had to be cut, so he had to keep one ear on the phone downstairs so as not to miss a call. While he was vacuuming alone upstairs, the phone rang. He ran downstairs to catch it before the fourth ring, when the answer machine clicks on. After taking the call, he returned upstairs to find that the vacuum cleaner had been unplugged and put away.

Numerous times Derick Frisch, who lives in and manages the house, arrives at the front door after working late, around 11:30 P.M., and hears voices of people talking coming from inside the house. It always happens when there are no guests staying in the house. He quickly opens the door and enters, but the voices immediately cease.

There is also a hat rack in the entry that contains at least twenty different hats. Several times Derick has entered the house to find a black top hat lying on the floor in front of the entryway. The hat is always found in the same place, as if someone removed it from the rack and gently placed it on the ground. Derick has also heard disembodied footsteps coming from unoccupied rooms in the house. There are times when the owner's favorite hat or other personal objects will disappear, only to reappear in another part of the house days later. The game of hide-and-seek is quite common for the otherworldly guests. A sense of being watched is also commonly reported upstairs near where an elderly gentleman in period clothing has been sighted.

Another time two people from the Texas Department of Transportation were staying in adjoining upstairs rooms. In the Roquemore Room the ceiling fan suddenly began to spin much faster. The guest got up to turn the fan lower. When the guest returned to her bed, she had the strong sensation that someone was sitting on the edge of the bed next to her. When she tried to get up, she felt as if someone was trying to hold her down. Finally making it to her feet, she ran into the other room to spend the night with her partner. Whoever was in the room with her could have it for the night. She wasn't in the mood to share it with a ghost.

On another occasion when Steve Frisch was alone in the house, he began hearing noises coming from upstairs. Thinking that one of the guests had returned for the evening, he went to the bottom of the stairs to greet him and see if the person needed anything. The upstairs area was completely dark. The closest he can come to describing the event would be to imagine two people having an argument and slamming a door for effect. A door would slam loudly, followed a few minutes later by another door slamming. This continued for about fifteen minutes. He phoned a neighbor and asked him to come over to document the event. By the time he arrived the noise had subsided completely. Both men sat downstairs for a few minutes before Steve got a phone call. While he was on the phone, the neighbor got up and walked upstairs. He saw something partially transparent descend the stairs and move within a few feet behind where Frisch was sitting and talking on the phone. The neighbor said the figure was of a portly man who walked behind Frisch, stood there for a short time, then walked back up the staircase.

The historic Wiffletree has a very welcoming atmosphere that whispers of pleasant memories of bygone days. Perhaps during your stay you'll come across Lyla Belle or the elderly gentleman. Both are said to keep a watchful eye on the place as well as the guests, making everyone who enters feel right at home.

Port Aransas

With 2,274 inhabitants at 20 feet above sea level, Port Aransas is one of the most popular tourist destinations on the Gulf Coast. An English settler built a ranch house on the site in 1855, and the area was later developed as a fishing village.

Beulah's Restaurant

Address:	200 East Cotter, P.O. Box 2283, Port Aransas, Texas 78373
Phone:	512-749-4888
Fax:	512-749-7022
Contact:	Guy Carnathan
Open:	Wednesday through Sunday from 5:00 P.M. to 10:00 P.M.
References:	15, 28, 36, 37

History

Beulah's Restaurant and the adjacent Tarpon Inn are located in the waterfront area of Port Aransas. Padre Nicholas Balli acquired title to the 100-mile-long strip of sand dunes and grass from King Charles IV of Spain in 1880. Originally christened Isla de Corpus Christi, over time the island became known as Padre Island. Balli established Port Aransas. During the Civil War, the site of the Tarpon Inn was a barracks for Confederate troops. In 1886 the Tarpon Inn was built from materials that had been salvaged from the old barracks.

The inn was named for the tarpon fish that were found in the waters around Port Aransas. The first Tarpon Inn was destroyed by fire in 1900. It was subsequently rebuilt in 1904, but was once again destroyed in 1919, this time by a hurricane. In 1923 it was rebuilt to its present form, a two-story frame building. Directly behind the inn is a garden area and two frame buildings that make up Beulah's Restaurant. The long building at the rear of the property was once the original location for the Tarpon Inn that burned down. Beulah's was the bar for the original Tarpon Inn then became the Silver King. It took on the name Beulah's in mid-1992, after the head housekeeper at the inn, Beulah Mae Williams. Beulah lived in the old building that stands on a side alley behind the restaurant.

Phantoms

A *Silver King Newsletter* article once stated that the Silver King (now Beulah's) was haunted. Although Beulah Mae never saw any ghosts, she reported a number of occasions where she could hear them. One day as Beulah Mae was walking outside the Silver King and passing by the kitchen area, she heard a lot of noise coming from inside the building. She knew the restaurant was closed, so she decided to see if someone had broken in. Once inside and after carefully inspecting all the rooms, she found that everything was in order. Beulah Mae locked up the restaurant and stood outside for a moment, trying to come up with a logical explanation for all the commotion—she couldn't.

Other employees over the years have remarked about the eerie, sometimes loud noises that come from unoccupied portions of the restaurant. There are the heavy, disembodied footsteps that make their way through the building, loud pounding noises that seem to come from inside the walls, muffled voices of people carrying on a ghostly conversation, lights that turn on and off by themselves, and other sounds that have no visible source.

A very spirited ghost inhabiting the kitchen has been blamed for turning lights on and off, making loud crashing sounds as if dishes or implements are being thrown, shaking pots and pans while helpless staff persons look on, following people, causing colds spots to suddenly manifest, and causing the kitchen door to suddenly fly open or slam shut.

A former employee witnessed a female apparition dressed in period clothing and sporting a hairstyle reminiscent of the late 1800s. A male apparition, believed to be a former cook, has been sighted in the kitchen area and other parts of the restaurant. A visiting psychic ran into a strong male energy (perhaps the spirited cook) and came away with the name Sam, Sammy, or Samuel. An evening cook looked on in horror as an eerie haze formed in front of him. Within seconds the mist became a middle-aged female of medium height. The two stared at one another until the friendly female abruptly turned and dissolved in front of him. On another occasion an employee began mopping the kitchen floor. Within minutes after completing this task, large footprints appeared in the middle of the floor, followed by a smaller pair, as if an adult were walking hand-in-hand through the kitchen with a child.

Spend the night at the adjacent Tarpon Inn, which is also rumored to be haunted, and have dinner at Beulah's, and perhaps you will catch a glimpse of many spirits who call this historic establishment home.

Rio Grande City

With a present-day population of almost 10,000, the city is a port of entry with an international bridge between the U.S. and Mexico and is the seat of Starr County. The area was included in Jose de Escandon's settlement colony of 1753. General Zachary Taylor established Fort Ringgold in 1848. Among the fort's distinguished landmarks are Lee House, once occupied by Colonel Robert E. Lee when he commanded the Department of Texas before the Civil War; and the old post hospital. Portions of the fort are now part of the Rio Grande City school system. The fort was deactivated in 1944. Rio Grande City was once a bustling steamboat port.

La Borde House

Address:	601 East Main Street, Rio Grande City, Texas 78582
Phone:	956-487-5101
Contact:	Margaret Meade
Accommodations:	Seven historic rooms and six efficiency apartments
Amenities:	A lounge; restaurant named Che's; tropical courtyards
References:	11, 15, 36, 37

History

Francois La Borde commissioned Parisian architects in 1893 to design a residence that would remind him of his hometown of New Orleans, which explains the fancy metalwork, the interior

courtyard, and the verandas. The La Borde House was completed in 1899. The oil boom of 1939 saw her restored at a cost of five times her original price. The subsequent bust found her housing ladies of the evening, one of whom wrote her clients' IOUs on the wall. The historic house opened as a luxurious full-service hotel in April 1982, and is now listed on the National Register of Historic Places. For the past ten years the building has been managed by the Starr County Historical Foundation.

Phantoms

Some believe that Francois La Borde is one of the friendly spirits who keep an eye on the building and clientele. He is a logical choice given the fact that he is the original owner and loved his house with a passion.

Reported paranormal phenomena include doors that will open and close on their own as startled witnesses look on in amazement and lights that turn themselves on and off in many of the guestrooms. Some guests have reported being fast asleep when a lamp in their room will inexplicably turn on. Cold breezes reportedly manifest in certain portions of the building, and when this occurs, people have reported feeling as if someone walked right through them or was following them. Occasionally laughter or giggling is reported coming from unoccupied areas of the inn. The sounds are most likened to children playing or a group of people having a party. Shadows are sometimes seen floating through corridors, along walls, and entering unoccupied rooms before disappearing.

The owner wants to assure everyone that the spirits of this charming house are very friendly and probably remain because the authentic restoration of the house has brought back memories of happier bygone days, which everyone including the afterlife guests thoroughly enjoy, and so will you!

San Antonio

San Antonio has a present-day population of almost one million people. It was nothing more than a small Indian village back in 1718. It was here, in a pleasant wooded area of spring-fed streams at the southern edge of the Texas Hill Country, that Spain established Mission San Antonio de Valero (later called the Alamo). The Presidio San Antonio de Bexar protected the functioning mission. Several other Spanish missions soon followed, but the city's real growth dates to its establishment as a civil settlement in 1731, which began Spain's first step to colonize Texas.

Original colonists were Spanish Canary Islanders, to whom many Texas families proudly trace their roots. San Antonio remained the chief Spanish then Mexican stronghold in Texas until the Texas Revolution. Now San Antonio is colorfully accented by its multicultural heritage. The Battle of the Alamo in 1836 provided the city with worldwide notoriety and eternal landmark status, and the construction of the River Walk helped make the downtown area into the tourist mecca it is today.

The Royal Swan Inn

Address:	236 Madison, San Antonio, Texas 78204-1320
Phone:	210-223-3776
Fax:	210-271-0373
Toll Free Number:	800-368-3073
E-mail:	theswan@onr.com
Website:	www.royalswan.com
Contact:	Renee Martinez
Accommodations:	Five guestrooms

Amenities:	A full, sit-down breakfast daily; complimentary sodas
References:	15, 30

History

Between 1890 and 1894 Dr. Jabez Cain constructed the houses at 234 and 236 Madison. He later purchased a third home nearby. In 1900 Cain left his home to his partner, Dr. James H. Graham, who lived there for a short time. Later residents were primarily renters. During World War II the house was converted into apartments, which slowly fell into disrepair. During the 1970s,

when the River Walk was being developed, people began renovating many of the King William Historic District homes. The Cain house was purchased by Mr. and Mrs. Egon Jausch, who restored the facade and reduced the number of apartments to two. In 1993 the house opened as an inn.

Phantoms

There were immediate indications after opening as an inn to suggest that one if not more spirits occupied the house. One spirit in particular is felt to be a female, perhaps Dr. Cain's wife. There were numerous reports from guests about lights mysteriously turning on in the middle of the night, heavy footsteps pacing in unoccupied rooms, beds being shaken by invisible hands, cold spots suddenly manifesting, and of furniture being moved by unseen hands.

One guest staying in the Veranda Suite, after climbing into bed next to her husband, felt the bed begin shaking back and forth as if she were in the middle of a ghostly tug-of-war. She ended up on top of her startled husband, which turned the evening from somber to romantic.

Once again in the Veranda Suite, a female guest decided to relax in the sitting room as her husband dozed off on the main bed. The woman was unable to relax for long, because she started feeling uneasy, as if someone else was next to her in the sitting room. Unable to stand the uncomfortable feeling, she ended up beside her husband. Other similar reports point to a phantom guest who enjoys joining the living in bed.

Staff has had encounters with the spirit while cleaning the rooms. One time the bathroom faucets mysteriously turned on then a few seconds later shut off, as if someone washed their hands and left. Also, a downstairs parlor radio will manage to turn itself on to a particular station. A housekeeper entered the Veranda Suite to clean the room after the guests checked out, or so she thought. Upon entering she glanced out toward the veranda, and there on the porch was a young lady comfortably ensconced in a rocker. After excusing herself the lady rose from the chair, and the housekeeper went down to see why someone was still in the room. Of course, the guests had checked out, and upon returning to the room, they found no sign of anyone in the room or on the porch. This spirited woman is said to most frequently appear to those of Hispanic descent.

There are times when the rocking chair in the Veranda Suite will be rocking with no one sitting in it. Also, the ceiling fans will often start spinning even though the switch is still in the off position. After a few seconds the fan will abruptly stop. Pictures hung on the walls have managed to fall off without breaking, landing in such a way as to suggest that someone invisible removed them and placed them gently on the floor. Closet doors will occasionally open and shut as if someone was checking their ghostly wardrobe. The temperature in the Veranda Suite has been known to drop as much as 30 degrees without the aid of the air-conditioning unit. On several occasions guests in the Veranda Suite have reported being awakened at 3:00 A.M. to a dark-haired woman resting comfortably in the sitting room bed, only to have her vanish a few moments after materializing.

If you don't mind spending some time with a spirit, we suggest you try spending the night in the Veranda Suite. The Royal Swan is always ready to provide their guests with every amenity they may ask for, and some they might not consider, like spirits!

The Alamo Street Theater and Restaurant

Address:	1150 South Alamo Street, San Antonio, Texas 78210
Phone:	210-271-7791
Contact:	Marcia Baer Larsen
Business Hours:	Call for hours and days open
References:	1, 15, 23, 27, 28, 30, 36, 37

History

The first level of The Alamo Street Restaurant houses the dining room and kitchen, while the second level hosts theater performances, concerts, and weddings (the theater area used to house the old chapel). Mr. Beverly Spillman designed the building, and construction was completed in 1912. The congregation disbanded in 1968 and merged with another congregation east of San Antonio. The building lay vacant for eight years, suffering deterioration and vandalism. In 1976 Bill and Marcia Larsen purchased the building to create the Church Dinner Theater as a bicentennial project and earned the coveted San Antonio Conservation Society award. The building is listed on the National Register of Historic Places. Bill Larsen died in 1996.

Phantoms

As the cover of their pamphlet states, "Great Food and Friendly Spirits, from the Most Haunted Eatery in San Antonio." According to the owner, "You can't see 'em, but our visitors have ways of letting us know they're around: Cold spots suddenly develop in the air; lights go on and off by themselves; cooks are shoved into the refrigerator; washed and draining dishes suddenly move back into the dishwater by themselves; doors open and close . . . or lock and unlock themselves; and unusual noises persist."

Regardless of who or what is responsible for these occurrences, the restaurant staff just seems to work around the ghosts. Once in awhile a cook will shout, "Now you just stop that!" and everyone knows there's an otherworldly visitor in the place. If you're skeptical, ask to see the photos of the "lady-in-white" caught on Polaroid film by an out-of-state guest one summer day in 1990! Larsen can't explain the visitors and is not sure she wants to. But they know for sure that their otherworldly visitors are definitely friendly spirits!

Psychics have confirmed that at least five resident spirits occupy the building. Management has taken the time to discuss each spirit in more detail as follows: Miss Margaret is a graceful lady and the restaurant's most frequent visitor. She is always spotted wearing a white Victorian-style dress, complete with high lace collar, leg-o-mutton sleeves, and a full-length skirt. She wears her hair swept up into a bun on top of her head. Because she is most often seen appearing during a stage production, she is believed to be Miss Margaret Gething, a charming, beautiful young singer and actress, who lived with her mother on Guenther Street. When a touring show came to San Antonio in the early 1900s, Miss Gething stepped into a part vacated by an ailing actress. She performed in New York and Europe, once starring on Broadway with Clark Gable. Margaret died in 1975, and the lady-in-white began visiting the building one year later.

Little Eddie is a mischievous spirit, playing pranks and practical jokes on the long-suffering kitchen help. He is less frequently observed than Margaret, and his age is thought to be between eight and twelve. Like most kids, he is known to get rather bothersome until he receives attention. One local psychic said his name was Edward (although he preferred Eddie), while another linked his death to a long-since vanished playground. A third psychic believes the youthful spirit came to the place by way of an antique rattan wheelchair, which was once used as a prop for a play.

Other apparitions include an elderly man and woman who appear on or near the stage or on the bell tower at the front of the building. Psychics have come up with the name of Henrietta for another of the female spirits. She may have been a servant or employee of Miss Margaret and did her sewing. She has been blamed for costumes appearing and disappearing. The elderly man is believed to be Alvin, an actor in one of the Alamo City Theater plays performed long ago. Alvin, who was a partner in a gallery at Blue Star, two blocks down from the theater, was cast in a performance of *Born Yesterday*. On opening night he thought he might have the flu and stayed home. The next evening he didn't show up for the actors' call. When the stage manager went to his home to find him, he was almost comatose. Days later Alvin passed away in the hospital from an unknown virus, never getting a chance to perform. Perhaps that's why he remains behind in the theater. The trouble is, Alvin's ghost is still late for many of the rehearsals—but at least he shows up.

The active spirits are responsible for a number of unexplained events including cold spots that suddenly develop, lights going on and off by themselves, cooks being shoved into the refrigerator, and shelves suddenly being pulled out of the refrigerator and microwave. The corroded and useless church bell mysteriously rang out. Silverware was lifted by invisible hands off the steam table, carried across the room, and placed on the carpeted floor between the dining tables. An occasional plate gets thrown from a waiter's tray while delivering food. Washed dishes are placed back inside the dishwater. Loud whistling comes from an empty lobby. The radio turns itself on and plays a Crosby, Stills and Nash song, "Southern Cross." Doors open and close or lock and unlock by themselves. The sound of pipes rolling across the floor are heard in the unoccupied set shop. There was the sounds of boxes being thrown down the stairway, but upon checking, there was nothing amiss. Discarnate voices whisper an employee's name.

Three men had a routine where they would close the theater after a performance. Beginning with the stage, they would turn off the lights, gather the trash, lock the front door, then return to the office to turn on the alarm before exiting the back stage door. One time a set of metal fire doors that were chained and locked from the inside were being forced open as far as the inside chain would allow, then they suddenly slammed shut. The men reacted quickly and went back inside. The alarm system and motion sensor detectors did not go off, there was no movement inside, no indication that anyone broke in, and after a chair by chair, room by room inspection, no one was found inside.

Some staff, while working alone, have heard their name called out or a disembodied voice calling out for help. An actress during rehearsal happened to glance up toward the old choir loft and saw the apparition of a woman dressed in a white Victorian-looking dress walk across the area and vanish. While setting up for a play, a technician was in the glassed-in booth, when a very real looking, tall, young woman with dark hair piled on her head appeared in front of him. She gazed at the technician for a few seconds then slowly vanished.

At the Alamo Street Restaurant and Theater, things are not always as they appear, or should we say, things appear seemingly out of thin air. There are plenty of spirits to go around at this historic, haunted hot spot in San Antonio.

Bullis House Inn

Address:	621 Pierce Street, P.O. Box 8059, San Antonio, Texas 78208-1425
Phone:	210-223-9426
Fax:	210-299-1479
Toll Free Number:	1-800-317-7143
Innkeepers:	Steve and Alma Cross
Accommodations:	Ten guestrooms
Amenities:	Continental breakfast; four rooms with private baths, six shared; television; air-conditioned
References:	8, 15, 30, 36, 37

History

A Texas historic landmark, this house was formerly inhabited by two army generals: General Bullis, a New Yorker who came to Texas after the Civil War, and General Jonathan Wainwright, who was captured by the Japanese in the Philippines. The house sits across the street from Fort Sam Houston. Construction on the house began in 1906 and was completed in 1909.

Brigadier General John Lapham Bullis moved in after the house was completed but was able to enjoy his new residence for only a short time, passing away in 1911. He was brought home to lie in state in one of the front parlors. The Bullis family lived in the house before selling it to General Jonathan Wainwright in 1949. For some reason Wainwright chose not to reside in the house. After 1949 the house was leased for office space, as well as a child care center. The inn has been owned by Steve and Alma Cross since 1983.

Phantoms

The Bullis House has served many contented visitors over the years, including a few spirits who refuse to leave. And who can blame them. A guest once reported that an invisible force prevented him from coming down the back stairs. It was as if someone was pushing on him for a few seconds before relenting and finally letting him pass. On another occasion, while upstairs, the owners heard men arguing downstairs near the entryway foyer. They were the only ones in the house at the time, so they assumed people had walked in. Upon checking, they found no one in the entryway, and the front door was bolted shut.

Another guest sleeping in a downstairs bedroom awoke to see the shadowy figure of a Native American standing beside her bed. The man had long, black hair, which was secured with a bandanna that was wrapped around the forehead. The figure was only visible to his waist. When the guest screamed, the spirit vanished into thin air.

Room G upstairs has a reputation for keeping some people out by the door slamming shut in their face, while letting others in by having the door swing open without assistance. There are also reports of disembodied footsteps walking along the hallway late at night when there are no guests at the inn. There are sounds of items falling yet nothing is ever found broken. On occasions, especially around Halloween, children's voices can be distinctly heard laughing and giggling in the house, yet there are never any children around when this happens.

The spirits of the Bullis House Inn are occasionally restless but never harmful. They like to play and amuse guests, while enjoying the run of the house. Perhaps it's the spirit of General Bullis, Genonimo, or children from the time when the former residence functioned as a day-care center.

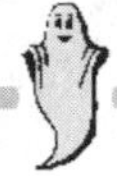

Cadillac Bar

Address:	212 South Flores Street, San Antonio, Texas 78204-1011
Phone:	210-223-5533
Fax:	210-223-5224 or 210-223-3746
Contact:	Jesse Medina
Open:	Daily from 11:00 A.M. to 2:00 A.M.
References:	15, 30, 36, 37

History

In 1870 Herman Dietrich Stumberg and his son George built a limestone building on land Herman had purchased in 1863. Mayo Besan owned the bar during the 1920s, calling it the White Horse Bar before changing it back to the Cadillac Bar.

The era of 1920s and early 1930s ushered in Prohibition, wild parties, the great Depression, and the end of the Stumberg General Store, which ceased operating in 1932. After closing the store the building was used for a number of purposes. A family named Carvajal once ran a popular saddle shop where John Wayne had a saddle made. Mayo Besan was succeeded by his son-in-law, Porter Garner, who retired in 1980 and left the bar to the employees, who in turn sold the place to "Chito" Longoria and Ramon Salido.

The buildings were restored and renovated as part of a redevelopment project known as Stumberg Square. In December 1991 George Stumberg, the great-great-grandson of the German immigrant, became the operating stockholder of the Cadillac Bar in San Antonio.

Phantoms

Psychics believe that at least two spirits reside in the bar. One is a tall, thin man sporting a handlebar mustache, who is spotted on the back steps leading from the kitchen to an upper storage room, taking his phantom stroll, as if by habit, then vanishing. The other is a young woman who has been described as thin, homely, with stringy dishwater blonde hair and protruding teeth.

Jesse Medina has seen and heard it all during his long stint at the establishment. He recalls numerous times cleaning up after parties where it sounded as if another party was beginning, this time with chains rattling and items like heavy saddles and bridles being dragged down the stairs. He has heard the screams and laughter of children playing inside when he was the only one around, as well as the frequent sounds of glass shattering as if someone drove a car through the front plate glass windows facing on South Flores Street, yet there is never anything out of place or broken. The alarm often goes on and off by itself before closing time. Large bowls and dishes will inexplicably fly off the shelves in the kitchen. The water faucet will sometimes turn itself on and off all day long. Staff members have watched as invisible hands slowly turned the faucet until the water flowed. When a plumber was called to find out what was going on, the man said there was nothing wrong with the spigot and no possible way it could turn on by itself; but it did, repeatedly!

A kitchen employee once saw the spectral shape of an older man on the back steps leading from the kitchen to a second floor storage room. The tall, thin man with the white handlebar mustache may have been Herman Stumberg. "Uncle Herman," the "black sheep" of the family, may have had a handlebar mustache and was known for carousing and spending time in the old Silver Dollar Saloon, now the old Frost Bank Building. Later a psychic was able to obtain the name of Herman or Henry for the elderly wandering spirit. The psychic also pinpointed a morose, young female spirit who remained in the building. Speculation is that she may have been a lady of the night who frequented the place, since the red light district was nearby. Once again the psychic came up with a name for the female wraith, Beatrice, who was rather homely, thin, and had stringy dishwater blonde hair.

Several of the employees have spotted a woman fitting the description of the psychic's Beatrice. She is most often sighted upstairs near the glassed-in portion of the party room, just looking down at those who spot her. Some see her as an angry spirit, others, a sorrowful specter who seems lost or forlorn. A security guard, serving staff, and waitress have seen the spectral lady staring down from the second floor windows before turning, walking away, then turning back and peeping out of the lower portion of the window.

The spirits of the Cadillac Bar seem determined to stay, and given the lively atmosphere inside, they fit right in. Oftentimes you can't tell the dead from the living when a party-like atmosphere is in session—unless they vanish before paying their bill. Even then it may be a friend or an acquaintance short of cash.

Crockett Hotel, Holiday Inn

Address:	320 Bonham Street, San Antonio, Texas 78205
Phone:	210-225-6500
Fax:	210-225-6251
Toll Free Number:	1-800-292-1050
E-mail:	crockett@travelbase.com
Website:	www.travelbase.com/destinations/san-antonio/crockett/
Accommodations:	206 guestrooms, 5 junior suites, 2 suites

Amenities:	Private baths; television; air conditioning; outdoor swimming pool; 7th floor sun deck with Jacuzzi, Landmark Restaurant; Ernie's Bar and Grill
References:	15, 20, 30, 34, 35, 36, 37

History

Situated directly across from the Alamo, the Crockett is listed on the National Register of Historic Places. The land on which the Crockett Hotel sits is located between the two branches of the Acequia Madre, just south and east of the mission property. The grounds of the Crockett were part of the Alamo battlefield. During the night before the battle, hundreds of troops moved into the area where the hotel pool and courtyard are now situated. The southeast palisade was defended by the colorful Davy Crockett, for whom the hotel is named.

A prosperous French-born merchant, Augustese Honore Grenet, purchased the property in 1874 and operated a general merchandise store on the site. G.B. Davis bought the land in 1887. It changed owners three more times before being sold to the International Order of Odd Fellows on January 30, 1907. This fraternal organization built the lodge hall and hotel (now the Crockett) in 1909. The 275 brothers dedicated the top two floors of the six-story structure for lodge purposes and the first four for a hotel. The hotel's first proprietors were F. Peck and William Nagel. In 1927 a west wing was added. The Independent Order of Odd Fellows maintained ownership until 1978 when it was purchased by an investor from British Columbia. In 1982 San Antonio native John Blocker bought the Crockett. At that time the property was renovated.

Phantoms

The ghostly activities in the Crockett center in the lobby where the entrance doors occasionally open and close without being triggered by a human being, the bar area, and in certain guestrooms in the hotel where faint whispers, colds spots, and a variety of unexplainable events have taken place over the years. The figure of a man has also been sighted in the executive offices section of the

hotel by several staff persons. The offices are located in the modern two-story section of the Crockett that encompasses the swimming pool and patio.

Docia Williams, who toured the Crockett in 1996, relates the following: "Dave Mora, the reservations manager, decided to tag along. He had actually seen the figure of a man clad in a dark blue jacket as he moved into the small kitchen area adjoining the boardroom. He recalled the day he had come around the corner from the area where the offices are located and spied the figure of a sturdy man with dark brown hair as he moved into the kitchen. A quick check into that room revealed no one was there. Yet Mora was convinced he saw the man quite clearly. He added that other hotel staff members had seen him at various times."

According to psychics and staff, there is yet another spirit that haunts the Crockett.

The spirits of the hotel seem to affect the air-conditioning units, are responsible for whispered conversations that are heard in unoccupied areas of the building, cause curtains to move in rooms that are being cleaned, open the electronic doors at the front entrance, and are responsible for disembodied footsteps throughout the building and for fooling around with the electricity.

Considering its proximity to the Alamo and the fact that the hotel lies in the heart of the 1836 battlefield, it's not surprising that the hotel is haunted. But who are these restless spirits? Soldiers, defenders, or ordinary people who spent memorable times in this timeless place?

Emily Morgan, The Ramada

Address:	705 E. Houston Street, San Antonio, Texas 78205
Phone:	210-225-8486
Fax:	210-225-7227
Toll Free Number:	1-800-824-6674
E-mail:	ramadaem@ix.netcom.com
Website:	www.the.ramada.com/sanantonio05097
Accommodations:	13-story tower with 177 guestrooms
Amenities:	Private baths, air conditioning; cable television; hair dryers; irons/ironing boards; coffee makers; Yellow Rose Cafe; and Emily's Oasis.
References:	15, 20, 34, 35, 37

History

Legend has it that after the Battle of the Alamo, while encamped at San Jacinto, Emily West, a twenty-year-old mulatto girl, detained General Santa Anna in his tent long enough to contribute to the victory by the Texas army over his forces in 18 minutes, securing Texas Independence. Thus, the legend of the Yellow Rose of Texas was born and lives on. Construction of the Medical Arts Building, now the Emily Morgan Hotel, began with much fanfare in November of 1924. J.M. Nix, who would later build the Nix Hospital and

the Majestic building, was the developer of this building. The most prominent San Antonio physicians of the era established their offices in the new building. In 1976 the Medical Arts building was converted into a modern office building. In 1984 the building was adapted for use as a hotel, and the Emily Morgan Hotel was founded. The building is listed in the National Register of Historic Places.

Phantoms

The hotel is located across the street and north of the Alamo at the intersection of 705 East Houston Avenue and 'E' Street. Sightings, according to staff, management, and guests, have occurred on the seventh floor, as well as in the lobby where ghostly manifestations, cold spots, and mysterious noises have taken place over the years. The property is also said to contain a well where a maid's body was reportedly dumped. Her apparition has been sighted in the hotel.

According to ghost hunter Martin Leal, most of the ghost activity reported to date is confined on the twelfth and seventh floors. Actually the twelfth floor is the thirteenth floor because the first floor is considered the ground floor. People have complained to the front desk that their room smelled of alcohol and other scents that are associated with a hospital. The twelfth floor was reportedly the floor used for operations and such. One of the engineers told Leal that one day when he was walking through the hallway, he heard a woman's voice calling for a nurse. People on that floor have reported being touched by someone or something when there was no one else around.

Much of the activity on the twelfth floor is related to noises, smells, and being touched. On the seventh floor people have witnessed human shapes walking around or walking through walls or doors. A number of years ago a German family was staying in one of the rooms on the seventh floor, and about 2:30 A.M. they said that everything in the room suddenly turned on full blast. The television started blaring, the clock radio went on full volume, and all of the lights went on simultaneously. There are two beds in the room, and as the family of four sat up in bed, they all saw a human shape move across the room and through the wall. They checked out about ten minutes later.

The basement was used as the morgue and crematory for the medical building, and there are regular reports of activity in this area including disembodied voices, footsteps, and strange orbs of light. The elevators represent another area where frequent paranormal activity is reported. One time, late at night, calls started coming to the front desk every few minutes, but no one would speak on the line. After about ten calls, the engineer was able to trace the calls to the elevator phones. As the night manager and engineer walked over to the elevators, the elevator floor indicator kept going from the sixth to the seventh floor repeatedly. When they used the fireman's key to bring the elevator down to the first floor, there was no one inside. When they let the elevator go up, the mysterious calls began coming once again from inside. They finally had to disconnect the elevator phone. The phone system was inspected the next day, and no problem was found with the phone.

At the Emily Morgan, you get preferential treatment, a great view of the historic Alamo, and a few spirited former occupants from days when the building served as a medical center.

The Camberley Gunter Hotel

Address:	205 East Houston, San Antonio, Texas 78205
Phone:	210-227-3241
Fax:	210-227-3299
Toll Free Number:	1-800-222-4276
E-mail:	gtober@gunterhotel.com
Website:	www.viewone.com/gunterhotel
Contact:	Sue Baker
Accommodations:	320 guestrooms
Amenities:	Private baths; televisions; heated pool; Jacuzzi; sundeck; dining; Gunter Bakery

References: 15, 20, 27, 30, 31, 34, 35, 36, 37

History

The Gunter Hotel, when completed in 1909, was the largest building in San Antonio, a veritable palatial structure with marble floors, walnut paneling, and chandeliers. The history of the Gunter Hotel began in 1837 when the Frontier Inn was built on the site of the present-day hotel. In 1851 the site became the United States Military Headquarters; from 1861 to 1865 it served as Confederate Headquarters, in 1872 as the Vance House; and in 1886 it was renamed the Mahncke Hotel. In 1909 the *San Antonio Express* declared, "Out of the ruins of he Mahncke Hotel will rise a palatial structure."

The Gunter Hotel became reality because of real estate developer L.J. Hart and twelve local investors, including Jot Gunter, who purchased the site from Mary E. Vance Winslow in 1907. The Gunter survived the major floods of 1913 and 1921; a ninth story was added in 1917; in 1926 three more stories were added; the Seiterle Group acquired the Gunter in 1979 and began restoration, which was achieved from 1982 to 1984.

Phantoms

With its fame and notoriety came the inevitable stories of hauntings. Room 636 (now changed) became legendary as the location of one of San Antonio's greatest unsolved mysteries, which tragically concluded at the St. Anthony Hotel in room 536. The murder room at the Gunter is reportedly haunted. Briefly, the event involved a blonde, a man registered as Albert Knox, and a body that was there one minute, then gone the next. Blood was found everywhere in room 636, indicating someone had been brutally murdered, even butchered, but no body was ever found. The only suspect during the investigation, Albert Knox was found at the St. Anthony Hotel in room 536, the victim of an apparent suicide. In the end there were two people dead, blood everywhere in room 636 of the Gunter but no woman's body, no motive, no confession, and no missing person report for the woman. The case

remains open and is considered one of the most bizarre crimes in San Antonio's history.

The Ballroom is another area where psychic activity is strong. Photographs of employees and guests have been developed at a variety of functions, showing guests from another time appearing as transparent images partying alongside the living. There have also been a number of peculiar disturbances reported in the elevators. Other strange events include phantom voices coming from unoccupied rooms and hallways of the hotel, ghostly parties being reported in rooms that have not been checked into, and mysterious shadows appearing on corridor walls as startled guests and staff look on in stunned silence (especially true in the vicinity of room 426).

A man named Buck, a long-term tenant who died in the hotel, is still seen wandering near his former room, picking up the paper and just taking life—or death—one day at a time. A Lady in Blue and a Lady in White have also been seen floating through walls, as well as following staff and guests down hallways and into rooms.

These are only a few of the hundreds of ghost stories pertaining to the Gunter. Dine, drink, relax for the night, or take a stroll through this historical hotel, and perhaps you can add to the ghostly legends.

Inn on the River

Address:	129 Woodward Place, San Antonio, Texas 78204
Phone:	210-225-6333
Fax:	210-271-3992
Toll free number:	800-730-0019
E-mail:	adz@swbell.net
Contact:	Kevin A. Hughes
Accommodations:	12 guestrooms
Amenities:	Private baths; private porches and balconies; cable television; Jacuzzis
References:	15

History

The main house was built in 1916 by Homer Gibson. It was a three-bedroom house without indoor plumbing. The Gibson family lived here until the 1930s when the house was converted into four small apartments. The current owner, Dr. A.D. Zucht III, acquired the building in 1974 and rented it as apartments until 1985. After the River Walk improvements, Dr. Zucht completely restored the house. The first guests arrived on June 23, 1990.

Improvements were continued into 1955 when the Cottage House across the street was acquired and became part of the bed and breakfast along with the house next to it and the parking lot.

Phantoms

Rooms 11, 13, and the dining room are reportedly haunted. A female ghost is believed to be a previous resident of the house, which was built in 1916. She is a friendly ghost and is known for dropping in on guests in room 13. Guests in the room report an intense coldness in the room despite the fact that the heater is on. The phantom female is also known to shake the table lamps, the bed, and the armoires. She is also responsible for changing the positing of various items in the room.

Rebecca Huston, who is a mystery novelist, stayed in room 11 and reported similar paranormal experiences as those described for room 13. When you visit the inn, be sure you ask about what happened to Rebecca during her stay. This is one recently opened inn that is sure to produce more stories as time goes by!

The Menger Hotel

Address:	204 Alamo Plaza, San Antonio, Texas 78205
Phone:	210-223-4361
Fax:	210-228-0022
Toll Free Number:	1-800-345-9285
E-mail:	menger@ipsa.net
Website:	www.mengerhotel.com/
Contact:	Ernesto Malacara
Accommodations:	350 guestrooms
Amenities:	Private baths; air conditioning; Colonial Room Restaurant; Menger Bar; Victorian Lobby; Renaissance Room; swimming pool; gardens.
References:	12, 15, 20, 27, 30, 31, 32, 34, 35, 36, 37

History

The original two-story, fifty-room hotel built out of limestone quickly became so popular that a three-story addition was built directly behind it. A list of major events in the history of the Menger Hotel follows: 1871—William A. Menger died; 1874-75—additional property was acquired to the north; 1881—the hotel was sold to Major J. H. Kampmann. The kitchen was relocated and a third story added to the Alamo Plaza portion, along with a three-story addition to the north. In 1887 a fourth story was added to the Blum Street side, and improvements included the addition of an artesian well, steam laundry, electric lights, and a steam elevator. In 1897 the kitchen was remodeled and new fixtures and furnishings were added to the dining room; 1899—a fifty-room addition was built; 1909—noted architect Alfred Giles made extensive changes to the hotel. An ornamental marquee of ground glass and iron was added to the interior, and the original (south) lobby was embellished with a new marble floor. In 1912 architect Atlee B. Ayres was commissioned to renovate the dining room and add thirty rooms.

In 1943 the hotel was purchased by W. L. Moody Jr. From 1949 to 1950 a four-story, 125-room addition, new lobby, and pool were added. The historic bar was installed on the Crockett Street side. In 1953 the Menger Patio Club and a swimming pool were added.

From 1966 to '67 a five-story addition was built. Restoration of the hotel was completed in 1988. A new ballroom, several meeting areas, and thirty-three rooms and suites were added. In 1990 the Colonial Dining Room was restored. In 1992 there was extensive renovation and restoration of the original 1859 building.

Phantoms

Throughout its illustrious career as one of San Antonio's premiere hotels, rumors of ghosts have always been a hot topic of conversation. Odd occurrences have frequently been reported, particularly in the old section of the hotel, such as mysterious gusts of cold air and unexplained voices and knocking sounds. Cigar smoke has suddenly materialized in the no-smoking bar. The smell is said to come and go and is most noticeable in the early morning hours. Lights inexplicably turn on and off; doors open or close by themselves. There are frequent sightings of ghostly figures and pervasive feelings of being watched or followed.

A former security guard, while patrolling the hallways of the older section of the hotel, witnessed a man walking down the hall late at night. The man wore western-type clothing, including a broad-brimmed black hat. The curious guard pursued the man to where the hallway turned. The startled guard watched as the man walked right through the wall! On other occasions, the same guard stated, while riding up the elevator, it frequently stopped on the third floor, no matter what button he pushed.

A hotel manager is convinced that Teddy Roosevelt's spirit visits the Menger Bar. Maintenance men have frequently discussed how doors will suddenly open or mysteriously close even after being locked. Staff members have also heard musical sounds and marching footsteps coming from unoccupied portions of the hotel.

A woman in blue is occasionally spotted walking silently through the hallways, as well as appearing to housekeepers who are busy cleaning rooms. One housekeeper in particular, while performing her daily routine, began sensing someone in the room with her. Thinking it was a co-worker or a guest, she turned around quickly to see an attractive woman with blondish shoulder length hair worn in a style of the 1930s or '40s, and wearing an old-fashioned, long blue dress, sitting in a chair a few feet away from her. The awe

struck employee was still gazing at the phantom woman when the apparition vanished—along with the housekeeper who quit.

Another restless spirit who roams the third floor halls in the older section of the original building has been sighted wearing a full, floor-length skirt, with a scarf or a bandanna tied around her head and a long necklace of beads around her neck. She is sometimes seen sporting an apron. The ghost is said to be Sallie White, a chambermaid who worked at the Menger in 1876, who was shot by her jealous husband on March 28, 1876. Clinging to life for two agonizing days, Sallie died on March 30. An old hotel ledger entry says that Frederick Hahn paid $32 cash for Sallie's burial: $25 for a coffin and $7 for a grave.

A famous ghost guest was Captain Richard King, founder of the famous King Ranch, south of San Antonio. The King Suite is still furnished with furniture used during his visits there. King died at dusk in August of 1865 in the hotel he called home. He loved the hotel so much that his funeral service was conducted in the front parlor. His love for the hotel is also evident by the fact that his spirit refuses to leave his former room.

A bell at the front desk, though disconnected, periodically rings. Some are convinced it's the ghost of Teddy Roosevelt, demanding the prompt service he enjoyed while he was visiting the Menger. Teddy Roosevelt as well as one or two of his "rough riders" have been sighted in the Menger Bar, a favorite hangout and place Roosevelt used for recruiting purposes.

One morning in April, before the bar opened, a young custodian entered the double doors to the Menger Bar to clean up. After placing a doorstop to hold the heavy entrance doors in place, he glanced over toward the bar. Sitting at the end of the bar was a patron he assumed had eluded the staff. The employee suddenly froze in his tracks when he realized that the man was wearing an old-fashion military uniform, and worse, he could see right through him. When the man beckoned the young man over, the young man ran toward the entry doors, which suddenly slammed shut before he could reach them. The frantic custodian raised such a ruckus that a manager and security guard rushed to his rescue. The distraught boy, who explained he had seen a ghost, was in such bad shape that 911 was called. After the boy was taken to a local clinic as a precaution, the night manager and security guard searched the bar for an intruder, or ghost. No one was found inside, and the young man never returned to the Menger.

Another custodian, working in the bar around 1:30 A.M., glanced up at the balcony area and noticed a man dressed in a dark gray suit and wearing a small hat. The strange-looking man stood near the railing on the side closest to the Alamo before vanishing. The employee quit rather than meet another Menger spirit.

On another occasion a couple remained in the Menger Bar until closing time. As they got up from their table to leave, a man entered the bar and began walking toward the woman. Since the man appeared to ignore the husband and continued approaching the woman, the husband intervened. To their amazement, as the husband stepped in the path of the man, the visitor vanished!

Four men once watched in silence as the heavy brass front doors to the bar suddenly swung open, yet no one walked in. Another time a women operating the gift shop off the main lobby witnessed shot glasses lift off the counter, move from the left side of the counter to the right side, then return to their original spot on the counter.

A female guest reported seeing a male figure appear just before stepping into an elevator on the top floor. She had pressed the elevator button, while glancing at the strange-looking man wearing a jacket with large, puffed sleeves and a hat from another era. As the man was about to enter the elevator, he vanished.

A man who was checking out of the hotel questioned a number of telephone calls billed to his room. He swore that he had made no such calls. Upon closer inspection, the phone number seemed familiar. Then he remembered that it belonged to his mother. Unfortunately, his mother had passed away ten years before! Was his mother trying to reach him for an otherworldly emergency or just calling to see how his stay was?

A waitress working the early morning shift in the Colonial Room restaurant saw the figure of a man the staff called "Mr. Preston." He is described as an elderly man who frequents a bench in the patio area, always wearing a top hat and a dapper dress suit of the late 1800s era.

During a recent convention, a woman and her husband were assigned a room in the original building. Upon entering the room the woman immediately felt a presence watching them. While taking a nap she had a vivid dream about two skulls. Later that night, while in bed, "something" began pawing at the bed sheets, and she felt as if she were being touched all over her body. She woke up her husband, told him what had happened, and said she wanted to move to another room. He refused and so she took her credit card and checked into another room. She wasn't bothered again by the pesky spirit. She decided it was better to spend the night alone than with an amorous spirit.

While checking out, a woman lodged a complaint. Apparently the night before the television had suddenly come on. After getting up to turn off the set, she climbed back into bed. Once again the television turned on by itself. This happened several times before she could finally rest in peace.

On another occasion a repairman was busy working on the hotel's video system. There are three steel lockers that house the video players, with eight units per locker. As he was working on one locker, the door to an adjacent locker mysteriously opened, and the movie *The Devil's Own* flew out.

Several PBX operators complained that they felt as if someone was watching them while they worked. On numerous occasions they have turned in the direction of where they felt a presence and have encountered a face that seems to dissolve before their eyes. No one has a clue as to the identity of this mystery person.

Two women spending the night in one of the "haunted" rooms said that one of them was awakened at 6:30 A.M. by the sound of someone walking across the carpet at the foot of her bed. The woman who was abruptly awakened described the sound as a heel-to-toe walking motion making its way slowly across the floor. Sitting upright in bed, her friend fast asleep, she focused in on the area where the sound was coming from. Since she couldn't see anyone in the room, she did the only rational thing a person could do when confronted by the unknown, and that was to quickly pull the covers over her head and pray that whatever it was would go away—it did!

On your next visit to San Antonio, make sure you sample the food, have a drink in the bar, spend the night, or simply browse this historic wonder in search of its legendary spirits. Or you can take a fabulous tour of the Alamo and local haunts given by Martin Leal, renowned ghost hunter and member of the International Ghost Hunters Society. Leal's Hauntings History of San Antonio ghost tours are offered every day of the year (call 210-436-5417 for times and reservations). By the time this book goes to press, renowned writer Docia Schultz Williams will have a new book out that deals solely with the Menger called *The History and Mystery of the Menger Hotel*. Be sure to carry a copy with you as you wander through the hotel!

The Oge House Inn on the Riverwalk

Address:	209 Washington Street, San Antonio, Texas 78204
Phone:	210-223-2353
Fax:	210-226-5812
Toll Free Number:	1-800-242-2770
E-mail:	ogeinn@swbell.net
Website:	www.ogeinn.com/
Contact:	Patrick and Sharrie Magatagan
Accommodations:	Five guestrooms and five suites
Amenities:	Private baths; full breakfast
References:	15, 30

History

This Texas Historical Landmark (pronounced O-jay) was built in 1857. The landmark plaque in front reads: One of early stone residences of San Antonio. First Floor and basement were built as early as 1857 when place was owned by Attorney Newton A. Mitchell and wife Catherine (Elder). Louis Oge (1832-1915) bought house in 1881, after migrating (1845) to Texas with the Castro Colony, serving in Texas Rangers under W.A.A. (Bigfoot)

Wallace, and making a fortune as a rancher. He was a San Antonio business leader and served as alderman and school board president. He had leading architect Alfred Giles enlarge and remodel the house in neo-classical style. Louis Oge died in 1915, with his family retaining the house until a short time after Oge's widow passed away in 1942. The house was purchased by Lowry Mays and converted to apartments, and numerous other owners followed. The Magatagans purchased the house in 1991 and completely refurbished it.

Phantoms

It was during the renovation of the house that "unusual" things began occurring. Eerie images began appearing on the dark tile in the kitchen, and shadows were spotted out of the corner of their eye darting in and out of rooms, particularly the kitchen area. Sharrie Magatagan would often cook in the kitchen and would look on in awe as the condiments she was trying to use to flavor her dishes often seemed to intentionally avoid landing in what she was preparing. It was as if an invisible hand was directing the flow of seasoning. The spices would suddenly be blown on the counter, stovetop, and even the floor, usually missing the food. A spooky phantom with a fetish for food preparation was competing with Sharrie for kitchen duty!

Psychic visitors immediately picked up on a presence in the house and said this was a friendly, yet concerned female. A clairvoyant said the spirit belongs to a ten- or twelve-year-old girl who had drowned in the river adjacent to the house. So far there is no historical evidence to substantiate the claims about the young girl, but research is ongoing.

Most guests who have sensed something in the house have pointed to the Mathis Room as a focal point for the unusual. There are reports of lights turning on and off on their own, disembodied footsteps, and an occasional cold spot that suddenly manifests in a particular area. Other guests frequenting the Bluebonnet Room have recorded numerous unusual events in the guest books (you'll just have to visit and see what they report). An upstairs room is also known for the door that opens without keyed access in the middle of the night.

The benevolent spirit or spirits in the house always put their best disembodied foot forward when guests arrive. So while sipping some O.J. at the Oge, ask the Magatagans to fill you in on the latest sightings. Or perhaps you'll be telling them your story in this spirited house.

The Riverwalk Inn

Address:	329 Old Guilbeau Street, San Antonio, Texas 78204
Phone:	210-212-8300
Fax:	210-229-9422
Toll Free Number:	1-800-254-4440
E-mail:	innkeeper@riverwalkinn.com
Website:	http://www.riverwalkinn.com/
Contact:	Tracy and Jan Hammer, Johnny Halpenny
Accommodations:	11 guestrooms
Amenities:	Private baths; continental breakfast and evening desserts
References:	15, 30

History

Five two-story log homes relocated from Tennessee have been combined to form the Riverwalk Inn. The log homes were built from cottonwood trees and date to around 1842. The homes were brought to San Antonio and authentically reconstructed in 1994 by San Antonio entrepreneur Tracy Hammer and his wife, Jan. The two traveled the byways of Kentucky and Tennessee, found just the right 1830s-1840s structures, bought them, had the lumber shipped to San Antonio, restored them at 329 Old Guilbeau Street, and furnished them with period bedsteads, rugs, spreads and

quilts, and artwork. Hammer and property manager Johnny Halpenny said the main house is from Edmonton, Kentucky.

Phantoms

Sometimes when people buy old "things"—be it antiques, furniture, jewelry, and even lumber that's disassembled and then reassembled—spirits sometimes attach themselves to these treasures. This seems to be the case with the Riverwalk Inn where everything is a part of someone else's past. That's probably why guests have witnessed a female spirit, who has been affectionately named Sarah after a portrait of a young woman hanging over the fireplace. Others say there are several ghost guests who came to the place courtesy of the myriad items that were brought there when it was assembled.

Disembodied footsteps are often heard walking on the steps that connect the upstairs guestrooms with the common room, which is in the old Kentucky cabin part of the inn. The television in the common room often turns itself on and off. Certain rooms will suddenly register a marked drop in temperature. Guests frequently report feeling as if they are being watched. Doors will sometimes open or close by themselves when there are no drafts or wind. Unexplained whisperings, as if someone is softly talking, have been heard coming from unoccupied areas in the building.

A young couple who were married at the inn and had their reception there had a strange encounter via the camera. During the wedding and reception, which called for everyone to dress up in period (Victorian) clothing, a number of photographs were taken. The couple revisited the inn and brought the photos and showed management one shot of the bride and groom cutting the wedding cake. There in the photo is a man dressed in period clothing who was not in the wedding party. No one to this date has a clue who the party crasher is, although most suspect it's one of the friendly spirits at the inn who couldn't pass up a chance to be in a wedding.

The Riverwalk Inn is always a great place to stay, because you feel as if you've stepped back into another time. You also have the rare opportunity to mingle with other interesting people who come to visit, including guests who have never left—the spirits of the inn.

The Crowne Plaza St. Anthony

Address:	300 East Travis Street, San Antonio 78205-2411
Phone:	210-227-4392
Fax:	210-222-1896
E-mail:	stanthonyhotel@internetmci.com
Website:	www.stanthonyhotel.com
Accommodations:	350 guestrooms, including 42 suites
Amenities:	Private baths; television; heating and air conditioning; telephones; heated rooftop pool; fitness center; the Madrid Room for dining; Pete's Pub; ballrooms.
References:	15, 30, 31, 34, 35, 36, 37

History

Named after a city and a saint, San Antonio de Padua, the Crowne Plaza St. Anthony Hotel was built in 1909 by two prominent cattlemen, B.L. Naylor and A.H. Jones, mayor of San Antonio from 1912 to 1913. In 1935 the hotel was purchased by Mr. Ralph W. Morrison, who maintained the hotel's position as a truly elegant social center for San Antonio. From the 1920s until 1941 many of the nation's top big bands entertained in what was then known as the Starlight Terrace Nightclub, situated on the roof section of the hotel. While entertaining the hotel's guests, the band concerts were broadcast live nationally every week. In 1971 Mr. William Ochse purchased the hotel from the R. W. Morrison estate. It was purchased in 1981 by the Intercontinental Hotel chain, which renovated the property. Park Lane Hotels International purchased the hotel in September of 1988, and now the hotel has become part of the Crowne Plaza hotel chain.

Phantoms

The hotel boasts a number of friendly spirits. On the roof the sounds of children playing have been heard late at night by staff and guests. Additionally a woman wearing a white ball gown has been frequently sighted on the roof. According to management, there are times when you swear there's a party on the roof, with people dancing, drinking, and having a grand time. However, when you open the door in the evening and walk outside onto the roof, a silence engulfs you, and the experience chills many to the bone—it is considered a "hotbed" of paranormal activity.

Other strange sightings have been reported along a fourth-floor corridor, the men's locker area in the basement, a kitchen corridor, which is haunted by a ghostly woman, and various rooms throughout the hotel. Allegedly, a tragic event and unsolved murder connected to room 636 at the nearby Gunter Hotel ended in tragedy for the man accused of the murder in room 536 at the St. Anthony. Staff have on a number of occasions reported seeing a woman in ghostly attire in the hallways and rooms, as well as an elderly woman in a long, white gown in the Knox suicide room.

Drop in for an unforgettable dining experience or spend the night, and while you're there ask about the spirits of the hotel. Or better yet, pick up one of the books mentioned later and conduct your own self-guided tour, and see what kind of vibrations you pick up. It just might be that the staff person you think you see or the guest who breezes by you in the hallway might not be all that he or she seems. Some of the descriptions of the ghosts of the St. Anthony Hotel sound as if the only way you'd really recognize them as spirits is if you walked right through them, or vice versa.

Schilo's Delicatessen

Address:	424 East Commerce Street, San Antonio, Texas 78205
Phone:	210-223-6692
Fax:	210-229-9525
Contact:	Bob Lyons, general manager
Business Hours:	Monday through Saturday 7:00 A.M. to 8:30 P.M.
References:	15

History

Schilo's Delicatessen is situated only paces from the river and has been dishing to a mixed crowd of locals and travelers since 1917. The building, however, actually dates to the late 1800s when it served as a bank building. Just below Schilo's is the famed Mexican restaurant Casa Rio, which was once part of a Spanish hacienda dating to the late 1700s. Situated on Commerce Street, the adjacent bridge is the exact location where the first wooden bridge was built crossing the San Antonio River in October of 1736. It was also the only access to the Alamo during the siege from February 23 to March 6, 1836. Schilo's rests on a spot that became one of the focal points for the famed battle. Schilo's, a crown jewel of San Antonio's old downtown, is known as a businessman's friend, a historical landmark, and the best place in town to sip soup or homemade root beer.

Under the building are some foundations of old buildings believed to date back to Spanish Colonial times. One of the support poles seen in the rear actually rests on a limestone rock wall underneath. There is a stairway there that disappears into the dirt basement below. When excavating for more kitchen space in 1992 for Casa Rio Restaurant, an old fireplace was discovered in an exterior wall. There is an old well between the kitchen and restaurant area, and other wall remnants below that were once part of a Spanish hacienda, which floodwaters over the years have filled in with mud.

Phantoms

The great-grandson of Papa Schilo, Tommy Huntress, stated he remembered as a child around age six being inside Schilo's late one night after a family meeting. As family members were leaving and turning the lights out, a beer mug that was left on the countertop slid unassisted across the bar and fell to the floor.

In 1995 long-term employee Ursula Curde, known to all the regulars for her antics and serving style, died of lung cancer. Sick and going through therapy, she came back to work for several weeks before becoming ill again, because the place was home and the people were her only real family. When she died, private services were held at the restaurant, and her request for having her ashes scattered at Schilo's was honored. It was later discover that Ursula was actually Hitler's step godchild but was never a Nazi sympathizer. To this day there are those who knew Ursula, who claim that the feisty waitress never left, and they often feel her presence in the dining area, watching over the place.

A Mr. Valdez, who has worked for Schilo's for over twenty-five years, claims that there are "phantasmas" (spirits) in the building. One night Valdez and another employee had turned off the lights in the back Trophy Room and restrooms. As they were performing a final check of the restaurant, Valdez went in the back room and immediately felt apprehensive. It didn't take him long to notice that both restroom lights were back on. He felt chills, turned the lights off quickly, and left the building, locking the doors behind him. To this day he doesn't want to be the last one out of the building.

A former server named Pam recalls being pinched while walking behind the bar. It was a particularly stormy night, and she immediately turned around to find no one there. She asked the other servers if any of them had been playing a prank on her, but none had. She remembers feeling a strong chill at the time of the incident. Another server named Lucy, who is seventy-six and has worked at Schilo's for twenty-six years, occasionally gets chills in certain areas of the restaurant. There were other instances over the years where the servers have felt someone following them and have turned to find no one there. There are also recollections of staff seeing something move, like shadows, in the restaurant late at night out of the corner of their eyes.

According to general manager Bob Lyons, "Our 'spirits' do not have any reason to be in conflict with us. They probably do not want us to be frightened so we will not move elsewhere and will continue to serve our great eats! I am sure there are many customers who have passed on to the other side in our eighty-three years that still meet here regularly to conduct business and socialize."

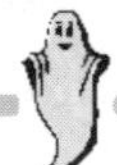

Terrell Castle Bed and Breakfast Inn

Address:	950 East Grayson Street, San Antonio, Texas 78208
Phone:	210-271-9145
Fax:	210-527-1455
Toll Free Number:	1-800-481-9732
E-mail:	smilgin@aol.com
Website:	www.bbonline.com/tx/terrellcastle/index.html#top or www.geocities.com/southbeach/pier/9656/
Contact:	Victor & Diane Smilgin
Accommodations:	Nine rooms on the second and third floors
Amenities:	Private baths; air conditioning; full breakfast served
References:	15, 31, 37

History

Terrell Castle was built in 1894 as the residence of Edwin Holland Terrell. Terrell was a lawyer and statesman who served as ambassador to Belgium during the presidency of Benjamin Harrison in the early 1890s. Terrell and his first wife, Mary Maverick Terrell, had ten children, four of whom died young. Terrell had his house built by English architect Alfred Giles after the castles and chateaus in Belgium and France. The residence was called "Lambermont" after a business associate. Unfortunately, Mary succumbed to pneumonia while in Europe, and after her death Terrell returned to San Antonio, giving up his stately duties. Some speculate that Terrell returned to San Antonio with the six children because Mary's influential family provided moral and emotional support to Terrell and the children during his time of mourning.

Eventually Edwin remarried, and the Terrell family consisted of Edwin Terrell, his second wife Lois Lassiter, his six children, and Lassiter's three children. The Terrells lived in the house until Edwin's death in 1908. It has had a succession of owners, operating as a bed and breakfast since 1986, including Katherine Poulis and Nancy Haley. In September 1997 it was purchased by the present owners, Victor and Diane Smilgin. The Terrell name is known statewide, and Terrell County and the city of Terrell bear the family name.

Phantoms

The inn is reportedly loaded with friendly spirits still enjoying life in this grand building in the afterlife. One woman, alone in the house and relaxing in the downstairs den just off the main entry hall, began hearing footsteps that sounded like a woman's high-heeled shoes making their way across the upstairs hardwood floors. The woman was in no frame of mind to see who it was.

Several housekeepers have heard unexplained footsteps and shuffling sounds in the house while they were cleaning. They have also reported glimpsing a shadowy figure walking along the hallway outside the upstairs room. A door or two has been known to open by itself, the lights in some of the rooms seem to have a mind of their own, and personal items have been known to move from one location to another—all in the spirit of having fun!

A couple who stayed in the Giles Suite reported that they heard a loud sound in the middle of the night that sounded exactly like a toilet seat had been intentionally dropped down. When they went to check the bathroom, everything was in place. This noise kept them awake the rest of the night, and they never did find the cause. Moving to the Americana Room on the fourth floor, because someone else had reserved the Giles Suite, they settled in and moved the television set to a small coffee table near the foot of the bed. All of a sudden the ceiling fan began moving by itself with the switch still in the off position. The fan continued to operate by itself the rest of the evening. As if this wasn't enough, after they were able to actually go to sleep, the television set flew off the table and landed upside down on the floor!

A psychic visiting the inn confirmed the fact that at least two friendly and harmless spirits were responsible for all the activity in the house including the ghostly footsteps, spectral noises, and apparitions that are frequently sighted at Terrell Castle!

Two rumored deaths were reported in the house. The first was the original building contractor, who leapt to his death from one of the upper balconies during the construction of the house rather than be exposed for illegally using contract laborers. A second death involved a soldier and his fiancée, who were occupying a third-floor apartment. The soldier caught her in bed with another man and either pushed her or she accidentally fell over the stair railing. She fell three floors to her death, leaving a large bloodstain on the floor that was finally removed when the floors were redone.

A recent conversation with the Smilgins confirmed that their beautiful, historic treasure is still filled with friendly and playful otherworldly guests. According to Diane, she was standing in the foyer with a friend, her daughter, and granddaughter, who came for a brief visit to view the house. During their stay, the granddaughter became excited and started pulling at her mother's arm excitedly, saying there were children in the house and they wanted to play with her. The child insisted that they were upstairs. Diane suggested that the child and her mother visit upstairs to see what they could see, and she continued talking with her friend in the foyer.

The four-year-old and her mom walked up and down the hall on the second floor, looking for the children, when the child pointed to the third-floor stairs and said that the children were up there. As they reached a landing on the third-floor staircase, the child pointed to a closet and said, "They are in there and are playing on the stairs." Thinking that the closet was locked, the mother and child returned to the foyer and relayed the results of their search to Diane. She was amazed since she had only recently discovered that the third-floor staircase had been altered and that the original stairway did indeed ascend along the side wall of that closet to the original ballroom on the third floor.

The child's story about the phantom children had a ring of believability because some of the nine Terrell family children would have been playing on these stairs at some time while the adults were in the ballroom. Diane, the mother, and the child climbed to the closet door with the child still excited about seeing the children. As Diane placed her hand on the door to open it, the disappointed child said, "Oops they're gone." Later, while the adults were chatting about this incident, the child once again became excited and stated that the children were back and wanted to play with her. When asked where they were, the girl pointed to the back kitchen staircase and stated they were coming down the stairs. This was puzzling since the child had never been in the house before and was not aware of the back staircase. As Diane approached the stairs, the child again said, "Oops they're gone"!

Were the Terrell children playing a ghostly game of hide-and-seek with their new friend, the only member of the group who could see them? And how did the young child know about the hidden stairs? These are only a few of the many playful antics that the unseen guests of Terrell Castle continue to bestow on those fortunate enough to sense their presence.

Victoria's Black Swan Inn

Address:	1006 Holbrook Road, San Antonio, Texas 78281
Phone:	210-590-2507
Fax:	210-590-2509
Website:	knot.com
Contacts:	JoAnn Rivera
Business Hours:	Tuesday through Friday from 9:00 A.M. to 5:30 P.M., full service catering; seminars; luncheons; private parties; weddings; receptions; complimentary wine with any meal; dinner by appointment only.
References:	15, 22, 27, 30, 36, 37

History

A number of artifacts have been discovered by archaeologists over the years, illustrating the Native American occupation of Salado Creek for several thousand years. On September 19, 1842, a battle took place on Holbrook Road in proximity to the Black Swan Inn between a Mexican army of 1,400 soldiers, directed by a French general, and 200 Texans, along Salado Creek. Sixty-one Mexican soldiers and a lone Texan died in the battle. Heinrich Mahler and his wife, Marie Biermann Mahler, built their first house overlooking the creek and moved there in 1901. The Mahlers had four children: Sam, Daniel, Louise, and Sarah. Marie Mahler died in

1923 at age seventy-three, and Heinrich was eighty-three when he passed away in 1925. Both are buried in the St. John's Lutheran Cemetery.

Heinrich left Daniel the house, silo, and milk barn while Sam was given the corner property. Each daughter received one of the houses the Mahlers owned in San Antonio. During the mid-1930s Sam's property was purchased by Paul F. Gueldner, father-in-law of Sophie Mahler Gueldner, and was later again resold. Daniel's property was bought by the Woods and Holbrooks. Since both families planned to reside in the house, changes were made. The main portion of the house was converted into one extremely large drawing room, which looked out onto the long front porch. Several walls that had divided up smaller rooms in the original residence had to be knocked out. Two long wings were added to either side of the center section, each wing having one large and one smaller bedroom. Each wing had a large bathroom and numerous closets. A kitchen and dining room were added, and the remodeled house was now called White Gables.

The Holbrooks had no children; the Woods had a daughter, Joline. She lived in the house with her parents, aunt, and uncle until she married. Her husband, Hall Park Street Jr., was well known locally. After the Holbrooks and Mr. Woods passed away, Mrs. Woods remained in White Gables with Joline, Park Street Jr., and their children, Hall Park Street III and Joline. A second story was added and the house expanded to sixteen rooms and 6,000 square feet of living space. Joline Street died of cancer in her late thirties. Mrs. Woods continued to live in the house after the death of her daughter, with her son-in-law and the grandchildren.

Park Street finally remarried and lived in the house with his new bride. On August 4, 1965, at age fifty-five, Street was found dead by his wife—strangled, a belt looped around his neck and tied to a bedpost. After Park Street's death, his daughter, Joline Wood Street Robinson, and her family moved into the house with her grandmother. They remained there until she passed away. Finally, in 1973, the house was sold to Mrs. Ingeborg Mehren. She decided to sell the property and take on other endeavors in 1984. Today the residence is known as Victoria's Black Swan Inn.

Phantoms

The Black Swan is definitely haunted: Doors that have been securely locked will unlock themselves. Lights in the outside hallway turn on unassisted. A man dressed in a white shirt and wearing dark trousers, usually with his hands on his hips, has been frequently sighted standing at the foot of one of the beds before disappearing. An elderly, wrinkled man with an unpleasant demeanor peers into an upstairs bedroom window, even though it is physically impossible for someone to climb up to that part of the house. There are numerous reported cold spots. Bathroom doors will lock themselves from the inside. An oversized closet located in the largest room of the house, at the end of the wing, is so eerie that people are reluctant to go there alone.

A beautiful lady is frequently seen in the largest of the upstairs bedrooms wearing clothing reminiscent of the 1920s. Could it be the ghost of Joline Woods, who once traveled to Washington, D.C. to represent San Antonio at a gala ball? A period photograph showed Joline wearing clothing similar to the apparel her ghost often wears.

There is a pervasive feeling of being watched inside. During a television filming, all the lights in the south wing came on by themselves. A grand piano in the drawing room has been known to play a few notes by itself. The sounds of an unattended music box can be heard echoing throughout the house, and the distinct sound of hammering is often heard downstairs, although the source has never been found.

Then there is the gift shop on the premises, which has a number of dolls on display. On more than one occasion the dolls have been mysteriously rearranged and the doll buggy moved from its original position, as if an invisible child has been playing. A beautiful dollhouse, which the Streets built for their daughter, Joline, when she was young, still sits toward the back of the house. Perhaps the daughter's spirit likes to play with the reminders of a more pleasant time in her life.

A crew from the Sci-Fi Channel's television show *Sightings* visited the Black Swan Inn during December of 1996. Peter James, a renowned psychic consultant, agreed that the place is literally overrun with spirits. During his investigation, James was able to pick up the energy of a woman on the stairway, another energy form in the main reception room, two spirits in the south wing, and another force in a hallway. He also witnessed a man looking in the house from an outside window. James finally remarked that the spirit of a little girl who pulls the pranks with the dolls at the shop is named Sarah but commented that she was always called "Suzie." The renowned psychic also told JoAnn Rivera that former owner Park Street Jr. has been trying to contact her for quite some time. It seems he wants her to find something important he left hidden in the house.

A segment of *Haunted History, San Antonio* by the Discovery Channel dealt with the Black Swan, and a visit by famed psychic Kathleen Bittner Roth confirmed the continuing spiritual energy within the building and directly adjacent to it. Sarah, Joline, and the other resident spirits still make life exciting at the inn and help to confirm that Victoria's Black Swan Inn is one of the most spirit-filled places in Texas, if not in all the United States.

Seguin

The community of Seguin, located roughly 25 miles east of San Antonio, was established in 1838 by members of Matthew Caldwell's Gonzales Rangers but was not incorporated until 1853. It was originally called Walnut Springs for the nearby fresh water sources. Just six months later the name was changed to honor Colonel Juan N. Seguin, one of Sam Houston's ablest lieutenants during the struggle for Texas's independence. Later Seguin served as a Republic of Texas senator and as mayor of San Antonio. Fishing, swimming, and water sports are popular in the area, with five hydroelectric power dams on the Guadalupe River. The giant pecan marks Seguin as a major cultivator of the nut.

Weinert House Bed and Breakfast

Address:	1207 North Austin Street, Seguin, Texas 78155
Phone:	210-372-0422
Fax:	1-830-303-0912
Toll Free Number:	1-888-303-0912
Website:	www.texasbedandbreakfast.com/weinerthouse.html
Contact:	Tom and Lynna Thomas
Accommodations:	Four guestrooms
Amenities:	Private baths; full gourmet breakfast
References:	15, 30

History

During the mid-1990s Tom and Lynna Thomas opened the first bed and breakfast in the historic community of Seguin. The two-story Victorian house was built in 1895 by F.C. Weinert for his wife, Clara Maria Bading Weinert, and their four boys and three girls. The house remained in the Weinert family for almost a century before it was finally sold out of the family. The guestrooms are named for members of the Weinert family who all passed away in the house that is reserved for guests and ghosts.

Phantoms

Several friendly, spirited members of the Weinert family including the senator, his wife Clara, and a spinster sister named Miss Ella have been sighted in the house. The spirits seem to prefer showing themselves to families, who are visiting or celebrating a special occasion, and lone staff or guests. The spirited Weinerts are blamed for ethereal music that occasionally comes from unoccupied rooms in the house. Also the piano has been known to play a tune or two when no living soul is near it. A travel writer visiting the house was awakened by the sounds of a timpani during her visit. No one has a clue who the kettle drummer might be. According to Tom and Lynna Thomas, lights are often turned on and off by the spirits, and doors will gently open and close unassisted.

The senator's spirit, strong in life, likes to remain "in charge" even from the other side. Sometimes Lynna feels F.C. Weinert accompanying her as she does her chores. There are other times when she senses that the ghost guest wants to be alone. When that feeling comes over her, she usually locks up and goes home since she doesn't reside in the house.

One time a female guest witnessed a beautiful young woman dressed in a white gown, bringing a breakfast tray into her room. By the time she was able to wake her husband, the figure vanished. After telling the innkeepers about her nocturnal visitation, she was shown a picture of Clara Maria Bading Weinert. The guest positively identified the woman as the ghost.

A gentleman guest also witnessed Mrs. Weinert, standing at the top of the staircase one evening smiling down on him. Another startled couple staying in Clara's Room saw a blackout shade suddenly fly up and continue spinning on its roller. Perhaps Clara, who probably didn't have blackout shades when she occupied the house, doesn't appreciate them in her room.

Other guests have reported they've had the sensation of being gently tucked into bed at night, a task the Weinert women probably did repeatedly in life. Miss Ella is blamed for moving items around in some of the rooms, with one housekeeper constantly complaining that small accessories, clocks, vases, and art objects were always being relocated. A visit to the beautifully restored Weinert House inn will certainly produce a relaxing vacation, as well as a few Weinert family spirits only too eager to please as they did in life!

Spring

Spring has a present population of almost 35,000 inhabitants. It was originally settled by German immigrants in 1840. Spring served as a railroad center in the early 1900s, but the population declined until it became caught in the surging growth of Houston. Old Town Spring offers over 150 shops, restaurants, galleries, quaint and elegant lodging, tours, trolley rides, and two wineries to sample Texas wine.

Puffabelly's Old Depot Restaurant

Address:	100 Main Street, Old Town Spring, Texas 77373
Phone:	281-350-3376
Contact:	Seth Sanders
Open:	Tuesday through Sunday, Closed on Monday. Tuesday and Wednesday from 11:00 A.M. to 3:00 P.M.; Thursday through Saturday from 11:00 A.M. to 9:00 P.M.; Sunday from Noon to 4:00 P.M.
References:	15, 38

History

The name Puffabelly's comes from a childhood song about little black steam engines huffing and puffing out white smoke. The restaurant is a 1900-era train depot. The original Spring train station located across from the Wunsche Bros. Cafe & Saloon burned down in the late 1950s. The present building was originally constructed in Lovelady, Texas, a small town located near Crockett, on the Galveston-Spring-Palestine rail line operated by the Great

Northern Railroad. The Lovelady structure, built of board and batten pine siding, contained a passenger waiting area, baggage and cargo areas, and small offices. It was purchased by brothers Bob and John Sanders in 1985 and cut in half and moved aboard two separate large house-moving trucks to its present site. The station arrived in Spring at 3:00 A.M. May 15, 1985. Until 1994 the facility was used for storage and a small leather goods retail shop before being reconditioned, restored, and renamed "Puffabelly's" in 1994.

Phantoms

According to local residents, strange apparitions and ghostly happenings have been witnessed over the years at Puffabelly's. Its association with Lovelady seems to connect the building to numerous tales of ghosts and the sightings of eerie lights near the depot. History suggests that shortly after it was constructed in 1902, a railroad yard switchman was involved in a tragic accident as he was attempting to flag down an engineer whose train was headed down the wrong tracks. As the switchman ran toward the oncoming train, waving his lantern and yelling frantically, he suddenly tripped on the rails and fell underneath the train. The accident decapitated the poor railroad worker, whose mangled and bloodied body was taken inside the train station by his co-workers.

For years people in Lovelady reported strange apparitions near the terminal. Several said they could make out a headless man waving a lantern and moving up and down the front of the station near the tracks, presumably looking for his lost head. The story was all but forgotten when the depot was moved to Spring, but shortly after it was reassembled on its present site, there were reports of similar sightings.

One man, Ralph Hutchins, who used to live off Riley Fussel Road, reported to police that as he was returning home late one evening, he noticed eerie lights coming from the area of the east side of Puffabelly's (nearest the tracks). He at first thought it might be an oncoming train, so he stopped at the crossing, expecting a slow moving freight to pass. But there was no sound nor was there a train, only the slow moving lights that seemed to cross perpendicular to the railroad tracks. Mr. Hutchins also said he felt a sudden rush of cold air, even though the incident occurred in August, and he made out what he described as "a headless man in overalls," waving a lantern. As the man approached, Hutchins said he feared for his life and gunned his car across the tracks and away from the lantern-waving apparition.

The story of the strange sightings in Old Town Spring eventually made their way back to Lovelady and connected to the original ghostly appearances there. It is worth noting that since the removal of the Lovelady depot, there have been no more reports of the headless switchman at that East Texas town.

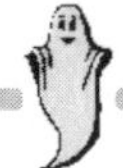

Wunsche Bros. Cafe and Saloon

Address:	103 Midway Street, P.O. Box 2745, Spring, Texas 77383
Phone:	281-350-1902
Fax:	281-353-4465
Business Hours:	Monday, 11:00 A.M. to 3:00 P.M.; Tuesday through Saturday, 11:00 A.M. to 10:00 P.M.; and Sunday, 11:00 A.M. to 8:00 P.M.
References:	6, 15, 28, 31, 36, 37, 38

History

Jane and Carl Wunsche were children of German immigrants who first settled Spring, Texas. Two of their sons, Charlie and Dell, who were former railroad men, acquired a piece of property near the railroad depot, and along with brother "Willie" constructed a two-story frame structure on the property. The new establishment, which opened in 1902, was named The Wunsche Bros. Saloon and Hotel. Spring prospered, and so did the Wunsches, until the Houston and Great Northern (now known as the Missouri Pacific) moved the Spring rail yard to Houston in 1923. By 1926 most of the town's frame buildings were torn down, but the Wunsche Saloon and Hotel continued to operate. The saloon was the last one to close in Harris County when Prohibition hit.

In 1949 Viola Burke leased the building, renaming the establishment the Spring Cafe. She was known for her homemade hamburgers, which sustained the railroad workers who passed through town. In time the reputation of the Spring Cafe spread far and wide. When Viola died in 1976, her daughter, Irma Ansley, inherited the business and continued making hamburgers. It was during this time that a gift shop was opened for cafe customers who were waiting for a meal. As the cafe clientele grew, so did the number of shops that were designed around the restaurant. The building was sold to Brenda and Scott Mitchell in 1982, and after the building was carefully restored, it became a Texas Historic Landmark and popular restaurant. They renamed the establishment the Wunsche Bros. Cafe and Saloon, which now serves only food—no overnight lodging.

Phantoms

In addition to great food, there is a ghost or two occupying the building. One spirit is Charlie Wunsche a.k.a., "Uncle Charlie." A former cook once went to retrieve a hand towel from the linen closet. As she opened the door she was startled to hear the sound of a man's voice mumbling something from inside the deserted closet. She quickly shut the door and left.

A former employee, Alma Lemm, was having coffee with a friend when they observed a candle burning on the far side of the room. The restaurant routine included lighting all the candles on the tables prior to the dinner rush and then extinguishing them at closing time to ensure that the old building wouldn't burn down. The two women would arrive on Saturday, grab a cup of coffee, and go into the dining area to relax before work at their favorite table. Over the next few weeks and only on Saturday morning, Alma and her friend noticed that the lone candle was making its way closer and closer to the women. Finally Alma decided to call "Uncle Charlie," who she surmised was responsible, over to join them. The next Saturday when the women arrived, the candle was resting on their table and burned down to the little metal plate in the bottom of the cup. When discussing the incident with other employees, the women found out that the spirited candle-lighting ghost had visited others with the same routine.

The most intense period of paranormal activity took place when restoration was concluded and the establishment opened for business. Changes seem to upset the delicate balance between the living and dead. It was during this time that staff noted unexplained footsteps coming from the unoccupied upstairs area, cold spots, doors opening and closing by themselves, furniture being moved to a different location, and chairs that would rattle or shake. Packets of sugar and salt and pepper shakers would be found on the floor when the place was opened in the morning. And although dozens of pictures adorn the walls, the same few pictures would frequently be found tilted or off center. All of the disturbed photographs belonged to the Wunsche family members!

Several times in the upstairs area the apparition of an elderly man wearing a black hat and black suit, with long white hair that reached over his collar was seen. The man looked somber and forlorn, and the witnesses reported being overcome by an immediate feeling of sadness. Some people have tried to communicate with the phantom man but to no avail. He simply vanishes, leaving a chilly gust of air in his wake. He loves his privacy.

Recent events include doors that mysteriously swing open and the sounds of items dropping in the kitchen when, upon inspection, nothing is ever found on the ground. An upstairs room is a paranormal hotspot where Uncle Charlie hang outs. Items are sometimes moved, and the computer seems to turn on by itself. A seance held in the "haunted" room ended abruptly when the candles set out for contacting Uncle Charlie all suddenly lit by themselves. An artist who rented an upstairs room found his painting supplies askew. Cafe workers have heard the sound of a sweeping broom when they were alone. One former worker was shaken when the pots hanging from hooks in the kitchen began swaying back and forth. And people have heard chains rattling.

A former waitress, working upstairs near the waitress' station after opening, suddenly felt intense sadness engulf her. As she was trying to shake off the feeling, she noticed a man attired in derby and black coat, crouched over the table with his face in his hands. Concerned, she approached the despondent man, who got up, turned, and ran from the room, passing right through the frightened woman.

We suggest that when you visit this historic building, you keep one eye on your food and the other eye on the lookout for the restless yet harmless spirit of Uncle Charlie.

Trinity

Trinity is a small East Texas lumber and railroad town where you can relax and enjoy shopping for antiques, gifts, fashions, and more in this quiet town of 2,500. Lake Livingston and the Trinity River are less than five minutes away, and the pine forests that once attracted loggers and timber barons now call to nature lovers.

The Parker House Bed and Breakfast

Address:	300 North Maple, Trinity, Texas 75862
Phone:	936-594-3260
Fax:	936-594-0329
Toll Free Number:	1-800-593-2373
E-mail:	styler@lcc.net
Website:	www.bbonline.com/tx/parkerhouse
Contact:	Mary Anne and Steve Tyler
Accommodations:	The Parker Suite, The Rose Room, The Gold Room
Amenities:	Access to snacks and soft drinks; full breakfast served in the dining room; available for weddings, anniversaries and special occasions
References:	15

History

A recorded Texas Historic Landmark, The Parker House was built in 1888 by Isaac Newton Parker. Parker, born in 1841, was the son of Jesse Parker, a pioneer who came to Spanish Texas in 1822, served as a delegate in the Mexican Convention of 1832, and later settled on his land grants in Montgomery and Walker Counties.

"Ike" Parker, as Isaac was known to his comrades in arms, served as a private in Company D of Hood's 5th Texas Infantry during the Civil War, fighting in twenty-seven battles. He was wounded at Gettysburg and again at Chickamauga. Parker eventually bought a home in Trinity in 1889 that now bears his name; he added the classical style porches around 1911. Parker's first wife, Mary Ashley, died in 1905. At the age of sixty-five Parker married Miss Lou Palmer, a forty-year-old clerk in his store. Parker died in 1918, and Miz Lou, as she was known, resided in the house until her death in 1955.

Phantoms

A number of strange occurrences point to the presence of spirits in the Parker House. Some believe that the spirits of Mary Ashley and Lou Palmer Parker, Isaac Parker's first and second wives, have joint custody of the house. A local Methodist minister, who had known Parker's daughter Linda well, swore that he had witnessed the apparition of Mary Ashley floating through the house.

While Mary Anne and Steve Tyler were working on renovating the house, they would continually return to find the balcony door either unlocked or completely open when they knew they had locked it before leaving. Lou Palmer's spirit has also playfully opened and closed the master bathroom doors (Parker Suite), causing quite a few midnight collisions with the unexpectedly closed doors by those using the room. Other events include lights that frequently turn themselves on or off in the master bedroom and dressing room (Lou Palmer Parker's rooms).

A friend of the Tylers found her three-year-old carrying on a conversation with an invisible someone in the master dressing room. When the boy was asked who he was talking to, he said "The lady in the wall."

One morning a young mother from Seattle came to breakfast puzzled and asked if the house had spirits. Never knowing exactly how to respond, the Tylers asked why. The woman recounted an experience she had the night before. She awoke to the feeling of someone stroking her forehead followed by a female voice telling her in a soothing manner, "Good morn, good morn." Mary Ashley loved women and children in life and continues to show affection toward them from the other side

A friend of the Tylers staying in the Parker Suite came to breakfast asking Mary Anne why she had awakened him in the middle of the night. She told him she had done nothing of the kind. He then told the Tylers that someone shook him and said "Tommy get up. Get up Tommy." Perhaps it was Mary Ashley. Many times when staying in the Parker Suite the Tylers have been awakened by someone tapping on the glass of the front door. Upon investigation there is no one there.

To date the only actual sighting was made by Mary Anne Tyler. While she was brushing her hair in the mirror of the Parker Suite bath, she sensed someone near. Thinking it was her husband, she glanced over her shoulder and caught a glimpse of a misty female figure standing behind her. After quickly turning around, she saw there was no one else in the room with her. Whether you come for the ambiance, fabulous breakfast, or for a chance to see the spirits of Mary Ashley or Lou Palmer Parker, you will not be disappointed.

Turkey

Turkey, with a population of around 500 people, is located about 100 miles northeast of Lubbock and 100 miles southeast of Amarillo. Wild turkeys discovered along a small creek gave this town the name of Turkey Creek, and the settlement that grew up there was known as Turkey Roost. The introduction of a post office resulted in the name being shortened to Turkey. The town was a shipping point for cattle, grain, and cotton.

Hotel Turkey

Address:	Box 37, 3rd & Alexander, Turkey, Texas 79261
Phone:	806-423-1151
Toll Free Number:	1-800-657-7110
E-mail:	suziej@caprock-spur.com
Website:	www.llano.net/ turkey/hotel
Contact:	Gary & Suzie Johnson
Accommodations:	15 guestrooms; seven with private baths.
Amenities:	Country breakfast; conferences; corporate meetings; weddings
References:	15, 29, 37

History

The Hotel Turkey was built in 1927 at a cost of $50,000, and it has never closed its doors since opening. It was bought by Jane and Scott Johnson in 1988, and they undertook its restoration. Eventually Jane and Scott sold the inn to cousin Gary Johnson and his wife, Suzie.

Phantoms

The spirit of the Turkey is reportedly a restless, western type. Stories have circulated for years about a force that likes to keep house in the upstairs portion of the building. On a number of occasions locked doors seem to have opened by themselves, and one of the beds, though freshly made, would a short time later appear as if someone had bedded down for the night. In this case the guest was a nonpaying ghost.

Numerous other events convinced past and present owners that something otherworldly was at the hotel. The front desk bell would ring when no one was near the desk. After being made, the bed in room 20 would exhibit an impression of a body form with a boot heel, as if someone had come in and had a quick nap. This happened often when the room was unoccupied or guests were absent from the hotel. When the nights were stormy, the front desk bell would usually ring, signaling the arrival of the ghost guest. Shortly after the bell rung, the upstairs bed would show signs of being slept in.

The phantom guest doesn't usually like the company of other guests, preferring to visit the hotel when most if not all of the guestrooms are empty, especially his favorite room, number 20.

The ghost seems to like his privacy and prefers a clean bed when he comes calling. The obliging owners don't seem to mind that he doesn't pay, so long as he doesn't cause any problems, stays to himself, and doesn't frighten guests. The mutual understanding between the phantom cowboy and the owners of the Hotel Turkey continues to this day. If you see a "do not disturb" sign on the door to room 20, there's a good chance the room's reserved for the Hotel Turkey's ghost guest.

A year or two ago a lady in her twenties was staying with her dad and brother in one of the rooms. During the middle of the night she sat up in bed and witnessed a man standing in the doorway between the bedroom and the bath, swinging a railroad lantern back and forth before suddenly vanishing. It makes sense, because the hotel was built in connection with the railroad (Fort Worth to Denver Line) spur coming through Turkey in 1927, located two blocks north of the hotel.

Waxahachie

Located 40 miles south of Dallas on I-35, the current population is under 20,000 inhabitants. The name derives from an Indian word meaning "cow creek." Presently the seat of Ellis County, the town was once squarely on the Chisholm Trail. Waxahachie is noted for its abundance of Victorian-style homes and the movies that have been made in the city featuring its old buildings and homes.

Bonnynook Inn

Address:	414 W. Main Street, Waxahachie, Texas 75165
Phone:	972-938-7207 (Dallas phone)
Fax:	972-937-7700
Toll Free Number:	1-800-486-5936
Contact:	Bonnie and Vaughn Franks
Accommodations:	Five guestrooms including the haunted Morrow Room
Amenities:	Air conditioning; five guest baths; breakfast
References:	15, 31, 37

History

Built circa 1890 by Waxahachie merchant Nathan Brown, who purchased the lot on Main Street from the R.P. Sweatt family, the Queen Anne Victorian home was later sold to W.T. Hunt. Hunt kept it only a year and sold it to Dr. W. E. West. West, his wife Gertrude, their baby son, and Gertrude's sister moved into the house. The resulting move played a significant role in a family tragedy. West, nearing completion of the house, provided Gertrude with a

new, up-to-date kitchen including the latest in wood burning stoves. Gertrude's treasured new stove accidentally exploded in her face, cutting her life tragically short. West wasted little time marrying his wife's sister a few months later. The family lived in the house until 1914, when it was sold to Mary Wyatt. The current owners bought the home in 1983 and, after restoring it to its former splendor, opened the former Brown/Hunt/West residence as an inn.

Phantoms

The Murrow Room is said to be a focal point for paranormal activity, and the presence of a woman has often been felt by those who frequent the room. There are those who believe that the spirit belongs to Gertrude West, who died tragically and of a suspicious nature in the house built for her. Others believe it could be any one of several former owners.

There are frequently reported cold spots in the Morrow Room and the apparition of a woman standing at the foot of the sleigh bed. The phantom woman seems to be checking up on the occupants and occasionally has put a good scare into guests. There have been reports of visitors waking to the shimmering form of an otherworldly figure standing nearby. Sometimes the woman has been sighted wearing a white gown, as she floats between rooms, along the hallway, or in other parts of the house.

When Gertrude, or whoever, is not drifting through the house, her footsteps are clearly heard upstairs and downstairs in unoccupied rooms. Other times the female phantom has been known to move furniture or relocate the guests' suitcases onto the floor. This harmless spirit seems to be a watchful presence. Guests have even recorded their encounters in the guest books, and psychics visiting the establishment have confirmed that this ghost wants to remain in her home.

Catfish Plantation Restaurant

Address:	814 Water Street, Waxahachie, Texas 75165
Phone:	972-937-9468
E-mail:	FoodCo2000@aol.com
Contact:	Jeff & Alice Hagemann
Open:	Thursday from 5:00 P.M. to 8:00 P.M.; Friday from 11:30 A.M.-2:00 P.M., and 5:00 P.M.-9:00 P.M.; Saturday from 11:30 A.M. to 9:00 P.M.; Sunday from 11:30 A.M.-8:00 P.M.
References:	7, 8, 13, 15, 17, 31, 33, 36, 37

History

The house was constructed in 1895 by a man named Anderson. His daughter Elizabeth, according to legend, was strangled in the house by either her lover or the groom on her wedding day in the early 1920s, in what is now the ladies room. A second woman, named Caroline Jenkins Mooney, died in the house in 1970. Another occupant was a farmer named Will, who lived in the house during the Depression and passed away in the 1930s. All three are said to haunt the restaurant.

Phantoms

The sign at the entrance to this quaint restaurant reads: "If you have a ghostly experience, please tell us!" Three spirits are rumored to inhabit the house: Caroline enjoys throwing and slamming things, since she spent a major portion of her life in the kitchen, preparing dinner for her family. If people do not respond when she wants them to sit at the table, she throws a tantrum. Caroline has been known to break wine glasses, slam doors, and throw coffee cups. Elizabeth is a quiet soul who often appears standing in the front bay window that looks out on the street. And Will is known as the quiet one who frequents the porch area. Police have reported seeing a man standing on the porch. When they walk up to investigate, he vanishes. He is also responsible for occasionally triggering the security alarm system.

The ghosts are blamed for numbing cold spots that suddenly manifest throughout the house, slamming doors, lights that go on and off by themselves, and refrigerator doors that open and shut unassisted. A big stainless steel iced tea urn was found sitting on the floor with all the coffee cups removed from the shelf and piled inside the urn. Coffee cups fly across the rooms. People are hit by an invisible hand. Freeze-dried chives floated off a shelf and were tossed across the room onto the floor. A fresh pot of coffee was brewed by the ghostly staff. Shadows move along the walls, and a stereo in the dining room frequently changes stations on its own.

A psychic once held a seance in the restaurant. Members of the assembled group began trembling, grew very pale, or began crying. There was tapping on the walls, dishes rattling in the kitchen, the candle on the table lit by itself, and the kitchen door flew open, exposing the apparition of a young girl identified as Elizabeth, who was wearing a wedding gown.

One psychic investigator picked up on the names Elizabeth, Caroline, and Will and said that Elizabeth's last name was Anderson and that her father built the house. Caroline was said to have died from a stroke, and her last name was Mooney, but her maiden name was Jenkins. The spirited Will was said to be an old farmer who lived on the land during the 1930s and likes wearing overalls.

There's the story of a lady who drove by the restaurant on one of her monthly trips to the area and found the patio furniture gone. After looking through the stained glass windows, her worst fears were confirmed. Everything had been removed, and her favorite place was no longer in business, so she left. Months later she decided to revisit her old haunt with her husband. Surprisingly, the restaurant had reopened. She excitedly approached the owner and asked what had happened. Did they renovate, sell, what? To her amazement, the owner calmly told the woman that she had never closed the place, not in the twelve years she had owned it!

During Halloween season three teenagers came to the restaurant with high hopes of inciting the spirits to manifest. They went into the ladies restroom and turned off the lights and chanted "Elizabeth, Elizabeth, Elizabeth." Just then the bathroom stall doors began to swing wildly, hitting them in this small, cramped two-stalled bathroom. They panicked as they all tried to escape from the bathroom. A waitress heard their screams and came to open the door to let them out. They tested the ghost all right, but Elizabeth proved that she could handle the challenge.

We challenge you to visit the Catfish Plantation for some delicious food or just to browse around, but don't fool with Elizabeth, Caroline, or Will, the otherworldly threesome.

References

1. "Alamo Street Restaurant and Alamo Street Theater," Great Food and Friendly Spirits: A Collection of Private Recipes, and "Spirited Tales from Marcia Baer Larsen's Alamo Street Restaurant," Talkin' Texas Productions, San Antonio, Texas.
2. Roy Bragg, "Supernatural Guests Welcome at Boerne Restaurant," *San Antonio Express News*, Metro Section, Wednesday, January 7, 1998.
3. Tim Carman (http://houston.sidewalk.com/detail/2488).
4. Charlie Chitwood, "Wispy Images," *Longview News-Journal*, October 30, 1994.
5. Catherine Cuellar, "Favorite haunts: When ghosts seem to inhabit your business year round, Halloween is no big deal," *The Dallas Morning News*, Lifestyles Section, October 31, 1999.
6. The Debra Duncan Show, Haunted Houston, KTRK-TV (ABC Channel 13, Halloween Special).
7. Dennis William Hauck, *The National Directory: Haunted Places—Ghostly Abodes, Sacred Sites, UFO Landings, and Other Supernatural Locations* (1996), Penguin Books, New York.
8. Dale Kaczmarek, *National Register of Haunted Locations*. Ghost Research Society, P.O. Box 205, Oak Lawn, Illinois 60454-0205, 708-425-5163, e-mail: dkaczmarek@aol.com
9. Bud Kennedy, "Building's ghosts manage to keep business at bay," *Fort Worth Star-Telegram*, October 31, 1996.
10. Randy Mallory, "Haunted Places in Texas," *Texas Highways*, October 1997.
11. Robin Mead, *Haunted Hotels: A Guide to American and Canadian Inns and their Ghosts* (1995), Rutledge Hill Press, Nashville, Tennessee.
12. The Menger Hotel. "Welcome to the Historic Menger Hotel: Historic Hotels of America, A Self-Guided Tour, San Antonio."

13. Arthur Myers, *The Ghostly Gazetter: America's Most Fascinating Haunted Landmarks* (1990), Contemporary Books, Chicago.
14. Leon Netardus, *Ghosts of Gonzales* (n.d.), Reese's Print Shop, Gonzales, Texas.
15. Personal communication
16. Jeanine Plumer, Austin Promende Tours and *Wierd Austin*, (E-mail:plumer@io.com/ website:www.promenadetours.com)
17. Lissa Proctor, "Three Ghosts Haunt Catfish Plantation," *The Antique Traveler Newspaper*, February 1990.
18. Carol Rust, "Holding Down the Fort: All of eight people live at Fort McKavett, a dot on the map where the trading post is the hottest spot in town and the ruins of an old army post play host to ghosts," January 16, 1994, *Houston Chronicle* Sunday edition, Texas Magazine.
19. Michele Chan Santos, "That's the Spirit: Local Ghost Hunters are on the trail of otherworldly beings in some of your favorite Austin Haunts," October 31, 1999, *Austin American Statesman*.
20. Jen Scoville Ghost City Texas (www.texasmonthly.com/travel/virtual/ghostcity/hunt.html)
21. Jo Ann Shaw, Planning Director and Originator of the Haunted El Paso Ghost Tours.
22. *Sightings* (1996), Paramount Studios, Ann Daniel Productions, Hollywood, California.
23. Allan Turner and Richard Stewart, *Transparent Tales: An Attic Full of Texas Ghosts* (1998), Best of East Texas Publishers, Lufkin, Texas.
24. Bert M. Wall, *The Devil's Backbone: Ghost Stories from the Texas Hill Country* (1996), Eakin Press, Austin.
25. Edward Weissbard, El Paso Ghost Research.
26. Mitchel Whitington, Dallas, Texas (www.whitington.com)
27. Docia Schultz Williams and Reneta Byrne, *Spirits of San Antonio and South Texas* (1993), Republic of Texas Press, Plano, Texas.
28. Docia Schultz Williams, *Ghosts Along the Texas Coast* (1995), Republic of Texas Press, Plano, Texas.

29. _________. *Phantoms of the Plains: Tales of West Texas Ghosts* (1996), Republic of Texas Press, Plano, Texas.
30. _________. *When Darkness Falls: Tales of San Antonio Ghosts and Hauntings* (1997), Republic of Texas Press, Plano, Texas.
31. _________. *Best Tales of Texas Ghosts* (1998), Republic of Texas Press, Plano, Texas.
32. _________. *The History and Mystery of the Menger Hotel* (2000), Republic of Texas Press, Plano, Texas.
33. Judy Williamson, "Spirited: Restaurant Offers Remarkable Fare," *The Dallas Morning News*, Sunday, December 6, 1987.
34. Robert Wlodarski and Anne Powell Wlodarski, *The Haunted Alamo: A History of the Mission and Guide to Paranormal Activity* (1996), G-HOST Publishing, West Hills, California
35. _________. *Spirits of the Alamo* (1999), Republic of Texas Press, Plano, Texas.
36. _________. *Southern Fried Spirits: A Guide to Haunted Restaurants, Inns, and Taverns* (2000), Republic of Texas Press, Plano Texas.
37. _________. *Dinner and Spirits: A Guide to America's Most Haunted Restaurants, Taverns, and Inns* (2000), iUniverse, New York.
38. Randy Woods (rwoods@infohwy.com), Souvenir Tours and *The Spring Souvenir.*

Other Haunted Hotspots In Texas

The following information comes from: (www.haunted-places); (www.lonestarspirits); (www.theshadowlands); Real Haunted Houses (www.realhaunts); Myers (1990); Williams and Byrne (1993); Mead (1995); Hauck, (1996); Williams (1995, 1996, 1997, 1998); Wlodarski and Wlodarski (1996, 1999, 2000); Randy Mallory (1997); Turner & Stewart (1998); and Kaczmarek (1999).

Abilene

Fort Phantom Hill: Built in 1851, ghostly soldiers and American Indians have been spotted at the fort.

Alice

U.S. Hwy 281 at Farm Road 141: During the 1700s Doña Leonora Rodrigues de Ramos, wife of Don Raul Ramos, was hanged at this site by her husband's hired hands after she was accused of adultery. Her spirit, called the Lady in Black, is frequently sighted along U.S. Highway 281 wearing the same black dress she wore the night she was hanged. Numerous motorists have pulled off the road to help the forlorn phantom, only to see her vanish.

Alpine

Sul Ross University: In a dormitory room at Fletcher Hall, showers mysteriously turn on and doors open and close by themselves. A female apparition named Beverly has been spotted in room 308.

Delores Mountain: The mountain is named for a tall, dark-haired servant girl, whose lover was reportedly killed by Indians during the 1800s. Her spirit is often sighted on the mountain.

Angleton

Bailey's Prairie: Brit Bailey homesteaded the land, died in 1833, and was buried upright so he could continue walking the land he loved from beyond. His restless spirit is frequently spotted as a ghostly shape or glowing ball of energy.

Anson

Anson Lights: The cemetery is a focal point for the disturbances. Legend has it that the lights are caused by a female spirit who carries a lantern while searching for her missing child, who froze to death one cold winter.

Arlington

Six Flags Over Texas: Near the entrance to the "Texas Giant" is a yellow candy store, the oldest building in the park. During the early 1900s a young girl named Annie drowned in Johnsons Creek. She haunts the store, turning lights on and off and opening and closing curtains and an upstairs door.

Austin

Austin State School: Several buildings in the school, which was built on top of an old cemetery, are haunted. Littlefield dorm is haunted by the daughter of Littlefield, who loves to manifest and play jokes on the students.

Bertram's Restaurant: Located on 14th and Guadalupe, the building used to be a general store and contains a ghost who has no intention of leaving. The restaurant no longer exists.

Capitol City Playhouse: Located at 214 West 4th Street, an unidentified spirit rearranges furniture, moves stage lighting, and displaces small personal items.

Eanes-Marshall House: The ghostly voice and mysterious laughter of former owner Howard Marshall has been heard in the house, and the specter of Marshall's wife Viola Eanes has also been spotted along Eanes Creek.

Governor's Mansion: Built in 1853, the north bedroom is haunted by Governor Murrah's 19-year-old nephew, who committed suicide in his bedroom in 1864 when Mrs. Murrah's niece refused to marry him. Reports of unexplained banging sounds and the boy's apparition forced Governor Hamilton to seal off the room after the Civil War. It reopened in 1925, and the boy is still heard crying, especially on Sundays, the day he killed himself. The Houston bedroom is rumored to be haunted by Sam Houston, whose apparition is seen in the corner of the room.

Logan's: Located on 6th Street; the spirit of a man who died when the building was a coffee plantation refinery moves items and causes doors to open and close unassisted, and unexplained noises come from the unoccupied second floor.

Littlefield Home: Located on the University of Texas campus; the spirit of Mrs. George Littlefield is rumored to haunt her former home. Footsteps are often heard in the upper floor, a piano in the living room sometimes plays by itself, and her apparition is occasionally sighted.

Metz Elementary School: Built in 1915; demolition in 1990 stirred up the ghosts. Reports included equipment failure, men being pushed off ladders, ghosts of children writing on blackboards and talking in the hallways, and mysterious shadows floating inside. After an exorcism, a worker was killed. A transplanted tree from the former school site is now haunted by the ghostly school children.

Old Stone Ridge Road: Some say a lady killed in an auto wreck haunts the area and protects the small children buried in the nearby cemetery.

Peyton Colony: This historic ranch owned by the Coffee family outside of Austin was settled as a slave colony in 1864. The old church and schoolhouse have been the site of four apparitions, frequent electrical problems, moving or disappearing objects, faucets turning on by themselves, ghostlike drum beats, ghostly photographs, balls of light, and sounds of children playing inside.

University of Texas, Austin: In the Jensen Auditorium, professor and pianist Dallis Franz, who taught on the campus during the 1930s-40, is frequently seen by faculty and students.

Westlake Hills: A phantom wagon driven by a ghostly cowboy, who was murdered by three men in the 1860s, passes through the hills of this housing project.

Zachary Scott Kleburg Theater: Several feisty spirits relocate props, turn lights on and off, take personal objects, and appear on stage.

Baird

Baird Cemetery: A woman's ghost has been spotted guarding her husband's grave.

Ballinger

House on 8th Street: The spirit of a Lady in White who died in the house during the 1920s is responsible for cold spots, ghostly laughter, apparitions, and a sense of being watched.

Rheem Air Conditioning Company: Formerly a saloon and dress shop, the old building was the site of a murder. Inside, objects are moved by unseen hands, there are ghostly footsteps, and people are gently shoved.

The Texas Grille: The former restaurant on Hutchins Street is haunted by a ghost named Norton. Events include unexplained footsteps, moving objects, opening and closing doors and windows, electrical problems; a scent of men's cologne, frequent manifestations, and photographs that turn up with a ghost in them.

Beaumont

Saratoga Road: A ghostly light appears, hovers for a moment, then speeds away, and it's not a UFO!

Beeville

Charco Road at Highway 181: A ghostly child's cry and flying heads have been reported in the area.

Belle Plains

Belle Plains Cemetery: A young couple in love had their romance cut short by a father who decided the boy wasn't good enough for his daughter. He killed the boy, and the bereaved girl hanged herself. The spirit of the boy is spotted and the loud cries of a young girl are heard in the cemetery built on sacred Indian grounds.

Belleville

Highway 36: A ghostly steam locomotive emerges from a fog pulling a string of freight cars at the junction of County Road 949 and Highway 36.

Ben Wheeler

A mobile home at the Van Zandt-Henderson County line has a ghost child named Buddy, who was run over by a tractor driven by his father. Buddy materializes and causes electrical equipment to go haywire.

Big Bend National Park

Bruja Canyon: Flickering lights and orbs and the apparition of a Mexican man wearing a serape and
sombrero have been reported for over 100 years. Photographs taken here often cannot be developed.

Los Chisos Mountains whose name means "the ghosts" harbor the Apache Chief Alsate, who was executed by a Mexican firing squad in the early 1800s; a sobbing Indian maiden, who drowned herself in a mountain pond rather than be raped; and a ghostly bull that forewarns of a death when sighted.

Terlingua Abaja: Several former residents have been seen near the stone church and cemetery in this ghost town.

Boerne

Public Library: A ghostly light is seen inside the building at night.

Brazoria

The Hanging Tree: The spirits of two men hanged at this spot are said to prevent people on horseback, car, or carriage from riding past.

Brazosport

Brazosport Little Theater: A female spectre, possibly Tallulah Bankhead, walks the theater.

Brazoria County

Lily Brown: The daughter of a white man and black woman disappeared one day on her palomino pony. Shortly afterward her ghost was sighted, suggesting that she was murdered. Her body was never found, but her ghost is frequently witnessed.

Brownsville

Channel 23: Several spirits have appeared to the custodial staff at this television station after hours.

Former Community Development Building: Located along Price Road, unexplained organ music, furniture that shakes violently, mysterious lights, strange shadows, items that disappear, phantom footsteps, and a black, hooded figure have been reported inside.

Glaevecke Residence: A brick-throwing spirit occupied the house in the early 1900s.

Local Strip Mall: The ghost of a man who died in the Mexican War haunts the building.

Old Brownsville Graveyard: The scene of a strange fog, unearthly lights, and ghostly figures.

University of Texas/formerly Fort Brown: Established in 1846 by General Zachary Taylor, an outbreak of yellow fever cost many lives. The fort was occupied by Union and Confederate troops. Gorgas Hall, the former barracks hospital, is part of the administration building. Doors mysteriously open and close on their own; ghostly horses and marching soldiers are heard; phantom soldiers confront people, and a female phantom appears to janitors.

Brownwood

Keys Crossing: Three ghosts kneel on the edge of the riverbank throwing roses. Some say the three spirits are in constant mourning for a family member who passed away. The spot was reported cursed by Native Americans.

Bryan

3602 Hawks Street: A ghost with no face, red eyes, and a cloak over his head haunts this house. People have been yanked out of bed, knocked down, locked in a bathroom without a lock; lights mysteriously turn on, objects move on their own, and ghostly images appear. An exorcism was said to be unsuccessful.

Buffalo Gap

Old Buffalo Gap School: On this site in the 1800s a farmer accidentally shot and killed his wife. Going insane, he burned down the house and killed himself. People have reported hearing the woman's favorite mantle clock chime.

Burnet

Joppa Bridge: Trolls, fairies, or ghosts reportedly haunt this bridge built in the 1800s.

Castroville

House on Gentilz Street: A ghostly lady frequents this two-story limestone structure. Visitors report cold spots, tobacco smells, and ghostly footsteps inside.

Choate

Knox Crossing: Located near Goliad on Highway 239, the ghost of a young female holding a light with a knife imbedded in her chest, soaked in blood has been sighted here before disappearing.

Christoval

Residential area: A ghostly Indian warrior and his family appeared to witnesses.

Cleburne

Wright Place: Constructed in 1874 as the 25-room Hamilton House Hotel, the south half was destroyed by fire in 1916. Purchased by A. J. Wright and converted into a dry goods store, the building is now used as a real Halloween haunted house with a restaurant. People see a young woman near a window and smell oranges when it is not being used as a haunted house. Legend reports that the woman was pushed out of a window by an angry boyfriend.

Clifton

St. Olaf's Church: Built in 1886 and abandoned in 1917, the church, located in Cranfills Gap west of Clifton, is home to disembodied voices and singing.

College Station

Texas A&M Campus, Agricultural Building: A worker bled to death when he accidentally opened a major artery. Since then a haunted elevator sometimes carries people to the floor he died on whether they like it or not.

Corps Dining Hall: Poltergeist activity has been reported in this building.

Colony

Crider Road: A three-story mansion, allegedly the site where a serial killer murdered numerous victims, burned down recently. Some report, when driving down Crider Road, the screams of the victims can be heard, and apparitions are frequently seen.

Coppell

Cemetery on Moore Road: A devil worshipper buried near the corner of the cemetery haunts his tombstone. People filming the gravesite often have their pictures turn out blank.

Copper Canyon

Goat Man's Bridge: Legend has it that a goat herder was decapitated by a motorist while herding his flock across the bridge during the 1920s along Copper Canyon Road. It is said that if you reach the bridge at midnight, the Goat Man, with a goat's head, will try and chase you.

Corpus Christi

Aviation Street: Located near a naval base, spectral wolves and misty Native American forms greet many visitors.

Fort Lipantitlan State Historic Site: Located along County Road 624, this old Mexican fort is haunted by a Lady in Green, believed to be the wife of Marcelino Garcia; he died from wounds suffered when Texians captured the fort. She is seen walking through a door leading to the room where Marcelino died.

Headless Horseman Hill: The ghost of a horse thief captured by a posse and beheaded because the men could not find a suitable tree from which to hang him reportedly appears on a horse in front of startled witnesses.

The USS *Lexington*: The boiler room holds the spirit of a young sailor who answers questions. Now a museum, workers have reported the sounds of chains being dragged across the deck, unexplained banging sounds, doors that open or close on their own, and the ghost of an engine room operator who died in battle.

Corsicana

Navarro County Courthouse: Late night visitors to the law library and people using the courthouse hear disembodied footsteps descending from the third and second floors. One ghost is rumored to be a former district clerk who was shot by the county sheriff after a political dispute on the courthouse steps.

Crosby

Williams House: Subject of a novel and the movie *The Black Hope Terror,* starring Patty Duke, the neighborhood was constructed over an old slave cemetery called the Black Hope Cemetery. Numerous residents were terrorized by angry spirits. Most of the activity is centered at the east end of Poppets Way and the side street that connects at the east end. There were frequent apparitions, poltergeist activity, disembodied voices, moving shadows, and much more reported. Before the Williams family moved out, several family members died under mysterious circumstances.

Crosbyton

Stampede Mesa: In 1889 over 1,500 cattle stampeded in the middle of the night. The spooked cattle went over a hundred-foot cliff at the southern end of the mesa. The cattlemen took a homesteader they thought had caused the stampede, tied him to a blindfolded horse, and sent them over the edge of the cliff. By 1891 the sights and sounds of ghostly cattle stampeding over the mesa at night were reported.

Dallas

LBJ House: Reportedly there is blood on the walls where a wife and children were sacrificed, and cold spots, apparitions, and ghostly voices are often heard coming from the house.

Millermore Mansion: This 1860s mansion was the home of the same Dallas family for over 100 years before becoming part of the Old City Park Museum. A female spirit near the former nursery and master bedroom on the second floor has been frequently sighted.

Mt. Pleasant Cemetery: Investigations have revealed wandering ghosts and abundant paranormal activity.

Oak Cliff: A little girl who was struck by a train while riding her bicycle across the tracks reportedly haunts a deserted street called Combs Creek, located near the railroad tracks. She is seen near the tracks before vanishing.

Baccus Cemetery: Located off Legacy and the Toll Road; ghosts are seen wandering through the graves, and strange lights suddenly appear.

White Rock Lake: The lake contains the mysterious Lady in White, who reportedly visits couples who park in the area. The adjacent DeGolyer estate is also haunted by the same spirit, who sometimes appears drenched.

DeKalb

Cry Baby Creek: While driving over the bridge on a clear night, you can hear the screams of an infant who was killed along with its mother in a tragic accident. The baby drowned in the creek.

Del Rio

Devil's River: During the 1850s a child was born to Mollie Pertul Dent. Mollie and her husband were killed by wolves, who adopted the child. The apparition of the wolf child has been frequently seen roaming with wolves in the old San Felipe Springs area, along the banks of Devil's River.

Denton

Mills Commune: This small community of fourteen homes is located on sacred Indian grounds. Residents report the appearance of a ghostly dragon in clouds in the smoke from campfires.

Dickinson

List Mansion: Now demolished, the mansion was the home of a Mr. List, who abused boys to the point that they murdered him and ransacked the house. While it was standing, reports of a spectral List were frequent.

Duncanville

Ninth grade school: The ghost of a teacher murdered in 1993 on the way to the girls' locker room is sighted after sporting events.

Eagle Pass

La Chimeneas Ranch: Now the Chittim Ranch, located twenty miles from Eagle Pass, the old 1800s ranch lies on the ruins of a

Spanish fort. Ghostly screams, sounds of people fighting, and misty figures are frequently reported here.

East Columbia

Old Sweeney House: Now demolished, the former Sweeney house; a spectral woman in a gray taffeta dress wanders the grounds. A woman was murdered by her husband and her body dumped into a cistern on the property.

Edgewood

Van Zandt County Road: Located north of Edgewood, the shell of a burned bus is all that remains of a tragic accident that killed several children and their driver. Ghostly screams of children are still heard along the road.

Egypt

Captain Heard House: Built in 1850, the house has a headless ghost, clocks that run backwards, balls of fire shooting through the house, ghostly voices, and disembodied footsteps.

El Paso

El Paso Museum of Art: Initially located on Montana Street, the museum was moved downtown. An elderly woman has often been sighted looking down from a window on the top floor. Lights have been known to flicker on and off, doors open and shut on their own, and unexplained moaning sounds come from the basement.

Fort Bliss:

Building 4: An elderly army cavalry soldier is often seen in the upstairs window, and other male and female specters have also been seen inside Building 4, which was once used as a secondary morgue to hold the bodies of slain soldiers.

Building 13: Built in 1893 for soldiers of the 18th Infantry, a calvary soldier hanged himself in the rafters of the building and is frequently seen inside, and doors swing open by themselves.

Asa P. Grey Recreation Center/Tumbleweed Tavern: The stage is the scene for unexplainable noises and specters.

Franklin Mountain: Spanish padres from the Paso del Norte Mission hid all their gold and valuables in a mineshaft and sealed it with red clay. Today visitors see ghosts of Catholic priests near the mines.

La Hacienda Restaurant: On the banks of the Rio Grande, this building has a female apparition of a woman who is seen walking nearby, weeping and asking for her children, who drowned in the river.

Loretta Academy: A nun imprisoned in the tower after becoming pregnant wanders the tower.

Plaza Theater: Built in 1929, the site once contained a residence where a jealous husband murdered his wife. The phantom female waters the theater's artificial plants, while a male specter appears in the balcony when someone lights a cigarette. There are cold spots, ghostly footsteps, disembodied voices, and lights that turn on by themselves.

Transmountain Road: There are numerous reports of a ghostly monk and his donkey walking along this road, which causes many car accidents. The monk guards a lost gold mine.

University of Texas: Semon Hall and the Cotton Memorial contain disembodied footsteps, ghostly screams, and apparitions.

Ennis

The Raphael House: Located on Ennis Avenue, the house was built in 1906 and named for the director of the railway, Cornelius Ennis. The former inn hosts the spirits of Raymond and Julia, and reported events include doors opening and closing on their own, windows closing by themselves, ghostly imprints appearing on freshly made beds, disembodied footsteps pacing on hardwood flooring upstairs even though the rooms are now carpeted, personal objects disappearing, and apparitions.

Fabens

Alameda Road: The apparition of a man in white is often seen running toward oncoming cars on Alameda Road between the cities of Clint and Fabens.

Farmers Branch

Manske Library: Haunted by the spirit of a construction worker killed during the renovation of the library in the 1980s or a Native

American from the burial ground that lies beneath the library. People see the figure of a man with red eyes pass through a wall.

Floydada

The Lamplighter Inn: Built in 1912, the inn, currently closed, contains the spirit of a man who was killed by his wife's lover in the 1970s. Also sighted is Mr. Cornelius, an elderly gentleman who died when the hotel served as a boardinghouse. Perfume and cologne often permeate the building; a man from the waist down runs up the stairs before disappearing; a woman from the 1930s or '40s floats down corridors; there are phantom voices and lights and doors with a mind of their own.

Fort Davis

Fort Davis National Historic Site: The ghost of Alice Walpole has been sighted since 1861. Walpole was abducted by Apache Indians and her body never found. She is seen outside the quarters where the women did their needlework. The odor of her favorite rose cologne presages her appearance.

Fort Leaton

Inner Courtyard: Founded in 1759 as Presidio de San Jose, the fort is noted for cold spots, feelings of sadness, and several apparitions.

Fort Stockton

The Sutlery: A dark, foreboding figure of George Garcia, who loved dressing in black and frightening people, is seen in the building. The spirits of Aniseto Peno, who died around 1837, or Manuel Ramos are also sighted inside.

Fort Worth

Armstrong House: Built in 1906, Gussie Armstrong, who died in 1923, is frequently witnessed inside.

Old Barbers Bookstore: Now called Greene's Antiques, this establishment is noted for disembodied footsteps, apparitions, unexplained shadows, and mysterious sounds including voices.

Del Frisco's Steakhouse: The Del Frisco's Steakhouse building was a bathhouse where a man was murdered while bathing. His spirit frequents the downstairs banquet room and wine cellar.

The Doop House: Built in 1916 by a wealthy oil baron for his musically inclined mistress, the resident spirit is nicknamed Mattie and he breaks appliances, suddenly materializes in front of people, and hates change.

Fort Worth Books and Video: This now defunct business was in a building that is home to mysterious lights, ghostly forms, unexplainable footsteps, and lights that turn on unassisted.

Log Cabin Village: Log cabins donated to the city in 1950, now a museum village, are host to a female wraith, a scent of lilacs, moving objects, strange voices, and unexplained footsteps.

A Mistletoe Heights Home: Ghost hunters attribute the hauntings here to a woman wearing an ivory-colored blouse, who sings and frequents the house.

Peters Brothers Hats: When the place was a pizzeria the ghost of dishwasher Jack Martin sprayed staff with water. Now another spirit named Tom Peters moves hats around. Apparitions and disembodied footsteps occur inside.

Schoonover House: Built in 1907, the basement is noted for cold spots, apparitions, mysterious voices, disembodied footsteps, and lights that turn on by themselves.

Texas Wesleyan University: The Fine Arts Building is haunted by a feisty female phantom named Georgia, who sits in the audience during rehearsals and roams the building at night.

Fredericksburg

Fort Concho: Established in 1867, ghosts of soldiers and Native Americans roam the area. Hazy shapes, ghostly voices, and disembodied footsteps occur with frequency. In Quarters #7 apparitions are frequently sighted.

Freeport

The *Mary Ann*: This ghost ship has been known to guide hapless boats caught in storms into safe harbor.

Galveston

Ashton Villa: Built in 1859 by James Moreau Brown; his daughter Rebecca Ashton Brown is frequently witnessed on the center stairway, in the hallway on the second-floor landing, in the Gold Room, and near an alcove in the living room. Objects move unassisted, clocks suddenly stop, and there are disembodied footsteps and voices in the house.

Avenue K Boarding House: Several people have died of natural causes in this house, and visitors report items moving on their own, doors that open and shut unassisted, and apparitions.

Fire Station #6: Captain Jack, a former fireman who died in the line of duty, frequents the former fire station in the form of ghostly smells, unexplained noises, and moving objects.

Flying Dutchman: This ghost ship was sighted in Galveston Bay twice in 1892. Captain Bernard Fokke, who made a pact with the devil, is seen at the helm.

Julia Ideson Building: This 1926 former Galveston Public Library building is haunted by a caretaker named Mr. Cramer, who is seen or heard playing the "Blue Danube Waltz" on his violin.

The Oaks: Built in 1838, the spirit of young Clara Menard, who died after falling down the stairs, has been heard and seen in the house.

Old Skinner House: Located on Sealy Avenue, apparitions and strange noises have been frequently reported.

Samuel May Williams Home: The spirit of Samuel May Williams is sighted in his rocking chair on the L-shaped front porch and in his upstairs bedroom, walking on the narrow balcony that surrounds the third-floor observation room.

University of Texas Medical Branch: The face of a fisherman who owned the land is still seen on the walls of the building.

The Virginia Point Inn: Currently closed, the inn is home to the spirits of Sarah Hawley and her husband. Windows and doors open and close by themselves, there are disembodied footsteps, rocking chairs move on their own, unexplained voices call out to guests, and Sarah's apparition has been sighted.

Witwer-Mott House: Built in 1884 by Captain Marcus Mott; the ghost of the captain's son, who was reportedly murdered by his father, roams the building. Loud voices and banging sounds come from the attic, and an apparition of a bearded man occasionally appears to visitors.

Garland

Garland High School: The ghost of school hero John Isom has his name mysteriously placed on the ballot for school president every election.

Goliad

La Bahia Presidio: Built in 1721, it was the site of the massacre of James Walker Fannin and his men on Palm Sunday, March 27, 1836, on orders from General Santa Anna. Ghostly crying sounds, unexplained music, an invisible woman singing, a ghostly padre, a lady in black, and spectral soldiers are all sighted here.

Gonzales

Courthouse Clock: The tower clock is haunted by Albert Howard, who was hanged behind the county jail on March 18, 1921. Howard cursed the clock that would toll his death. Since his death it has never worked properly.

Harlingen

Harlingen Insane Asylum: Now deserted, people hear screaming and see apparitions.

Hempstead

Liendo Plantation Ranch: Renowned German sculptress Elizabet Ney, her husband, and the ashes of their only son, Arthur, are buried in a family plot on the ranch. Arthur's gasping ghost is sighted and heard in the guesthouse.

Henderson

Howard Mansion: Constructed in 1851 by James Howard; his wife's spirit is seen on the stairway. There are also reports of disembodied footsteps and mysterious voices.

Hereford

Victorian House: Built in the late 1880s and relocated; a spirit named Jack haunts the building. Ghostly music, cigar smoke, faint voices, disembodied footsteps, and objects that move on their own have been reported.

Houston

Alief Cemetery: Apartments were built over a portion of this 100-year-old graveyard. Many occupants report apparitions, ghostly cries, and strange shadows in their apartments.

Alley Theater: The spirit of managing director Iris Siff has never left the site where she was murdered. Her spirit materializes, floats around, then disappears.

Barnard Street House: In the Montrose area, former owner Mr. Cowen was murdered by a friend. Owners have reported cold spots, strange animal behavior, and unfriendly apparitions.

Battleship *Texas*: The ghost of an unidentified sailor has been spotted on the second deck. Other spectral sailors manifest below deck.

Bookstop: Located in the old Tower Theater, the place is rumored to be haunted by several ghosts.

Cactus Moon: Located in Humble, the ghost of a young woman sits on patrons' laps and tosses objects.

First Pagan Church: Once inhabited by cults, an unseen force pushes some people, and unexplained sounds, cold spots, and disembodied footsteps come from inside.

Hillendahl Cemetery: Also called "Blue Light Cemetery," because of the blue glow that emanates from the markers. When someone disturbs the cemetery, the houses bordering it experience poltergeist activity.

Hogg Middle School: During the mid-thirties or forties a notorious gangster was excavated and hanged from a flagpole as a practical joke. Since then staff have reported shadows and disembodied footsteps inside.

KLOL: The former Jones family residence has apparitions, telephones jumping off their hooks, stuffed animals moving on their own, shadowy figures, malfunctioning elevators, cold spots, and disembodied footsteps.

Lovett Hall, Rice University Campus: Ghostly voices and the sound of phantom typewriters have been heard late at night. An apparition hurled a chair at a janitor, and there are reports of shadows and unexplained voices inside.

Office Building 1011: Located along South Highway 6, reports of disembodied footsteps, elevators opening on their own, things moving by themselves, and ghostly voices are common.

Old Woman Hollerin' Creek: Located off Interstate 10 between San Antonio and Houston, this forested creek is haunted by a woman who drowned her two children in the creek and now walks the banks searching for them.

U.S. Army Medical Training Center: Located within Fort Sam Houston, Service Club #2 is haunted by a playful ghost nicknamed Harvey, who clears his throat, opens and closes doors and windows, tampers with unmanned typewriters, and plays ping-pong.

Huntsville

The Walls Unit/Texas Department of Criminal Justice: The oldest prison in Texas, built in 1848, is home to numerous apparitions of former inmates.

Hutto

Jakes Bridge: A man who killed his wife and child then hanged himself from the bridge haunts the locale.

Jacksonville

Lon Morris College/Fair Hall: Strange things have been reported in a dorm where a suicide took place. Doors open and shut by themselves, there are unexplained moans, spectral voices, and lights that turn on unassisted.

Pierce's Chapel Cemetery: Reports include unexplained footsteps; the ghostly silhouette of a man; an unearthly fog that only covers half the cemetery, rising to the level of the gravestones before disappearing instantly when headlights are turned on; mysterious orbs of light; disembodied voices; and numerous apparitions.

Jasper

Bishop Family House/Family Cemetery: Located about six miles from Jasper, a phantom woman and other apparitions have been sighted near the house and family plots.

Maund House: Built in the mid-1800s by William Maund; Lacy Merritt, who committed suicide in the house after a love affair went awry, is said to be responsible for ghostly voices, disembodied footsteps, and manifestations. The original house was demolished and rebuilt. The new house is also said to be haunted.

Mill House: Built in 1903, the house was part of the mill town that contained 143 buildings. Claude Walker was murdered in the house in 1974, and bloodstains continue to appear in the tile. There are unexplained wailing sounds, mysterious voices, and a phantom woman in a 1920s dress.

Jefferson

The Claiborne House: Haunted by the apparition of a well-dressed man.

Kenefick

Dayton Lake Estates: A woman who murdered her husband upstairs is considered the cause of frequent apparitions and poltergeist activity.

Kingsville

Texas A&M University: Apparitions have been reported over the years along with cold spots and feelings of being watched in Lewis and Turner Dormitory Hall. A male student committed suicide in Turner Hall, and a female student took her life in Lewis Hall.

LaGrange

Old LaGrange High School: A teacher named Rosa Mieneke haunts the second floor of the school. Books fly across the room, papers are torn in half, there are disembodied footsteps, and a woman's voice echoes through deserted hallways and rooms.

La Porte

Trinity Bay: La Porte residents are sometimes awakened at night by Laffite's ghost, dressed in a red coat and standing at the foot of their beds. Laffite built his headquarters, called Maison Rouge, at La Porte.

Lajitas

Bad Lands Hotel: Portions of the hotel were built on the site of an old cavalry post. The hotel was the site of a grisly murder in the 1940s. Strange noises, ghostly footsteps, and apparitions have been reported here.

Lake Jackson

Jackson Plantation: A fight between two Jackson brothers ended in the decapitation of one brother. His head was tossed into Lake Jackson and never found, and the body was buried. Witnesses report hearing a voice near the plantation asking for the location of his head.

La Marque

Weller Home: Mysterious noises, objects moving on their own, and frequently sighted apparitions have been attributed to the ghost of 15-year-old Elvie Weller.

Laredo

The Bracht-Fisher House: The former inn was built around 1881. There is a "glowing fog," unexplained footsteps, front porch lights that turn on by themselves, kitchen doors that suddenly swing open, and the spirit of Leopold Bracht.

The Hamilton Hotel: Several restless spirits move objects, turn the lights on and off, toy with the elevator, move the furniture around, and suddenly manifest.

Laredo Independent School District/Azios Building: The spirit of a former owner turns off lights, opens and closes doors, and appears to unsuspecting females.

United Middle School: A closed off section where a girl was killed after a basketball game is home to her spirit.

Liberty

Hardin House/Seven Pines: Built by Franklin Hardin and his wife Cynthia O'Brien; their son, Christy, died at the age of 24. The house is now a cultural center haunted by Christy's ghost.

Lockhart

Lockhart County Court and Jail House: Now a museum, the top three levels once held the old jail where people report cold spots, unexplained voices, and ghostly footsteps.

Lubbock

Shopping Center: The building, a hotel at the turn of the century, is home to ghostly voices, unexplained footsteps, cold spots, and apparitions.

Brick Building: Built in 1921, this building is haunted by the widow of a former professor where there are frequent cold spots, apparitions, and items moved by unseen hands.

Texas Tech University: On the third floor of the Chemistry/Geosciences building, a cleaning lady was killed by a student stealing a copy of a Biology final. Her spirit manifests during final exams. A chemistry professor haunts Holden Hall where he has been seen and heard clearing his throat.

Luckenbach

Kung Residence: Built in 1858 by Otto and Jacob Kung, the house is host to phantom whistling, disembodied footsteps climbing the stairs, faucets turning on by themselves, a man in a blue shirt who suddenly materializes, and doors that open unassisted.

Maxdale

Maxdale Cemetery: This old cemetery is haunted by an elderly man with a limp. An iron bridge leading to the cemetery is haunted by a man who hanged himself after his girlfriend drowned in the river under the bridge.

McAllen

Old McAllen High School: Built in 1913 and replaced in the 1970s; four former students killed during World War II return together to haunt their former high school. Witnesses described the four apparitions as a red-haired girl in a green print dress; a blond-haired, blue-eyed boy; a shy boy with large brown eyes; and a thin, dark-haired boy.

Mereta
The Delagarza House: Built in 1996 over the grave of a little boy; sounds of gurgling water below the house, scratching noises, clothes being moved in the closets, small objects mysterious falling from the ceiling, painful cries, the apparitions of a woman and a child named Manuel are a few of the paranormal events reported in the house.

Mineral Wells
The Baker Hotel: This 415-room, fourteen-story building opened in 1929 and ceased operations in 1972. The spirit of Douglas Moore, killed in an elevator accident, still roams the old hotel. A male spirit, a phantom prostitute, unexplained footsteps, and ghostly voices are reported inside.

Mineral Wells Mansion: This 22-room mansion is haunted by a young man and an elderly gentleman.

Mission
Roosevelt School Mission: The condemned school has apparitions and disembodied voices.

Neches River
Plains: From Real County to Lake Corpus Christi, ghost riders have haunted the area since the 1870s. A cattleman who stampeded his herd through a farmhouse, killing everyone, has left a lasting imprint on the landscape.

El Muerto: A grotesque-looking phantom cowboy named Vidal has been seen since the 1840s, with a headless torso, clad in buckskin and rawhide chaps, and riding a black, red-eyed mustang.

Nederland
Nederland House: Built around 1922 by Joe Lee who died in the house; his spirit shakes beds, has shattered a glass chimney, materialized, and is responsible for disembodied footsteps.

Old Waverly
Walker Cabin: Located in Old Waverly, mysterious coughing sounds, screams, and ghostly drumming and marching noises have been reported.

Paint Rock

Weldon Ostrander House: Also called Thornfield, the house was built in 1882 by Weldon Ben Ostrander and his wife, Sarah. During 1889 the entire family disappeared. Apparitions are seen and ghostly sounds come from inside.

Palestine

Courthouse: On certain nights people have heard a baby, who died in the house, crying or walking around as evidenced by the sound of tiny footsteps on the floor.

Payton Colony

Settlement: Ghostly photos, apparitions, moving objects, mysterious lights, unexplained voices, and doors opening by themselves have been reported here.

Pecos

Reeves County Courthouse: Unexplained footsteps descending the fourth floor stairs, objects being tossed or moved, and shadowy figures have been reported here.

Plainview

Plainview High School: The school is haunted by a ghost dubbed Herkie, who died in the auditorium. Herkie turns lights on and off and appears to some students and faculty.

Wayland Baptist University: A young female who was either killed in a car accident or committed suicide is rumored to haunt the third floor of Gates Hall, formerly the old parapsychology lab and music department. Doors shut on their own, a dark figure appears, and a ghostly voice echoes through the darkened hallways.

Port Isabel

Padre Island: The lingering spirits spotted along the beach are rumored to be in search of lost treasure.

Port Neches

Sarah Jane Road: Sarah Jane, a Union sympathizer betrayed during the Civil War, was reportedly shot by a Confederate soldier while trying to save her baby. Sarah is seen and her baby heard from the bridge at night.

Presidio

Fort Leaton: Edward Hall was murdered in his house by John Burgess. Burgess was murdered by Hall's stepson. The spirit of Hall and a female spirit have been spotted in the kitchen and a bedroom. Chairs rock on their own, and mysterious voices and disembodied footsteps are heard inside.

Reeves Thicket

Reeves Thicket Ranch House: Near Goliad, the former John Reeves ranch house, now a subdivision, has had ghostly figures appear, especially near the old cemetery.

Sutton's Mott: Near a dense stand of trees, ghostly figures are sighted hanging from trees or wandering aimlessly.

Rome

Deep Creek Cemetery: At a place called whispering bridge, children who fell to their death are heard crying at night.

Sabine Pass

Sabine Pass Lighthouse: Built in 1857, some kind of ghostly force haunts this old lighthouse.

San Angelo

Fort Concho: Operating from 1867 to 1889, the buildings are now residences. Ghosts of soldiers are heard in the barracks, and apparitions are seen walking the grounds. Mysterious lights are witnessed in the headquarters and court-martial room. The presence of Captain William Notson frequents the post hospital. The museum library, formerly Officer's Quarters No. 7, is haunted by several ghosts of those murdered in the building in the 1890s.

The University: Unexplained footsteps and the sound of a man and woman arguing are frequently heard late at night in the deserted second-floor hallways of the Administration/Journalism Building. On the ninth floor of the girls' dorm, the spirit of a young woman is seen near room 200, which is now the Housing Office.

San Antonio

Aggie Park Facility: A misty form haunts the building. Moving shadows, cold spots, problems with the electricity, items that move, and mysterious noises keep the place lively.

Alamo/Mission San Antonio de Valero: Originally established as Mission San Antonio de Valero in 1718, spirited activity dates back to its founding days. After the Battle of the Alamo, reports of ghostly soldiers in front of the chapel were said to have prevented the Alamo from being destroyed. You name it, apparitions of Native Americans, monks, soldiers, and defenders, unexplained footsteps, cold spots, disembodied voices, and ghostly reenactments continue to be reported.

Bexar County Medical Health Building: Here, toilets flush on their own, loud band music comes from the unoccupied warehouse, objects are moved by invisible hands, and doors open by themselves.

Botanical Gardens: The gardens contain the wandering spirit of a headless horseman.

The Chabot Reed House: This national register house was built in 1876 by George Starks Chabot and Mary Van Derlip Chabot both of whom died in the house. Unexplained footsteps, Roaring Twenties music, disembodied voices and laughter, and the apparition of a woman floating down the stairs in a full-length skirt are reported.

Brooks House: Run by the San Antonio Historical Society and built in 1890 by the Hertzberg family, reports of pipe smoke, disembodied footsteps, and a tall, mustached figure in an upstairs bedroom are frequent.

Cafe Camille: Constructed in 1910, the residence was turned into the Cafe Camille, now closed. Doors opening and closing by themselves, a strong sense of a presence in the front portion of the building, a mirror which was lifted off the wall by an unseen force, ghostly footsteps, and the sighting of an apparition or two have been reported.

Central Texas Parole Violator Building: The building served as a jail. Prisoner Hugo Saenz was murdered in the facility, and his spirit has been seen wandering through the facility before vanishing. Other spirits roam the halls.

Comanche Look-out Hill: Haunted by Native Americans and soldiers.

Denny's on 410: A past manger who suffered a heart attack and died in the store has been spotted on security cameras at night, standing in front of the cash register where he died.

Dienger Building: The spirit of Charley Dienger frequents the cellar. He is known to slam doors, turn lights on and off, and shake windows. There are reports of mysterious voices, water glasses turning up half empty, disappearing objects, disembodied footsteps, and apparitions of a man and woman inside.

El Camino Real House: A woman who was murdered by her husband and her body buried under this abandoned house is often sighted or her mournful cries heard by passers-by.

Fort Clark: Founded in 1852, a one-story building at one end of Officer's Row is reportedly haunted by a black cook and her cat. The cook was killed by a colonel before the turn of the century. Ghostly footsteps, apparitions, and disembodied voices are often heard coming from this building, which no one wants to occupy. Building No. 8-9 is haunted by the spirit of Ollabelle Dahlstrom, who enjoys grabbing and touching people. A voice yelling, "Help me" has also been heard, and beds have begun shaking for no reason. In Building No. 10 people often smell food cooking when no one is in the kitchen. The misty form of a woman is also sighted inside. Building No. 11 is haunted by a friendly spirit, where deep sighs are heard and people's names are called out by an invisible person.

Fort Sam Houston: Service Club #2 and a swimming pool are haunted by a ghost named Harvey. The Pershing House on Staff Post Road, built in 1881, has strange events including toilets that flush on their own, a doorbell that rings unassisted, lights that turn on by themselves, and disembodied footsteps that some say belong to "Black Jack" Pershing. Quarters #1 built in 1881 have toilets that are flushed by invisible hands, an unseen force joins people in their bed, and disembodied footsteps make their way up the stairs.

Fire Station #12: Built in 1925; the spirit of Captain Ike Bowman who died at age 61 is rumored to haunt the building. His dark, shadowy figure has been spotted with glowing eyes, as he confronts people.

Gatlin Gasthaus: This former inn has spirits who play with the plants, cause the electricity to malfunction, open and close doors, blow out or light candles, and suddenly manifest.

Hertzberg Museum: John McMullen was murdered in his house, which once occupied the site of the museum and former public library. It has reports of cold spots, a shadowy figure, ghostly footsteps, banging noises, items being knocked off of shelves, and shimmering lights.

Hope Farm: This 1871 residence built by Alphonse Perrin is the site of doors that open unassisted, disembodied footsteps, objects that disappear, windows that rattle, and fresh linens that are disturbed by an invisible force.

House at 1166 West Chavaneux Road: Built after the 1920s, the deserted house was reportedly the site of multiple murders. Unexplained cries of children in the night, ghostly music, apparitions, cold spots, strange lights, and a dark foreboding feeling encompasses the house.

Institute of Texan Cultures: The appearance of a workman who committed suicide is often sighted in the building. Other reported events include mysterious pipe smoke, disembodied footsteps, objects rearranged by unseen hands, doors opening and closing by themselves, and ghostly voices.

John F. Kennedy High School: A teacher named Gus Langley haunts the school. Cold spots, lockers suddenly banging shut, manifestations, posters being removed by phantom hands, and disembodied footsteps are reported.

John J. Wood Federal Building: Voices in the elevators saying, "Help me" and "Get me out of here," sounds of loud, unidentified hammering coming from the roof, doors opening on their own, an apparition in the courtroom, and lights turning themselves on an off are reported inside.

Jose Navarro's Former Homestead: Several buildings on South Laredo at West Nuevo Street were once part of Jose Navarro's estate built after 1832. Mysterious footsteps, cold spots, and the apparitions of a young man, Confederate soldier, bartender, lady of the night, and child are occasionally reported in this "very" haunted abode.

La Mariposa Inn: This former inn is now a private residence. Built by Benno Engelke in 1884 after he married Mary Elmendorf, the house is host to a gentle, female spirit who is responsible for unexplained footsteps and joining people in bed.

Lasses Boulevard House: Built next to an orphanage, the house contains the spirit or spirits of children. Eggs are mysterious cracked, ghostly music is heard, and strange shadows are sighted inside.

La Villita-Chamade Jewelry Store: At 504 Villita Street, objects that move on their own, voices of people arguing, shadowy figures including a woman wearing an apron, and cold spots are frequently reported inside.

La Villita-River Art Gallery: A female apparition dressed in white visits this establishment.

La Villita-Starving Artists Gallery: An 1800s woman with her hair pulled back in a bun, items that are moved or flung off shelves, and strange shadows are reported inside.

La Villita House: Built in 1864 by Cirius Gissi, the house and spirit of a little girl were moved to La Villita.

The Linden House: Built in 1902 by Judge Walter Linden for his wife, Martha, and their only child, Mary Ann; ghostly footsteps, moving objects, opening and closing doors, and electrical malfunctions are reported in the house.

Long Acres: Located on Vance Jackson Road, this haunted house has items disappear or move along with a female spirit named Elsie.

Midget Mansion: Built in the 1920s on Donore Street, a midget killed his entire family before killing himself. Moans, scratching sounds, and apparitions were reported before the house burned down. Some people still claim to see spirits and hear cries come from the undeveloped land.

Milam Square: Ghosts of phantom Spanish settlers and Native Americans are sighted here. Milam Square was also the site of a Catholic cemetery in the early 1700s.

Missions San Jose, San Francisco, San Juan Capistrano, and San Jacinto: Frequent reports of apparitions, unexplained footsteps, rapping and knocking sounds, disembodied voices, and chanting are reported in the missions.

North Star Mall: Shadowy figures suddenly appear, and mysterious voices whisper people's names in the mall.

Old Menger Soap Factory: Built by Johann Nicholas Simon Menger in 1850 and rebuilt after a flood, a restless spirit haunts the building. There are unexplained footsteps, apparitions, and cold spots inside.

Old Salinas Homestead: Built in 1874 on the corner of Nueva and Villita Streets, a phantom man and woman frequent the house.

Old Spanish Tower: Built in the 1920s, unexplained "ghost lights" have been reported near the tower.

Old Onion House: Built in 1848 by Joseph Heubner, the Onions occupied the place in the 1930s. The spirit of Joseph Heubner haunts the house.

Our Lady of the Lake University: This university is haunted by a janitor who frequents the basement of the library. Ghostly nuns and a headless apparition walk the halls of the former dorm.

Reed Candle Factory: The spirit of founder Peter Doan Reed frequents the building.

Rivercenter Mall: Cries of ghostly men have been reported inside. This is the area where the ashes of dead Texans were reportedly buried after the Battle of the Alamo. It was also part of the original battlefield.

San Antonio Academy: The ghost of Professor Jim Roe, who died in the building, haunts an upstairs area of the Stribling Building.

San Antonio College/McAllister Auditorium: Built on the site of two homes and a kindergarten, strange shadows, arcs of light, lights turning on by themselves, and ghostly voices are reported in the building.

San Antonio Express News: The phantom figure of a slightly built gentleman wearing a black jacket and a phantom woman have been spotted on the third floor. People have experienced dizziness on the third floor and hear their names called out by someone unseen.

San Pedro Playhouse: The spirit of an elderly, balding, stocky man and a man in military dress have been reported passing through the building. Objects are sometimes moved by unseen hands, and doors open and close unassisted.

Sartor House: This 1880s house on King William Street has a friendly presence in the parlor and central hallway.

Spanish Governor's Palace: Built in 1749, the spirit of a young girl who was tossed into the well behind the house by robbers roams the grounds. Unexplained voices and footsteps, lights that turn on, and doors that open unassisted are reported here.

Spanish Ranch House: Located near Mission Concepcion, misty forms, strange noises, cold spots, and unexplained footsteps are commonly reported.

Stinson Field Airport: An old hangar used for storage is haunted by a man who died while starting his plane.

Stinson Field Graveyard: This early cemetery is haunted by the ghost of an Oriental woman who committed suicide. Her spirit is said to hover near her grave. Mysterious blue lights have also been spotted there.

Tobin Estate/Apartment Complex: The original house by Salado Creek is now part of an apartment complex and is used as an office. A sea captain who built the house in the late 1890s and accidentally killed his wife haunts the office where ghostly footsteps, mysterious voices, apparitions, and electrical malfunctions are reported.

Ursuline Academy: The buildings, now part of the Southwest Craft Center, date to the early 1850s. People have been pushed by unseen hands, and the spirit of a priest and nun have been sighted.

Villa Main Railroad Tracks: The restless spirits of children killed when a freight train hit a school bus haunt this location. It is said that the spirits try to push cars across the tracks to safety.

Weiderstein House: Located on a golf course, the house is haunted by a man believed to be a former owner.

Whittier Middle School: Constructed in 1929; a young girl who fell to her death on the stairs is responsible for relocating personal items, turning doorknobs, and occasionally manifesting.

Witte Museum: Doors mysteriously unlock, personal items are moved, and a hazy, gray figure believed to be museum founder Ellen Schulz floats through the building before vanishing.

Wolfson Manor: The house is noted for slamming doors, ghostly footsteps, floating objects, and the shadowy figure of a woman.

Yturri-Edmunds Home: Dating back to the 1820s, the house is the site of cold spots and an apparition.

San Bernard River

The ghostly sounds of a fiddle can be heard playing the same tune over and over again by the side of the river.

San Juan

San Juan High School: A former custodian named Fred, who fell off a ladder while repairing the lights, frequents the auditorium.

San Marcos

San Marcos Bridge: The bridge is haunted by a Confederate soldier carrying a rifle. The restless spirit went off to war and never returned in the flesh.

San Patricio

Aransas River: Along the Aransas River the murder of John Savage was avenged by the hanging of Chipita Rodriquez, although some say her son killed Savage. Her apparition is seen near the river perhaps seeking justice for a crime she didn't commit.

Santa Rosa
La Llorona: The weeping woman's cries can sometimes be heard by those walking up the canal at midnight.

Saratoga
Bragg Road Light: A legend says the light is the ghost of Jake Murphy, a brakeman beheaded when he fell underneath a train. Others say the light belongs to the ghosts of four Mexican laborers killed by a foreman.

Scottsville
Scottsville Cemetery: Bordering this old cemetery on the west was a two-story house, which burned in the fifties. People talk of hearing a woman weeping down at the spring house near the cemetery.

Sealy
Sealy High School: Unexplained footsteps, doors that open and close unassisted, and an elevator operating by itself occur here.

Seguin
The Sebastopol/Joshua Young House: The 1854 Greek Revival house overlooking Walnut Creek is haunted by a lady in a white gown and long hair and a nine-year-old boy with short hair.

Spring
Doering Court: M.E. Hamilton built a large house on the property in 1917. Today part of the barn and its spacious loft is the home of the town's newspaper *The Old Town Spring Souvenir*. Sarah, a playmate of Henry and Ella Doering's youngest daughter, Marilyn, who died after complications from a fall in the barn, haunts the building. Playful sounds, footsteps running across the roof, and cold rushes of air are reported inside.

The Old Town Spring Historical Museum: Originally served as the courthouse; a 1900 Victrola originally owned by Marie Bailey starts playing by itself, and a ghostly young dancing couple appear inside.

Rose's Patio Cafe: A male spirit followed his favorite rocking chair to the building. He rocks back and forth in front of startled individuals. An extremely heavy iron will be moved by invisible hands.

The Spring State Bank: In the spring of 1932 the bank was robbed by Clyde Barrow and Bonnie Parker, and their spirits are seen in the bank.

Whitehall: Built in 1895, it became McGowen's Boarding House, a family residence, a funeral parlor downstairs, apartments, church schoolhouse, and the Hudson house. The spirits of a young couple make their home in one of the rooms and are referred to as the courting ghosts of Whitehall.

Springtown

Springtown Cemetery: A glowing tombstone and ghostly woman are seen in the graveyard.

Stanton

Academy of Our Lady of Mercy: Constructed by the Catholic Church in the 1880s, the home served as a convent/school. Weeping nuns, a priest who hanged himself, babies crying, and unexplained lights are part of this scene.

Sterling City

Landmark Hotel: A ghostly telephone operator still makes calls to the pay phone in the downstairs cafe. Disembodied footsteps, cold spots, door opening by themselves, and apparitions are also reported.

Sweetwater

Sweetwater High School: Disembodied footsteps are heard on stage in the auditorium, and a ghost has been sighted in the teachers' rooms.

Terlingua

Perry Mansion: A female apparition is seen inside, usually preceded by intense cold. There are unexplained voices, disembodied footsteps, and doors that open on their own.

Terlingua Cemetery: This old, abandoned cemetery is home to misty shapes, glowing forms, and icy drafts.

Thorndale

Snively-Pope Cabin: What remains of this cabin is haunted by the possessive ghost of a hermit who was murdered by outlaws and his body buried with their stash.

Tomball

Spring Creek Park: A munitions factory during the Civil War stood in what is now the back area of the park; 200 men died during an accidental explosion, and apparitions, screams, and cold spots are still reported there.

Uvalde

Fort Clark: A POW camp during WWII, the former officers quarters are haunted by ghosts who like to cook, move items, and make noise.

Victoria

Sutton's Mott: A picnic grove is frequently visited by the feisty ghost of William Sutton, a goat herder who was murdered in the 1850s while walking up the church steps in the nearby town of Goliad. Animals refuse to enter the grove of trees, and floating phantoms and ghostly bodies hanging from trees are reported here.

Waco

Baylor University: Elizabeth Barrett Browning's ghost walks the halls at night holding a candle and wearing a white gown. She also peers down from a top floor window.

Waxahachie

Ellis County Courthouse: Built of red sandstone in 1895; the ghost of Mabel Frame, a railroad telegraph operator, haunts the courthouse. Strange voices, materializations, and cold spots have been reported.

The Rose of Sharon Bed and Breakfast: This former inn, now a private residence, was built in 1892 by E. P. Powell. A man wearing a top hat, a woman wearing a long dress in the style of the late 1800s, and two playful little girls are responsible for unearthly music, disembodied footsteps and voices, frequent cold spots, and disappearing objects.

Wichita Falls

Grant Street Residence: Icy cold drafts, apparitions, and strange sounds come from inside this house.

White Sanitarium: Built by a Dr. White; unearthly sounds, ghosts playing cards, an invisible woman calling out for "Susan," and unexplained footsteps have been reported inside.

Wink

Oil Fields: The ghost of a Russian Cossack who was kidnapped is sighted in the oil fields. Roy Orbison saw the ghost on a dirt road east of town in 1950.

Texas Tourist Information

We recommend the following travel books:

America On Wheels Series (Southwest), Macmillan Company, New York

Texas, by Lone Star Books, Houston

The Great Stays of Texas by Sharry Buckner. Historic Accommodations of Texas, Fredericksburg

The Best Places to Stay Series (The Southwest), Houghton Mifflin Company

American Automobile Association travel guide for Texas.

Romantic Texas by Ken Christensen. fsquare creative Services Group, San Diego, California.

Recommended Country Inns (The Southwest), The Globe Pequot Press, Old Saybrook, Connecticut

The Annual Directory of Southern Bed and Breakfasts, Rutledge Hill Press, Nashville, Tennessee

A Texas State Travel Guide, Texas Department of Transportation, Travel and Information Division, 1101 East Anderson Lane, Austin, Texas 78752, or order a copy by calling 1-800-452-9292.

Texas Maps and Mileage Information

State and area road maps from Avis—(www.avis.com/maps_and_directions/road_maps/tx)

Texas Mileage Guide—mileage between Texas cities (www.window.state.tx.us)

General Information

Online Guide to Bed and Breakfasts in Texas—(www.ibbp.com/obb/texas.html)

Historic & Hospitality Accommodations of Texas (HAT), P.O. Box 1399, Fredericksburg, Texas 78624, 1-800-HAT-0368, email: info@hat.org (www.hat.org/)

Texas Hotel & Motel Association—List of lodging facilities from across Texas (www.texaslodging.com/)

Travel and Texas Tourism Information—(http://web2.airmail.net/danb1/Txtourism.htm)

Texas Travel Industry Association (TTIA)—(www.tourtexas.com/ttia/ttia.html)

TravelTex—From the Texas Department of Economic Development (www.traveltex.com/high/home.asp)

Texas Monthly—Comprehensive travel information for Texas Tour of Texas Vacation Ideas—lists events, tourist articles, information on all popular destinations, order brochures (www.texasmonthly.com/travel/)

@texas, a source for Free Texas Travel Information—(www.tourtexas.com/)

Wild Texas: Parks, Nature & Travel Guide—(www.wildtexas.com/index.htm)

Travel Ideas for Texas—Lists lodging, restaurant reviews, museums (http://travel.org/texas.html)

Internet Guide to Texas—Lists history and attractions for most Texas cities (www.iitexas.com/gpages/)

Winter Texans—Campgrounds, recreational ideas, and articles on South Texas cities (http://wintertexans.com/)

Texas Ghost Towns—A site highlighting Texas towns of the past (www.texasghosttowns.com/)

The Best Small Towns in Texas—Rural towns in Texas (www.bestsmalltowns.com/txtowns.html)

Texasescapes.com—All the history that's fit to print and then some (www.texasescapes.com)

Texas Highways—magazine articles and images from the highways of Texas (www.texashighways.com/)

Texas River Expeditions—Information on various river adventures (www.texasriver.com/texas.htm)

Texas Parks and Wildlife—Detailed information on Texas State Parks (http://www.tpwd.state.tx.us/)

Texas Hill Country—Maps, information and links to other Hill Country information (www.txinfo.com)

Texas Historical Commission—Tour ideas and historical points of interest (www.thc.state.tx.us/)

Little-known facts about the Lone Star State—(http://web2.airmail.net/danb1/Txfacts.htm)

State of Texas Government Information—(www.state.tx.us/)

TACO—Texas Association of Campground Owners—
(www.texasusa.com/taco/)

Texas Association of Convention & Visitor Bureaus (TACVB)—
TACVB was organized to enhance and encourage the convention and visitor industry in Texas
(http://www.texasusa.com/tacvb/)

Texas Festivals and Events Association (TFEA)—
(http://www.tourtexas.com)

Disclaimer

The stories appearing in this book are based on factual accounts of people who have owned, worked, or visited a particular establishment—some choose to remain anonymous. The authors take no responsibility for the veracity of each story except that we believe the storytellers. We have attempted to research each establishment and the paranormal encounters described in this book as accurately as possible. Although we have made every effort to ensure that the information was correct at the time the book went to press, we do not assume and hereby disclaim any liability to any party for any loss, damage, or injury caused by information contained in this book. Furthermore, the publishers disclaim any liability resulting from the use of this book.

We apologize if there is inaccurate information presented in this book, and will rectify future editions if we are contacted by mail, fax, or e-mail and provided with the correct information. Given the nature of businesses and the fact that many change ownership, names, and phone numbers, go out of business or become another type of business, we also wish to hear from those establishments where these changes have occurred. We regret that we cannot make any changes in this edition; however, we will address your concerns if and when a subsequent edition is prepared.

The authors would love to hear from readers about their paranormal experiences at an establishment mentioned in this book, or from those who know of other "haunted" locations. Address all inquiries or story submissions for future publications to G-HOST Publishing, 8701 Lava Place, West Hills, California 91304-2126; by telephone or fax to: 818-340-6676; or by e-mail to: robanne@ix.netcom.com, or we can be contacted through our publisher.

Index

F

G

H

I

J

K

L